THE DAYS OF ALKIBIADES

THE PARTHENON

The view is taken from the Propylaea. Many of the statues which line the way up to the great eastern door may be identified in Pausanias' guide-book. Near the end of the way up, the smoke of the great altar rises. On the right is the Chalkotheka adjoining the precinct of Brauronian Artemis.

THE PARTHENON

THE
DAYS OF ALKIBIADES

BY

C. E. ROBINSON, B.A.

ASSISTANT MASTER AT WINCHESTER COLLEGE

With a Foreword by

PROFESSOR C. W. OMAN

ILLUSTRATED

SECOND EDITION

NEW YORK
LONGMANS, GREEN, AND CO.
LONDON: EDWARD ARNOLD

FOREWORD

WHEN those of us who are interested in History, Ancient or Modern, come upon that common and depressing personage the boy or man who labels history as 'dull,' and conceives of it as a tedious string of names and dates, we are forced to ask ourselves how this pernicious attitude of mind comes into existence.

I am bound to say that I believe that it is mainly the result of a course of 'smaller manuals.' The shorter the history-book, the less human does it become. Those who have already some knowledge of a definite period may juggle with the names of Pericles or Caesar, Cromwell or Napoleon, because they have a notion of what those counters mean. To the victim of the 'smaller manual' they are only names, or at most have inadequate labels attached to them. It is hard to take much interest in Pericles if we have no longer definition of him than that he was 'an Athenian statesman of democratic tendencies, who was a great patron of arts and letters.' And even Napoleon may be tedious if we start with no more idea of him than that he was 'an ambitious Corsican general who succeeded in making himself despotic ruler of France.' It is absolutely necessary to rouse in the beginner an interest in the human and personal aspect of the historical figures with whom he comes in contact. I would pardon a reader who had never heard of the *Code Napoleon*, if he could tell me that the great emperor carried his snuff loose in his pockets, ate his meals too fast, and was accustomed to pinch the ears of his generals. There is some hope for that reader—none for the unhappy being to whom Napoleon means a string of battle-names and constitutional enactments. Whether illustrative anecdotes are absolutely accurate is a thing of almost secondary importance, for the 'legend' of a great man is sometimes quite as worthy of memory as his biography in the Smaller Historical Dictionary.

In dealing with Ancient History, the difficulty is decidedly greater than when Modern History is in question. It is, after all, not impossible to turn a reader who has developed an interest in the times of Elizabeth or Anne, or the Napoleonic wars, on to half a dozen interesting books which all but the most perverse can read for pleasure. With Greek and Roman history the task is far harder. For the life and manners of the classic world are far less comprehensible to the general reader than those of the sixteenth or the eighteenth century. We can not give him to read anything corresponding to *Westward Ho! Esmond*, or even *Brigadier Gerard*. And it is a very exceptional inquirer who will read Plutarch or Herodotus, in the crib, for pure pleasure. Even if beginner an interest in the human and personal aspect of the historical figures with whom he comes in contact. I would pardon a reader who had never heard of the *Code Napoleon*, if he could tell me that the great emperor carried his snuff loose in his pockets, ate his meals too fast, and was accustomed to pinch the ears of his generals. There is some hope for that reader—none for the unhappy being to whom Napoleon means a string of battle-names and constitutional enactments. Whether illustrative anecdotes are absolutely accurate is a thing of almost secondary importance, for the 'legend' of a great man is sometimes quite as worthy of memory as his biography in the Smaller Historical Dictionary.

In dealing with Ancient History, the difficulty is decidedly greater than when Modern History is in question. It is, after all, not impossible to turn a reader who has developed an interest in the times of Elizabeth or Anne, or the Napoleonic wars, on to half a dozen interesting books which all but the most perverse can read for pleasure. With Greek and Roman history the task is far harder. For the life and manners of the classic world are far less comprehensible to the general reader than those of the sixteenth or the eighteenth century. We can not give him to read anything corresponding to *Westward Ho!* *Esmond*, or even *Brigadier Gerard*. And it is a very exceptional inquirer who will read Plutarch or Herodotus, in the crib, for pure pleasure. Even if

FOREWORD

WHEN those of us who are interested in History, Ancient or Modern, come upon that common and depressing personage the boy or man who labels history as 'dull,' and conceives of it as a tedious string of names and dates, we are forced to ask ourselves how this pernicious attitude of mind comes into existence.

I am bound to say that I believe that it is mainly the result of a course of 'smaller manuals.' The shorter the history-book, the less human does it become. Those who have already some knowledge of a definite period may juggle with the names of Pericles or Caesar, Cromwell or Napoleon, because they have a notion of what those counters mean. To the victim of the 'smaller manual' they are only names, or at most have inadequate labels attached to them. It is hard to take much interest in Pericles if we have no longer definition of him than that he was 'an Athenian statesman of democratic tendencies, who was a great patron of arts and letters.' And even Napoleon may be tedious if we start with no more idea of him than that he was 'an ambitious Corsican general who succeeded in making himself despotic ruler of France.' It is absolutely necessary to rouse in the

he does, the customs and the surroundings of the
heroes of whom he reads are often unintelligible,
their motives and actions mysterious, for want of
what we may call ' atmosphere ' in the story.

There are really only two periods in the history
of the Elder World in which we can make for ourselves a detailed and lively picture of the daily life
of one of the great men whose names are familiar
to us in formal history. The one is the time of
the Fall of the Roman Republic, made real to us
not so much by the orations of Cicero as by the
private letters in which he tells us of his political
and literary tiffs, his financial misadventures, and
the discomforts of his travels. The other is the
short age of the Athenian Empire : and here we
are helped, not by Thucydides, who (with all his
merits) is almost the least human of historians, but
by the plays of Aristophanes, the dialogues of Plato,
and a bundle of the very best of Plutarch's *Lives*,
whose anecdotes are none the less valuable for side-
lights on the times, because they may sometimes be
inaccurate or even obviously untrue.

Between 430 B.C. and 400 B.C. we really have the
material for forming a picture of the life of Athens,
without being tied down to the philosophic narra-
tive of Thucydides, on the one hand, or falling
victims to the horrors of archaeological research on
the other (as do those who write romances about
Rameses or Sennacherib). We can not only visualize
the leading historical figures, but reconstruct their

manners and their motives, as we can do with men
of the sixteenth or the eighteenth century. Mr.
Robinson has chosen to hang his story around the
career of Alcibiades, the most freakish and fascinating of all the personalities of that wonderful age.
Fortunately there is a great deal to be gathered
together, from one source and another, about that
extraordinary youth—we never can think of him
as a middle-aged man even in his last years of
adventure. From first to last he was ' in the thick
of it '; it seems almost more than the story-teller
can reasonably expect, when we find that one
versatile personage was at once the ward of
Pericles, the favourite pupil of Socrates, the scandal
of the streets and supper-parties of Athens, the
victor at Olympia, the guiding statesman at the
crisis of his country's fate in 415 B.C., the traitor
who wrecked her policy two years later, the saviour
who won her a short breathing space of restoration
in 411 B.C. He was the greatest of adventurers,
the most perverse yet not the most unpardonable
of those who have sought to ' stand in the limelight,' rather than to work in the shade of duty.
Almost everything that he did or said has its interest, and I can conceive of no more fascinating
central figure for a study of Athenian life in the
Great Age.

C. OMAN.

AUTHOR'S PREFACE

THESE sketches conform to no strict canon of scientific history. They are rather intended to depict the manners, customs and general atmosphere of the times. Nevertheless the plots are in most cases based upon actual events and anecdotes, related in Plutarch and elsewhere. Nor are the characters fictitious ; nearly all of their names at least are on record. They are designed, however, to stand less for individuals than for general types. The farmer is such as Attic farmers would seem on the whole to have been. The Spartan is seen as he appeared to Athenian eyes : the sayings put into his mouth are attributed to various historical personages.

The materials from which the chapters are compiled have been drawn, whenever possible, from contemporary monuments and authors. Even the phrases used in the dialogues are based chiefly on the current language, as rendered by Aristophanes. In this way I have hoped to reproduce, truly and with fair completeness, the habits of an Athenian gentleman, how he dressed, ate, and spent his day, how he talked and what he thought, the scenes he saw and the places he visited.

I have not thought fit to fill the margin with references. There are manuals. To those readers who have no Greek, I have made two concessions.

From Mr. Zimmern I have borrowed the practice of referring to public offices, buildings and institutions in terms which may to some degree suggest their modern equivalents; from Mr. Rogers that of transcribing the language of non-Attic peoples into dialects suitably analogous. In translating the literary matter also, I have tried to suit the style of the translation to that of the original. The literature of Athens developed more swiftly than our own : but it passed through the same or approximately the same phases. Thus Homer becomes ballad-verse ; Alkibiades' speech has some flavour of Elizabethan rhetoric, the dialogues that of Elizabethan comedies ; the maturer style of Lysias finds its counterpart in the more rounded periods of Addison and Steele.

One last word upon the drawings. Vases have given evidence for costume, physiognomy and pose. The landscape of Attica cannot have differed materially from that of to-day ; though I doubt if I have clothed the hills with a sufficiency of trees. Some of the scenes must be largely conjectural. Those which represent the Theatre and the Galley deal with subjects which are still hotly debated. Wherever the ground is insecure, I have thought it better, whether in letterpress or illustration, to be bold and banish doubt. The tangles of controversy are for students to unravel. And to admit controversy in such a work as this would be but to dim the outlines of the picture, and to obscure the main interest which it is intended to awaken in the realities of living Greece.

CONTENTS

LIST OF PLATES

represents Plain-land
lying between the main
hill-masses.

SKETCH MAP OF GREECE

represents Plain-land
lying between the main
hill-masses.

SKETCH MAP OF GREECE

HISTORICAL INTRODUCTION

ALKIBIADES' manhood covered, with a strange and exact coincidence, those very years in Athenian history which were the most brilliant, the most troubled, and to ourselves the most interesting of all, I mean the twenty-seven years of the Peloponnesian War. He was a young man when the war broke out, but old enough to be serving in the ranks. He first took a lead in politics, when ten years' fighting had brought a truce and a breathing-space in the struggle. He died when the war was over, and Athens beaten.

In a sense, it was his uncle Perikles' war ; but I doubt if Perikles had wanted it. He was too great a statesman to be ignorant of its dangers. But soon or late war was bound to come for Sparta and Athens, as it was for Germany and Great Britain. From the day when, fifteen years before, Perikles definitely broke the old conservative clique of Thukydides and his timid pacifists, he must have seen it coming. He at any rate was able to measure with clear vision, but without flinching, the risks which his own policy involved. Nor were they to be regarded lightly. The Greater Athens, which was his ideal and exclusively his handiwork, was much more than a metropolis of art and wit, the hub of Hellenic culture. Perikles himself had called her the schoolmistress of Greece ; but she was, in a more material sense, its mistress too. Little by little she had turned to her own use that defensive union which the towns and islands of the Aegean basin had formed against the dangerous power of Persia. From chief partner in the alliance she had come to be its ruler; thus the Free League had turned into a Subject Empire; and such Perikles meant it to remain. But under a constraint of this character the 'allies' were already chafing. What if they should revolt? That risk Perikles had seen and faced. There was another. As head of a maritime empire, Athens' strength lay naturally upon the sea: but though not an island state, her very existence also depended upon sea-power no less than if she had been so. With the growth of a large industrial population, the soil of Attica ceased to be able to support its citizens. Naval supremacy therefore ensured to her not trade alone, but what was much more vital, corn. So it came to be an instinct with her to push her sea-power to its extreme limits; and this, as it was bound to do, brought her into collision with the interests of other states. Sparta, the head of a rival league in the Peloponnese, was a land power and a purely agricultural people: she could afford to ignore the Athenian menace. Not so her chief ally Corinth. This city, conveniently placed for trade in east and west, had watched with alarm her near neighbour's growing hold on the Aegean. But so long as her western outlet was left untouched, she had remained quiescent. When, however, Athens took the island of Corfu into alliance, Corinth's link with Sicily and South Italy was threatened. So in sheer self-defence she made vigorous representations at

Sparta and eventually pushed her somewhat unwilling partner into war. Once the plunge was taken, however, Sparta entered the struggle in grim earnest. All the old bitter jealousy of Athens rose in her; and she at once made a bold bid for victory (and, as it turned out, for Empire too) by declaring her cause to be the cause of all who suffered under Athens' tyranny. At the outset little came of this appeal, for neither Sparta nor Corinth had any fleet fit to send across the sea.

The first phase of the war lasted ten years. It gave Athens, as was natural, a still closer grip upon the trade-routes. The Corinthian Gulf was closely blockaded by Phormio's squadron at Naupaktos, which fought more than one successful action against heavy odds.

It also brought her one notable success on land. The Spartans, woefully misjudging the scope of naval power, landed a body of picked troops on a little island near Pylos. These were there cut off and forced into surrender. This (though in point of fact her men yielded only to overwhelming numbers [1]) was a terrible blow to Sparta's unique military prestige; and the loss of these prisoners for a time inclined her strongly towards peace.

Meanwhile Athens, for her part, had suffered too. Peloponnesian armies had made yearly invasions into Attic territory, destroying crops, felling trees and burning homesteads. All the country population was called inside the capital: and though her long walls from port to city secured Athens from

---

[1] Demosthenes and Kleon landed some thirteen thousand troops. The Spartans numbered only four hundred and twenty—together with some three thousand helots, if each Spartan was accompanied by his usual complement of seven.

starvation, she lived in a state of virtual siege. Neither Perikles nor his successors ever dared to meet the enemy in battle ; they even failed to send relief to their little ally Plataea, which lay just across the Boeotian border to the north-west. On land Athens was helpless. The invincible prowess of the Spartan army had become a legend. It was also in spite of Pylos an uncomfortable fact.

In the city one result of this wretched over-crowding was a serious outbreak of plague : it killed off many of her most brilliant men, and Perikles among them. The only reprisals she could make took the form of intermittent raids on the coasts of the Morea, and the seizure of the port of Megara which lay between Athens and the Isthmus. This last stroke, however, was not enough to bar the route to Northern Greece against the passage of Spartan troops ; and the ephors had the wit at last to send Brasidas with an expeditionary force to the coasts of Macedonia, where many of Athens' ' allies ' were only too ready to throw off her yoke and open their gates to the Spartan liberator. The Athenians made one bold attempt, which, had it succeeded, might have shut off Brasidas from all hope of reinforcements. They delivered a sudden attack in full force upon Boeotia, which lay between Macedonia and the Isthmus, and which had fought throughout the war at the side of Sparta. But this excursion ended disastrously at Delion, and Brasidas continued to spread disaffection along the northern littoral. This touched on the weakest spot in Athens' armour : and though Brasidas fell at Amphipolis, she was so thoroughly alarmed that she agreed to terms. But the truce (for it could be nothing more than that) was destined to last but a bare six years.

The time was now ripe for Alkibiades to play his part. No great figure any longer dominated the stage or united the state, as Perikles had done. And since his death, Athenian policy had begun to lose cohesion. Strictly speaking, there was no machinery in Athens which could be called Party Government.[1] But two main factions had, as the war went on, become more and more defined. Ten years of fighting was time enough for a man to learn where his interests lay. If he were a landowner, he saw that the renewal of the Spartan raids meant ruin. So feeling against the war hardened among the aristocracy, the farmers, and among that least articulate class of the community, the peasantry who tilled the soil. Their grumbling found vent, in the absence of a press, through the Comedies of Aristophanes. Their chief spokesman in the Assembly was Nikias, a man whose cautious moderation gave him more weight than his ability merited. But though he gained a brief success in establishing the so-called peace, he was never secure of a permanent majority. Over against him and his party was ranged another and a stronger interest. The industrial and commercial element—the workers of the pottery, the dock, the forge, the loom —dominated the Assembly. It had not of necessity a preponderance of voting strength—though this was formidable. But, what meant far more, it held the initiative in politics. The working population of Athens and Peiraieus contained (as did the

---

[1] Thus leaders of two opposing factions, such as Alkibiades and Nikias, often held office as 'generals' simultaneously.

town of Paris in eighteenth-century France) the brain and motive power of the community. With intellects practised in the business of the Courts and the Assembly, trained in the strict logic of their classic playwrights, and whetted to a keen edge by the 'Higher Criticism' of the new sophist-teachers, they were more than a match for the slow wits of country-cousins. The direction of such a mob called for adroit handling. To minds like these Nikias appeared a dull fool. They looked rather to whatever leader would flatter their sense of intellectual superiority and push to its furthest limit the principles of Democracy and Licence. Kleon, their most popular spokesman, succeeded not because he was a man of the people, but because he possessed the same violent enthusiasm and the same ruthless logic which marked many of the French revolutionary leaders. When Kleon died, Alkibiades, though an aristocrat both by birth and training, was able to place himself at their head, by virtue of similar qualities. Had he possessed the sanity and restraint of Perikles, he might have held the balance between the opposing factions, but he was singularly deficient in such restraint, and he threw all his weight upon the democratic side.

The party with which he now identified himself had never been averse to the war. On the contrary, they had everything to gain by it, nothing to lose. While the farms suffered, commerce flourished. The whole carrying trade of the middle seas, or at least the bulk of it, was little by little falling into Athenian hands : and at the conclusion of the peace the traders cannot but have felt themselves balked of the full fruits of a victory on which they had confidently counted. In the future, therefore, they looked for a bolder line of action : and they were resolved first to tighten the grip upon their refractory allies, and then, when opportunity offered, to try conclusions with Corinth and Sparta once more. From henceforward in all the tactics of aggression which Athens presently adopted, it was this party that led the measure : as it was Alkibiades that called the tune.

He it was in all likelihood who prompted the unscrupulous attack on the little island-state of Melos. This small defenceless people were summarily told to join the Athenian League. They refused : that was their only crime : and their punishment must have sent a thrill of horror through Greece. All males of military age were slaughtered, their wives and children sold into slavery. Other islanders whose ideas turned towards revolt were left to draw the moral for themselves.

Nor were Sparta and Corinth left long in doubt of Alkibiades' intentions. Since the peace had been concluded there had been some re-shuffling of the forces that held the balance against Athens. The town of Argos, hitherto a neutral, but an old enemy of her neighbour Sparta, had now formed a league of some of the minor states of the Peloponnese. Sparta was undisguisedly perturbed, the more so when Corinth herself joined in the League. She at once endeavoured to bring about an understanding with Argos ; in this she had all but succeeded when Alkibiades, by an adroit but unscrupulous diplomacy, turned the tables and brought Argos into line with Athens. His novel idea of forming a land combination against Sparta had one capital advantage. It enabled him to operate in such a way as to divide the forces of Sparta from those of Corinth. It only failed through the unrivalled fighting powers of the Spartan foot, who, though taken at a tactical disadvantage at Mantinea, transformed a doubtful day into a brilliant victory. This defeat put an end to Alkibiades' schemes in this direction, and he turned his thoughts towards the sea.

Of all the fields open to the enterprise of Greek traders, Sicily was perhaps the richest. Syracuse, its most prominent and prosperous city, had originally been founded by colonists from Corinth, and as we hinted above, it was in this direction that Corinth's chief trade lay. The plan which was now hatched in Alkibiades' swift intellect, was nothing more or less than to utilise Athens' sea-power for the conquest of this town. This accomplished, Sicily would be at their mercy, and Corinth too. The Peloponnese could be blockaded and forced into submission.

The story of that fatal enterprise cannot be told here. Alkibiades' own part in it was fated to be a strange one. He had carried the Assembly with him, in defiance of Nikias' warnings, and a great fleet was fitted out, when on the very eve of sailing a catastrophe occurred which wrecked all his ambitions, and altered the course of his whole life. An outrage took place which touched the superstitious citizens of Athens on a weak side. One night the sacred images known as the Hermae were mutilated by unknown hands. Suspicion fell on Alkibiades and his wild companions. Though allowed to sail, he was condemned in his absence and forced to flee for his life. He fled to Sparta. There he urged, in concert with the Corinthians, that help should be sent to Syracuse; this advice, more than anything else, worked the destruction of the Athenian expedition, which through Nikias' feeble generalship was lost to a man. Alkibiades also pointed out to the Spartans that the permanent occupation of some strategic point in Attica would do more harm than a dozen annual raids. The fortification of Dekelea was henceforward a perpetual thorn in Athens' side.

Meanwhile, however, Alkibiades had made things too hot for him at Sparta : and he moved to the south coast of Asia Minor where he made advances to the great King's satrap and was received at his court. As it so happened, the focus of the war now shifted in the same direction. When the news came from Sicily that the Athenian fleet was lost, it put heart into many of Athens' more distant allies, and she was soon faced with the danger of a general revolt. At home, moreover, her enemies had by now equipped a fleet strong enough to venture across the Aegean, and render invaluable aid to the rebels. Now it was that Alkibiades veered round once more ; for traitor as he was, his heart still turned towards his own town : and he was not slow to use this changed aspect of affairs to his own advantage. By a series of intrigues he first of all procured a *coup d'état* in Athens, by which the conservative party established a narrow oligarchical régime, pledged to recall the true author of its being. Then, when he foresaw the imminent failure of this short-lived government, he changed sides once more, declared himself a true democrat, proceeded to Samos and there joined the fleet, which had throughout remained loyal to the old political ideal.

He was now once again in command of his country's forces. He took up the war against her enemies to some purpose. After two or three brilliant victories in the Sea of Marmora he was re-called to Athens and received with a great ovation.

But his hold upon the populace was no longer what it had been. A naval defeat suffered in his absence, and in disregard of his orders, was turned against him and he was dismissed from his command. This time he retired to the neighbourhood of the Troad, and lived under the protection of a friendly satrap Pharnabazos.

Athens' fortunes now rapidly declined. Her fleet, no longer the invincible weapon of former days, and manned in part at least by slaves, was finally destroyed in the battle of Aigospotami. By this she lost her command of the Hellespont, and with it the power to import her indispensable supplies. Her coasts were unprotected, and she was forced to capitulate. The Long Walls were razed. A Philo-Spartan committee of thirty was put in control of the city, and a Reign of Terror set in. Amongst other crimes which the thirty com-mitted, they induced Pharnabazos to procure the murder of Alkibiades himself, so apprehensive were they even now of his power to harm. He died miserably at the hands of hired assassins,—a just fate.

I. ALKIBIADES' BOYHOOD

Each of you show
You what you taught their fathers of old,
You let us know
Your system untried, that hearing each side
From the lips of the Rivals the youth may decide
　　To which of your schools he will go.
　　　　　　　ARISTOPHANES, *Clouds*.
　　　　　(Translation by Mr. B. B. Rogers.)

IT is according to the fashion of these times that
the hero of a biography should be treated like a race-
horse and provided with a pedigree. And since this
is so, let us begin with Ajax. Alkibiades claimed
to be, and may for all that we know, have been, a
descendant of that illustrious warrior ; but when
all is said, that is much as if you or I claimed kinship
with Sir Launcelot of the Lake. So we may well
leave Ajax on one side and pass to a less shadowy
figure, old Alkmeon. Alkmeon has the best of rights
to be considered the founder of the great family to
which Alkibiades belonged ; for they all bore his
name. Along with it they seem to have inherited
something of his fortune and not a little of his wit.
For if Herodotos at least is to be trusted, he was a
man of no common shrewdness. Once upon a time,
so we are told, he was paying a visit to Kroesos in
Lydia, when that genial monarch out of the bounty
of his heart and the abundance of his treasure made

A

him an offer of ' as much money as he could carry about his person.' Thereupon Alkmeon clothed himself in his biggest tunic, and borrowing the widest pair of buskins available, entered the treasure-house so clad. There he stuffed as much gold dust as might be between the buskins and his legs, and pouching all he could inside his tunic, sprinkling some more on his hair, and taking a last consignment in his mouth, he came forth ' scarce able to drag his legs along, the queerest figure of a man, with his mouth cram-full, and his figure bulging out in all directions.' With such an ancestor the Alkmeonidae had plainly a reputation to maintain. They early did so. One of their number, Megakles, was in office at a time when faction was rife, and an attempt was made to overthrow the constitution. The insurgents, being beaten, climbed to the Akropolis and sat down at the sanctuary of Athena. This, after much parleying and upon an express promise of pardon, they were at length induced to quit ; not, however, until they had, as a precautionary measure, established communications with their divine protectress, by linking themselves with a rope to her Altar-stone. Keeping a firm hold upon the other end of the rope, they were venturing down the hillside, when Megakles had the rope summarily cut, and then butchered the suppliants to a man. This was a blot upon the family honour, which his descendants were never allowed to forget.

Under the Tyrants they suffered confiscation and exile ; but after an unsuccessful appeal to arms they won a bloodless victory and a reputation for patriotism to boot, by a somewhat dim manipulation of the Delphic oracle. There were ugly rumours too about their collusion with the Persians and stories of a shield flashed from the mountain above Marathon. But whatever truth there may be in the tales related of this entertaining family, a full measure of their ingenuity, high spirit and plentiful lack of principle descended to Alkibiades through his mother Deinomache, who must herself have been either a very astute or a very attractive lady : for she married three husbands, one of whom was no less a person than her kinsman Perikles.

Of the father of Alkibiades, Kleinias by name, less is known. He sailed as ship's captain in the Great Wars, sunk a Persian galley off the north of Euboea, and thirty years later fell on the stricken field of Koronea.

Such antecedents gave to his son a high standing at Athens and, since his mother's family had always stood for democracy, a decided political bias as well. Nevertheless we shall find that in making an estimate of him we look forward rather than back. He belonged to a New Age. For just now a new spirit, call it Individualism or what you will, was stirring in Greece. The apple of the Tree of Knowledge was once again between men's teeth, and the old order of comfortable dependence on tradition was passing away. The new order came, for a brief season flourished, and was, in its turn, forgotten ; and when after centuries of ignorance and superstition, Europe awoke and tasted again of that dangerous fruit, it was from the tomb of Greece that she took it. Athens and the Renaissance may stand two thousand years apart. But the spirit of both is essentially the same. The intervening changes, such as they were, are no great matter.

Alkibiades scoffed, it is true, at the prophecies of Apollo, not at the Bulls of the Pope : he could never have done a three-figure sum without the aid of a counting-board : he was even content to clothe his body in nothing more elaborate than two square lengths of cloth.   But, among the asphodel of the Elysian meadows, he must, I fancy, be loitering and lisping with Philip Sidney and Lorenzo il Magnifico upon either ghostly arm.

Of his infancy there is little to tell.   Upon his arrival in the world the Olive-wreath was duly hung at the street door, as was the custom when parents were pleased with their child.   Superfluous babies, especially girls, had in Greece but a cold welcome ; the truth being that, at Sparta always, and at Athens not infrequently, they received the shortest of shrifts, being summarily exposed, or as the phrase ran (in days when earthenware was more common than carpet bags) ' potted.'

Alkibiades, happily escaping the fate of little Spartan boys who were not wanted, stumbled upon the hardly more enviable fate of those that were. For he fell into the clutches of a Spartan nurse. His family frankly admired Spartan methods ; they had friends at Sparta ; and partly perhaps out of compliment to these, partly in memory of his great-grandfather, it was a Spartan name they gave him when his Tenth or Naming Day came round.

Amykla, for that was his nurse's name, knew how to train a baby.   Thanks to her, he was never converted into a miniature mummy by the cramping process of wearing swaddling clothes as most little Athenian victims wore them.   She watched over his physical development as only a Spartan could.

So that, when the time came that the hoop and the little go-cart should be exchanged for the dice and strigil,[1] his handsome face and perfect figure were the talk of the town. He won quite golden opinions from that impressionable old preacher, Sokrates; and even a master-potter seeking for a dedication to his latest bowl, wrote on its margin 'Alkibiades is fair.'

If his body bore the genuine Spartan stamp, his character certainly did not. After his father's death, he had passed to the care of two guardians, Ariphron and his own kinsman Perikles. He fell foul of both. Ariphron was a fussy man, and once, when the boy ran away from them, he would have sent the Public Crier crying him lost through all the streets of Athens. As for Perikles, he was mostly too busy to humour his troublesome ward, and on one occasion aroused his deep resentment by refusing him an audience. 'Doing accounts for the public audit, is he?' said the boy in a temper; 'the best accounts for him to give, you may tell him, are none at all.'

Every Athenian boy of any standing needed an attendant slave, whom they called a pedagogue,[2] and who served him as 'nurse, footman, chaperon and tutor' rolled into one. Perikles chose an incompetent fool: as a result Alkibiades led the old man a rare dance, and ended by breaking a stick across the fellow's back.

One of the pedagogue's chief duties was to escort his young master to and from the day-school, kept

[1] An instrument used in the gymnasium to scrape the body after violent exercise.

[2] The 'Pedagogue' or Boy-leader was a slave who looked after a boy, taking him to school and bringing him home again, and seeing that he did not fall into trouble by the way.

by one Zopyros. Here Alkibiades was a hero from the start. All the boys worshipped him, from the little seven-year-olds with nice manners and arms neatly tucked under their cloaks, to the young Hectors who took pet dogs to school with them and were just learning to lounge and gossip in the market-place. Every one petted and spoilt him. He it was set the fashions. And when, for instance, he led a revolt against learning the flute, every one agreed with him that making mouths was an unbecoming pastime only fit for Thebans and flute girls.

But the prescribed routine, reading, writing and arithmetic, he could not escape. And dull enough work he found it we may be sure, bending over the tablet on his knee, and tracing letters in the wax, or counting tens and hundreds on the counting-board. ' How many letters are there in Sophokles ? ' ' Alkibiades, it is vulgar to cross your legs.' ' What letter is like a curl of hair ? ' So the interminable catechism ran on, questions to which he knew the answer before ever they were asked. How much more amusing were those which he asked himself! Whence did the little imp hail that cleaned the desks ? Why was he born black ? Did the Muses really wear a sickly smile and leer through two eye-slits, like their statues in the corner ? and as he pondered over this, he would recall that the next day was their festival, and that meant a whole holiday and a ramble on Mount Hymettos. And now he thought of it, there was a preliminary procession at the Peiraieus that very afternoon. Most certainly he should not return to school after the midday break : and he fell to modelling little figures from the wax scraped off his ' slate.'

'Alkibiades, you are to take the letter Delta, for
that alone remains.' He woke from his dream amid
general derision ; a spelling drama was in progress,
and Zopyros had given him the letter that they
brand upon runaway slaves.[1] Still, in spite of
wandering thoughts he learnt quickly, and once won
fifty knuckle-bones ' for writing nicely.'

Progress, however, as far as he was concerned,
was a step from bad to worse. The letters known,
reading next ; reading without stops or divisions
between words to help you, and all in an Attic
accent most correct.

Then came repetition, hundreds of hexameters
to get by heart, till he loathed the very name of
Homer, and hated grown-ups who could repeat the
entire *Iliad*, and, what was worse, always let him
know it. But the time came when he could retaliate by innocently inquiring, whether they could
in that case explain precisely what the poet meant
by ' eldritch sprites.' [2] The first taste of the power
of words was like honey to the mouth.

About the same time that he made this last discovery, he also made a remarkable friendship. It
came about at the music school. Like all Athenian
boys, Alkibiades learnt the lyre ; for every gentleman was expected to be able to sing an after-dinner
song and to play his own accompaniment. It was
only an upstart like Themistokles that could afford
to boast ' I cannot fiddle but I can make a city
great.' So Alkibiades learnt the lyre at the school

[1] D for Δραπέτης. This may have been used as the letter K was
used at Rome for Kalumnia. On the other hand, slave-owners may
each have employed their own initials. There seems no clear evidence.

[2] An attempt to reproduce in old-fashioned English the Homeric
phrase ἀμενηνὰ κάρηνα.

of a well-known harpist. Among the pupils of this school was a middle-aged sculptor named Sokrates. He must have cut as odd a figure in this place as an elderly don at a dancing-class; but Sokrates had little fear of ridicule; and besides, he found there unlimited opportunities for conversation. He talked to the boys in season and out of season, upon politics and ethics, and Heaven knows what else, but invariably above their heads. If he was called up for his lesson, he would linger to finish a discussion on the morality of the gods in Homer; and when the master was fairly embarked on Lamprokles' 'Pallas, dread sacker of cities,' he would interrupt with a demand for some definition of harmony: and when it was reluctantly given, he would sit there on his stool arguing till the rest of the class had stolen away; then having forced the wretched lyre-master to the conclusion that what he called harmony was nothing else than discord, he would pursue his fellow pupils and cross-examine them all the way home about all manner of subjects, all the while lamenting his own deplorable ignorance. Many of the boys were bored, but Alkibiades drank in this as yet untasted knowledge like new wine.

And like new wine, it intoxicated his young brain. He learnt to quibble and split straws; he would have outdone Olivia's own fool at verbal jugglery. All that he had been brought up to reverence and obey, he now called in question with the zest of a third-year 'varsity cynic. Little wonder that when he left school, he had no fear for either God or man.

Already at fourteen he had bidden farewell to his

grammar-master; at eighteen he must enter upon his two years of military service. In the interim he was free more or less to kick his heels. At the moment the rank and fashion of Athens were crazy after Culture. The hero of the hour was the sophist of the powerful tongue and the narrow chest. Even the great Perikles counted among his friends many of these intellectual upstarts and condescended to argue with them. It was said that once he spent a whole forenoon discussing with Protagoras an accident which befell a horse at the races; one laying its death at the door of the man who threw the fatal spear, the other declaring the guilt to lie either with the javelin or with the President of the games. Alkibiades, who set the mode among his associates in everything from a lisp to leggings, 'went in' for culture with a vengeance. He attended lectures on the square root of three, and learnt to draw a proposition 'concerning circles' in the sand. He paid a high sum for a course on the 'whole duty of the citizen,' and argued a point with the lecturer. Whenever a ship put in from the West, he would send a slave down to the port to inquire what new savant was aboard. Whenever his cousin Kallias held his 'salon,' the doors were open to him and his friends; and on the day that his favourite professor left the town to tour in the Peloponnesos, he was mad to follow him, and was half way to Megara before the others could prevail on him to turn back.

Throughout such a bacchanalia of enthusiasms this strayed reveller had soon lit his torch at many a wayside shrine: but he never wholly forgot the high priest who first had drawn for him the curtain

from the mysteries of life.   Sokrates was never far
from his side, rolling his big serious eyes like an ox,
and sometimes drawing eager answers from his pupil
as they probed together some of the deeper problems
of philosophy.   Then the mood would change.
The boy would yawn over some discourse upon ' self-
control ' and be off to concoct some devilment with
a young blackguard called Anytos.   But Sokrates
had a tenderness even for the boy's delinquencies ;
and seeing him somewhat less than sober at the
Feast of Pots, vowed he was ' as fair as Love in the
picture with a crown of roses on his golden head.'
Some mysterious spell, too, was cast by the philosophic pipings of this uncouth latter-day Orpheus.
Affection indeed as deep as an old pagan saint might
well feel for a young pagan sinner, could not fail to
triumph in the end through its very manliness.
Then there would be real tears of repentance,
and a lecture that began by being very personal,
and strayed very soon to alien subjects, Alkibiades
knowing precisely when it was prudent to turn the
current and ask for a definition of ' Virtue.'

The friendship between this incongruous pair
was cemented above all at the Wrestling-School.
There it was that Sokrates, snatching chances for
conversation from the intervals of athletics, contrived
to ' lead the youth of Athens astray.'   The great
playground of the Academy lay out in the plain
on the western side of Athens.   It was a pleasant
place for lounging and gossip as well as for sport :
for Kimon had laid it out with shady avenues and
running streams.   And though it is now a parched
and dusty field and the Kephisos is clotted with
mud, it must once have been a spot of beauty above

all in the spring-time ' amid the fragrance of smilax
and of leisure and white poplar, what time the
plane-tree whispers to the elm.' Hither crowds
of demure little boys and sturdy youths would
make their way through the midday dust and
heat; and out under the glare of the sun in the
great cloistered court dozens of naked glistening
figures ran and jumped, learnt to swing the quoit
and aim the spear, or rolled and wrestled in the
sand.

Towards the cool of the evening, knots of bearded
men, too, filtered out from the Dipylon gate, to
watch the training, gossip about the coming games,
or take a turn themselves before their supper. One
night Sokrates and his friends repaired thither.
The philosopher was left behind at the bridge, for a
thinking fit had come upon him by the way; but of
his companions some immediately stripped for exercise, one stout burgess set to with a quoit, to get rid
of a tiresome headache; a second, finding that the
instructor was engaged, practised the cross-buttock
throw on imaginary opponents, to the great diversion of the less energetic. These intellectual lag-
gards took a turn or two up and down the shady
colonnade, and then, hearing the voice of Sokrates,
turned off into one of the undressing rooms. Here
the indefatigable talker had come upon the two boys
Lysis and Charmides as they were putting on their
cloaks, and he was plying them as usual with questions. ' Did they hope to be as fine men as were
their fathers ? ' ' How much did they pay for
their training ? ' Thus they were led innocently
on till there came the alarming, though perhaps
not wholly unforeseen inquiry, ' Why did they

pay nobody to train their souls too?' and they were at once floundering in the meshes of an argument.

At this moment Alkibiades entered; he was to wrestle with Autolykos, and the winner should enter his name for the great Games. As he takes off his cloak, a slave rolls it up and, disposing it in coils as one rolls up a hose, leaves it upon a neighbouring bench; a second slave, known by the elegant name of the 'oil and scraper' man, pours over him the contents of a narrow-necked, pot-bellied flask. Every one stops chattering to watch the match. Even Glaukon leaves scratching love-poems on the walls. Sokrates' victims are still kept well in hand, but they can hear the piper strike up to set the time. The trainer's voice says, 'Set your right hand so—shift your ground—engage.' Then there is silence except for the panting of the pair. Suddenly comes the crack of the trainer's forked stick on the bare flesh. 'You bite, Alkibiades, like a girl.' 'No, sir, like a lion,' says an angry voice, and its owner comes in fuming. He vents his ill-humour on the unlucky slave who scrapes him down with a bill-shaped implement from head to foot. After his water douche, he has hardly patience for the final oiling that should complete his toilette. 'When I am in my uncle's place,' he mutters, 'I'll pack that trainer about his business. Does he take Athens for a city of slaves?' As he made off, Sokrates followed him under the olives; the nightingales were singing clamorously round the mound of Kolonos; and in the dusk the sage, though little given to song, found himself humming over the lines of a chorus written long ago by a grim old poet.[1]

> ' They have stolen the whelp of a lioness,
>   Wean'd it and bred it at home,
>   The toy of the children's kindness,
>   The joy of the old man's blindness—
>   Till the fulness of time be come.
>
> Those soft eyes, who could have dreaded?
> Those large soft eyes that fawn,
>   On the hand of the friend that has fed it
>   While it lies in the arms that have bred it,
> As gentle as babe new-born.
>
> But the son of the old lion's daughter
> His debt shall at last make good ;
>   Will he stay for his master's order—
>   To be filling the folds with slaughter
> And the home with a welter of blood? '

---

[1] Aeschylos in the *Agamemnon*.

II. AN ATTIC FARM

Regum aequabat opes animis.—VERGIL.

IN the neighbourhood of Phlya—not many miles along the Kephisia road—there lived a farmer named Demokrates. He had been an intimate of Alkibiades' father : and Alkibiades well remembered seeing the old man often at their home. Then Kleinias had died; and soon after (for some reason which the boy had never fully understood) the visits to Athens had ceased. But although Demokrates came to the city no more, his friendship for the father was extended to the son; and Alkibiades, when he was old enough to go there, came to regard the farm at Phlya as a second home. Young fire-brand though he was, he took an honest pleasure in the old man's company; he would sit for hours listening to interminable tales of Kimon and Aristeides and of battles fought against the long-haired Medes. Even in his wilder moods, he felt something of an awe for his host's dignified old-fashioned ways, which were so different from the ways of the men he met in Athens. For the city (though Alkibiades was too young to know it) was changing in manners and morals and ideals. But the country, if it changes at all, changes very slowly; and, while a new restlessness of spirit was troubling the peace of Athens, while her streets were loud with noisy arguments of philosophers and quacks, and while the taint of foreign luxury already threatened to invade her homes, these quiet hamlets and secluded steadings preserved the old simple primeval innocence of rural life. The men who lived in them seemed almost the survivors of a long-forgotten age when kings and princes walked behind the plough, and when Odysseus came upon Laertes pruning the fruit-trees in the orchard plot.

It was a favourite saying of Demokrates that the farm had been in his family since Priam ruled in Troy. Though there is some doubt whether his pedigree could have been carried back a century, yet he seemed himself in his own person to support and justify this boast. For he was altogether of a piece with the past; and of this it was a kind of symbol that he retained like so many of his sort an antiquated style of dress, wearing at all times the finest linen (instead of wool, as others did) and binding his hair up in a large knob, which was held together by a golden pin shaped like a grasshopper. There was, too, an old-fashioned flavour about his speech, about the superannuated oaths he used, and about his simple piety. He was as strict as a Pharisee in his observances of feasts or sacrifices, and never did he let a new moon go by without anointing himself (and his wife) from a full flask of seasoned olive oil.

As was natural, his piety and honest character had won him a high place in his neighbours' esteem; and on more than one occasion they had elected him ' Headman ' of the parish.

Once, too, he had been chosen out and sent to Athens as candidate for the Magistracy of the year. The cast of the lots, as it so happened, had favoured him, but at the end of the year and from the day that he laid down office, he had forsworn politics altogether, and seemed to avoid every contact with the city. For this he would give no satisfactory reason ; and, if pressed, would declare that Athens might go her way to perdition without help from him. Sometimes he added, half in jest, that the blame should be laid in equivalent proportions on the sophists' lectures and the hot bath-house.

It was therefore only natural that he spoke rarely of current politics. His opinions, when he did so, were trenchant and strongly biased. The farmers of Attica were, as farmers are wont to be, of a conservative turn of mind, and Demokrates was no exception. He had never a good word to say for Perikles, ' a demagogue who does but tickle the people's palate.' Ambitious schemes of Empire frightened him. The levying of tribute on the allies he termed unjust extortion, the spending of it on monuments and temples, selfish pride. In this connection he would liken Athens to an idle woman spending her husband's money on the adornment of her person. ' But we shall reap, as we have sown,' was his conclusion. ' There will come a day of reckoning with these men across the sea.' For Sparta he professed open sympathy, admiring them for their rugged candour and stern self-discipline. His own philosophy of life lay in a studied moderation. The old saw, *Nothing too much*, was constantly upon his lips. He had for the sin of pride a special horror ; it was his firm belief that a Power above lay in wait against the insolent and boastful, and for this belief he would quote numerous proofs drawn from history and from his favourite poet Aeschylos. Zeus, as

Demokrates conceived him, was an unpleasantly jealous and vindictive being.[1]

Some said he had been soured by the ruin of his own ambitions, but there was more of resignation than of cynicism in Demokrates' philosophy. The truth was that during his year of office, he had done his utmost to stem the rising tide of democracy, and had been an active partisan of Thukydides [2] when that unlucky leader pitted himself against the growing power of Perikles. But the current was too strong for them. Thukydides had fallen in disgrace; Demokrates, losing hope, had retired to seek consolation on his farm.

Here by long industry and sound economy he had amassed a moderate fortune, and was able gradually to extend the boundaries of the estate. His olive groves were the pride of Phlya : his corn crops were never known to fail. But prosperity brought no change in his condition. He had a distaste for comforts, and often spoke bitterly of the growing luxury of the age. 'It is a shameful thing,' he would say, ' for Greeks to live like soft barbarians.' His own house was very unpretentious. Like other farmhouses it stood in a large courtyard, surrounded by high mud walls. Down two sides of this enclosure ran open sheds, in which agricultural implements were stored and which provided shelter for the oxen during winter, and on summer

[1] These opinions may be taken as broadly representative of the landed class in Attica, many of them the descendants of the old Eupatrids and heirs of the aristocratic tradition. Aristophanes himself often voiced their feeling.

[2] This Thukydides, who must be distinguished from the historian of that name, represented the old oligarchical faction who opposed Perikles' Imperial policy and favoured alliance with Sparta.

nights for the slaves. In the centre of the court stood an altar of charred turfs, and near to it, a stock of wood, carved at its upper end with a crude likeness of a human head, round which at festal seasons was hung a garland. The house itself (which, like the yard-wall, was built of mud) contained one roomy hall behind which, out of sight, lay the women's quarter. The hall or living-room was scantily furnished. In the centre four stout pillars, grouped round the hearthstone, supported the flat timber roof; on the pillars hung the pots and pans for cooking and the master's leathern shield. Half a dozen couches were ranged along the walls, together with a pile of sheepskin rugs, a chest or two, and in one corner a row of shapely oil-jars. As the room was without windows, the only light came through the smoke-hole in the roof, and through the door. But sunshine seldom penetrated there, even in summer ; for the doorway was covered by a loggia-porch, over which spread the leafy branches of a rambling vine.[1]

Demokrates had no children, but his wife was still alive, though now too old to do much else but sit by the doorstep spinning. If she ever went beyond the courtyard gate, it was because her stores of herbs and simples needed to be replenished, otherwise she stayed contentedly at home and supervised the work of the female slaves. The control of the men was the master's business, but in this he was assisted by the services of a faithful steward or bailiff. This was a man called Sakas, who had been in the farmer's service for more than forty years.

[1] It seems almost certain that the old type of the Homeric house survived in the country long after the Greeks had evolved the new type, in which the court was, as it were, turned inwards and set in the centre of the house.

Although his hoard of savings was enough to buy him his liberty, Sakas had preferred to remain on the farm as a slave. Indeed, Demokrates could ill have spared him; he would sooner (so he used to say) have parted with a nine-years' ox. The man was, in all respects, a model bailiff, and (what was most valued) he had the trick of planting olives better than any man in Phlya. His one great weakness was an exaggerated superstition. He had unbounded belief in the power of omens and charms and magic, his life was burdened by a constant terror of the ' evil eye,' which he studied to avert by wearing a large bunch of amulets about his neck. He was also particularly observant of the movements of animals and the flight of birds, trembling at the sight of a raven, and even abandoning an important journey if a weasel so much as crossed his path. Often these superstitions of his were something of a bar to good husbandry, for there was not a day in the calendar but was (for good or ill) coloured by some potent and mysterious influence. During the last quarter of the moon, for instance, one must on no account plant seed. Reaping had always to be begun on the twelfth of the month; at a pinch he might be brought to countenance the nineteenth evening; for then, by some inexplicable accident, conditions improved as the day wore on. These fanciful ideas he was thought, in part at least, to have brought with him from his home in Thessaly,[1] whence as a boy he had

---

[1] They were current there in Hesiod's time at any rate; and there is no reason to suppose that they were more short-lived than other rural superstitions. Compare the notion which prevails in some parts of England that it is lucky to plant seeds on Good Friday.

been kidnapped and shipped to the slave-market at Athens. With Alkibiades, Sakas was a special favourite. The boy took a great delight in crossing the bailiff's foibles—besides, nobody understood as well as he did the training of dogs or how to lime a twig for birds. The old man, so far from resenting the boy's pranks, was devoted to the young master (so he chose to call him) and seldom failed to find some trifling present for him when he came to Phlya, at one time a stick cut with curious patterns, at another a tame quail or a linnet.

Alkibiades had the run of the farm, where he could find amusement at all times and seasons, riding in a wagon, snaring a bird or watching the labourers at their work. Whenever city life seemed stale and monotonous, he was sure to meet with some novel experience out in the country. Once, in early autumn, he had played truant from school and gone to Phlya to see the vintage gathered. Away from the town and in the freedom of the fields, it was easy to forget he was a fine young gentleman, and he had mixed freely with the slaves, lending a hand with the heavy basket-loads of purple clusters, and even taking a turn in the winepress at treading out the grape juice. In the evening, when all was over, he stayed to see the peasants celebrate their Harvest Home. The boys had been busy preparing a huge wreath of olive sprigs and fruits and tufts of wool. When this was ready, they carried it off to the chapel of Apollo, to ask a benediction. Alkibiades followed the procession, and during the ceremony he caught a glimpse into the interior of the shrine. It was chock-full of offerings hung upon the walls, old rusted sickles, faded garlands, sham jewellery and terra-cotta dolls. Among all this trash he could barely at first distinguish the sacred image, a bright painted thing carved out of wood. When he saw it, it seemed so ugly that he would have laughed outright if it had not been for the serious faces of the worshippers, who approached it with awestruck veneration. When the priest [1] had finished blessing the Harvest wreath,[2] they all went off home in triumph to nail it up over the courtyard gate, chanting all the way the old thanksgiving song :—

> Wreath of the Harvest Home
> Bringeth prosperity.
> Figs, cakes and honeycomb,
> Fruit of the olive tree,
> Wine to drink deep, O !
> Drink and then sleep, O !

After that, there was feasting in the cool twilight, and dancing to finish the day. All the company linked hands and, when the piper struck up, began to move slowly round in a long serpentine, from which one pair and then another would break off and dance in the middle ; sedately at first, poising a foot in air and swaying the body backwards with a slow methodical rhythm : [3] but as night advanced, torches were lit and more wine was drunk and the

[1] The priest of this shrine was the father of Euripides the poet.
[2] The wreath was known as the Eiresione. The procession took place in June according to Miss Harrison, but I follow others who place it in October.
[3] This description is based upon a dance seen in recent years at Athens. Pose seems to play more part in it than step, and this must almost certainly have been true of classic times.

scene became more and more boisterous, till it had ended in a dance called the Kikynna, which was very wild indeed.

When Alkibiades returned to Athens, he was punished for his absence and forbidden to go again to Phlya; but this did not hinder him from paying an occasional visit on the sly, at one time to watch the oxen at the plough, at another to help at the olive picking in late autumn, when poor city folk came out in great hordes to lend a hand in return for a trifling wage. Above all, it was in the days of early summer, when the corn is in the ear and the first figs begin to ripen, that school-time seemed most tedious and the call of the country wellnigh irresistible. It was therefore the more provoking that Ariphron, his fussy guardian, chose this particular season to exert once more his authority. The mild, good-natured half-breed who had tutored him from childhood was dismissed, and his place taken by a more strict and brutal pedagogue. The man's chief duty was each morning to conduct his charge to the schoolroom door and then wait till noon to take him home again. He performed the duty with the vigilance of a Kerberos: there was no longer any loitering by pastry stalls, no game of dice at street corners; it was not even permitted to return home by way of the market-place. By degrees the tyranny became intolerable, till one day when Alkibiades issued from the schoolroom there was the fellow asleep at his post. The boy slipped past, ran down to the Dipylon gate and was soon shaking the dust of Athens off his feet, with a vow never to return.

It was not far to Phlya, and he was soon at the
farm. He found Demokrates out in the harvest
fields, standing, like the king depicted on Achilles'
shield, with ' staff in hand, and silent joy at heart.'
Two reapers were at work plying their sickles in
the standing corn. Others followed in their tracks,
and tied up the swathes in sheaves. By and by
these were collected and carried to the threshing-
floor among the olives, where they were spread on a
broad ring of beaten earth. A pair of mild-eyed
lumbering oxen were led to the floor and set moving
round and round over the scattered sheaves. A
small boy followed at their tail to regulate their
paces, which he did by shrill clucks of encourage-
ment and vigorous prods from a goad. Two
women were busy spreading out the corn under
their hooves till all was well stamped out. Then
the beasts having been led aside, and the straw
removed, a man stepped into the middle armed
with an instrument like a gigantic shovel with a
wide spreading mouth; this he waved to and fro
with a horizontal motion above the ground, dex-
terously fanning away the chaff to the edge of the
floor. Finally the grain was gathered up and
carried in large baskets to the granary. Meanwhile in the field the reapers put in the sickle,
the binders bound the sheaves, and soon another
batch was ready. The oxen lumbered up, the
boy clucked and prodded and the whole process
was repeated.

These tasks were performed with a servile obedi-
ence, but without energy or zest. Even when from
time to time the slaves broke into a song (for there
seemed to be a song appropriate to each agricultural

occupation [1]), there was about their singing, as about their work, a listless and mechanical monotony. Unlike the town-bred slave who is alert and cheerful, these men have been dulled by incessant manual labour, sharing their drudgery with the oxen and becoming, like the very olive stumps, mere creatures of the soil. The same soil, however, which gives life and vigour to the olive takes the virtue out of a man, turning him little by little to a thing. This is perhaps why Aristotle, that incorrigible snob, denied that any one who spent his life in such labour could ever be called a full man. It must not be thought, however, that they were downright unhappy, nor that Demokrates was a hard master. Indeed, as masters went he was indulgent, treating them fairly and without brutality. Many of them had grown up under his eye, born and bred on the estate. No slave of his was ever turned adrift in old age. Some even preferred, like Sakas, to forgo their liberty. Thus even captives, they say, are reluctant to leave their very chains and prison houses. Nor was the slave's life altogether without private interests and diversions. Each was allowed a trifling pittance—the reward of industry and good behaviour—which he might hoard or spend as he pleased. Working hours were long; but when at last the summer-day was over, they were free to amuse themselves with a game or a gossip like any other mortals. Then there was a sudden transformation; the weary harvesters became

---

[1] As, for example, the song of the Hand-mill :—

> Grind, mill, grind, round and round !
> So Pittakos his subjects ground,
> King in Mitylené crown'd.

a cheerful group of noisy gamblers, eager to risk their petty earnings at the Mora ;[1] fists whipped out fast and furious ; breathless shouts set the whole place ringing, with ' Pente-Hex,' ' Pente-Tettara,'[2] as they rang the changes on the numerals. While the slaves were thus busied with their game, the master, the bailiff, and Alkibiades set out for home, threading their way under the olives.

The sun had gone down on a brazen, cloudless sky, as he had done every day for four months past : four burning months with never a drop of rain, and with none to come for perhaps as many more. The country ached with drought, and welcomed, like a sick man, the refreshing interval of night. The tired dust-laden trees revived; flowers filled the air with scents unrecognised under the heat of noon. A luminous enchanted twilight spread under the olives, as the western sky turned swiftly from gold to orange, and from orange to blood-red, and then grew pale again. The shadows crept over the plain in a slow tide which left the hills like islands still bright with the afterglow. A last ray lit up the great Temple above Athens. For a moment some golden figure on the roof flashed, and then was suddenly extinguished. Dusk fell : the frogs began their croaking down by the river : an owl hooted ominously in the tree-tops, at which Sakas shuddered and spat in his cloak. Then the dogs

[1] The Mora is still popular in the South. It is played as follows: Two men confront each other with right hands behind their back. Each determines how many fingers he will show, and then both whip out their hands and simultaneously shout a number. A rapid addition is made of the *combined* number of fingers shown by both. If either has guessed right, he wins the stakes.

[2] 'Five-Six,' 'Five-Four.'

of the farm barked and the three came to the gate.

The old housewife was there to welcome them. She had prepared a simple meal, under the porch, of barley cakes, dried figs, and sour stiff curds.[1] Her husband brought out a jar of last year's wine, and mixing it with water offered a draught to Alkibiades, not, however, before he had first poured a few drops into the cup which he emptied out upon the floor.[2] When the meal was over, the old lady went on with her spinning, and Demokrates began to talk, grumbling, as farmers will, over the trivial annoyances of rustic life; the drought, the plague of insects, sickness among his bees, damage done in his vineyard by a neighbour's goat, a quarrel with the same vexatious neighbour over a boundary stone and the unscrupulous verdict given by a third party, who had been called in to arbitrate.

It was evident that this last incident had sorely hurt his pride, for he must needs go step by step through the whole argument for the benefit of Alkibiades, who, when it was over, gave a sigh of relief and asked for a story. Demokrates was never reluctant to enlarge upon the adventures of his youth, the days when he had gone campaigning in the far-off east, and he began to tell of Kypros and of the mainland beyond, where men dwelt in the midst of limitless deserts, in cities of fabulous wealth, and where human victims were sacrificed in ivory temples to the images of beasts. Then he

---

[1] This sort of junket or 'sour milk' is still popular in Greece. It is called jaorti.

[2] The pouring of a libation before drinking, which survives in our grace before meat, is a custom which may still be met with in central Italy.

went on to tell (it was his favourite tale) of a raid
upon the Lykian coast, how they had landed in a
bay where no trees grew, and how, finding no leaves
to make themselves garlands, the men had sat down
to a banquet with wisps of straw around their heads.
He was in the middle of describing the enemy they
there encountered, and the battle which they
fought in the defiles, when suddenly he stopped.
' This is the day,' he said, ' yet I had forgotten ;
there are spirits that call.' With that he went
out into the court where the altar stood, and long
after Alkibiades had fallen asleep on his straw pallet,
the old man might have been heard mumbling
prayers and incantations in the darkness.

A GYMNASIUM

Sokrates, seated under the colonnade, converses with two boys; the slave attendant sits in an ill-bred fashion on the ground; near him lie an oil-flask and scraper.

In the court are youths racing, quoit-throwing and wrestling. The trainer stands by, with his official forked staff in hand.

A GYMNASIUM

III. EPHEBES

Health is best of blessings far;
Next Manly Grace and Beauty are;
The third is Riches without reproof;
And the fourth to be Young with the playmates of Youth.
(GREEK ANTHOLOGY.)

'THERE is education and education,' as Plato once had occasion to remark; that sort which makes a good shopkeeper or a good ship's captain does not by any means make a man. Education in this mean and narrow sense, the Greeks, with Plato, heartily despised. They set more store by the truer type which trains a man 'in all a man's qualities, setting him in pursuit of the high ideal of perfect citizenship, and teaching him to rule and to obey.' If then, at his eighteenth year, an Athenian ceased to be a boy, his education was far from finished, for it ended only with his life—a life given in constant suit and service to his sovereign lady the State. Upon the active duties of that life he now at eighteen was definitely embarked. Now it was that, upon due satisfaction being given (in his own parish hall first, and then before five hundred solemn councillors at Athens) concerning his birth, parentage and bodily fitness, he was permitted to inscribe his name upon the Civic Register. True, when quite a child, his father had enrolled him as a member of his Brotherhood with much old-fashioned ceremony and great consumption of sausage-meat. That was at the feast of the Apaturia or All Kindreds'

Day.   But it had been purely a matter, as we might
say, of the Church, and had nothing whatever to
do with the State.   That exacting mistress, now
that her child was a full-fledged citizen, took him
formally under her wing, requiring first that before
he could enjoy the privilege of registering a vote
or even of paying a tax, he should serve two full
years in a special military corps.   He became, in a
word, one of the Epheboi.

Of this event the outward and visible sign was
the cropping of his hair (though that had, as a
matter of fact, taken place some time beforehand),
and, secondly, the wearing of a uniform.   This,
like Greek clothes in general, was of a simple sort.
Little boys and full-grown men wore as a rule two
garments—first, a short chiton, which resembled
nothing so much as the shirt described by Falstaff
as ' two napkins tacked together and thrown over
the shoulders, like a herald's coat without sleeves.' [1]
The second garment was a rough plaid or cloak,
which could be made to envelop the whole figure
or could be slung loosely round one shoulder leaving
half the body exposed.   Now, between the ages of
eighteen and twenty, the ephebes substituted for the
voluminous cloak a short dun-coloured riding cape,
whose ends hung down in a point before and behind,
leaving the spear arm free.   Besides this he wore a
broad-brimmed felt hat, usually slung at the nape of
his neck.[2]

[1] The difference was that the Greek shirt was a *single* napkin doubled
round the body and caught in by a band at the waist.

[2] When this hat was worn by a character in a Greek play at
Cambridge, every one was irresistibly reminded of the modern boy scout.
In many ways there is some similarity between the two institutions.
For the dress of an Ephebe see the reproduction of a Greek vase on the
cover of this book.

Thus arrayed, he was taken up the stairs at the northern foot of the Akropolis rock, near to that cleft by which the Persians had once made their way up the cliff side ; there, in the sanctuary of Aglauros, he took the following oath : ' I will not disgrace my Sacred Weapons nor desert the Comrade who is placed at my side. I will fight for things holy and things profane whether I am alone or with others. I will hand on my Fatherland greater and better than I found it. I will hearken to the Magistrates and obey the existing Laws and those hereafter established by the people. I will not consent unto any that destroys or disobeys the Constitution, but prevent him whether I am alone or with others. I will honour the Temples and the Religion which my forefathers established. So help me Aglauros, Enyalios, Ares, Zeus, Thallo, Auxo, Hegemone.'

It was all very solemn ; and no doubt the young ephebe felt vastly important. That sense of importance probably wore off at the barracks, to which he was now consigned, at the edge of the Great Harbour. The unfamiliar discipline, the mess dinners (at the cost of 4 obols per head [1]), the drudgery of drill in full armour, all this was a new experience. The drill masters were strict, and we hear of ' beatings with rods and ills innumerable.' If one of them, Pythodones, won the gratitude of the people of Aixone through the splendid order he kept, the ephebes of the Kekropid tribe no doubt had a different tale to tell. I could wish they had

---

[1] The Attic drachma (equivalent in weight to the modern franc, though of course possessing superior purchasing power) was divided into 6 obols.

inscribed it on the reverse side of that complimentary pillar which the citizens set there in his honour.

Not that there was, however, any scarcity of relaxation. At night it would be the after-dinner game of Kottabos that turned all Athens crazy over flipping wine dregs at a mark. By day they had their pets, their dogs and tame quails and fighting cocks. They would play at simple games; one was called Day or Night. A tile blackened underneath was thrown into the air: if it fell black side uppermost, one party cried 'Night' and ran to their 'Home'; if it fell otherwise it was the turn of their opponents to fly.[1]

There were many other sports and competitions besides the ordinary programme of the training ground. The rich were told off to ride, and learnt how to sit a mettlesome charger bareback,[2] and how to vault on to its back without wounding the animal with the spur (they wore but one). Competitions in swimming and rowing were held in the bay. But the great event of the year was the Torch races: some of these were run singly, some by teams who carried on the torch by relays. For these vigorous training was undergone. When some fat fellow waddled in half a furlong behind the rest, puffing up his torch to keep it alight, he got jeers and slaps from the crowd at the Dipylon gate, and a bad name among his messmates into the bargain.

[1] This ancient form of Tom Tiddler's ground (or whatever most resembles it) may seem to some too simple for grown youths, but not to those who have seen bearded Italians bowling wooden discs along a public road like children.

[2] The Greeks considered riding a very difficult accomplishment. Xenophon in a striking passage remarks upon the disadvantages which beset a cavalryman meeting a hoplite upon terra firma. Yet the riders of the Parthenon Frieze have irreproachable seats.

There was all the banter and rude wit and good humour that there is in a public school. Such nicknames as Ape, Bat, and Monkey followed their owners even into after life. There was, in short, a great spirit of camaraderie. Clubs were formed with fancy names such as the Sons of Herakles. Alkibiades founded one of these we may be sure, calling them perhaps the 'Wolf-foots' after those outlawed ancestors of his own.[1] Such clubs, like those of the boys of a modern school, outlived these two short years; and festive reunions took place long afterwards. There grew up great friendships too, less historic perhaps than those of the Sacred Band at Thebes, but not for that the less real; these were smiled upon by the authorities, and the friends were free to go off on days of leave to hunt the hare on Hymettos or visit some old retainer in his farm under the mountain. At other times they would clamber round the 'rocky brow that looks on sea-born Salamis,' spearing cuttles off the rocks or swimming out to Psyttalea for a bet, and finally climbing the hill to lie down among the cyclamen and anemones and watch through the pine branches the sun burning in the clear blue sky, till Salamis below them shimmered in the heat, one of the party piping the while old songs of war or new songs of love, and near by a cicada chirping in concert from a thorn.

There may yet arise a master to paint for us the 'sunlit air' in which Perikles 'delicately trod,' or the blue in which Phormio cruised, but the artist that could paint the Athenian boy as he was, the

[1] The Alkmeonids, being exiled in early days, formed themselves into a guerilla band under this title.

C

sculpture of his proud face, the keen thoughtful eye, and the free grace of sunburnt limbs—he is dead and buried long centuries ago. That glory has departed from the earth, and the only memorial that has been left behind of it is in the outlines drawn by forgotten hands on the surface of a few shattered pots.

With the end of the first year, this playing at soldiers with its various pleasures and hardships came to an end. There was a great review held in the Theatre—thirty thousand eyes focused upon them from the huge hollow semicircle—and at the end of the review each ephebe received a shield and a spear from the State : *his* shield and *his* spear for life or for death—and for the proud possessors realities had at last begun. They were divided according to their tribes, and sent out as ' patrols ' from end to end of Attica : it was their duty to garrison frontier forts and outposts. They were frequently moved from place to place that they might acquire a good experience of their native hills. Campaigns might often turn on the knowledge of a mountain track, as the victors of Pylos knew. They were posted for months together in those old grey watch-towers overlooking the Megarid. Life up on the bleak ridges was often stern—when the snow was falling up among the pines at Phyle, and one must go with one foot bare to get a grip in the slush. Time hung heavy ; a few old charcoal-burners were all the society they knew. Even these could spin a good yarn of old campaigns round the fire, and the young men would pray fervently that their own chance might come with the summer.

The only diversion that came their way was an

occasional man-hunt. Some slave would murder his master and make off with the valuables of the farm ; or some vagabond treason-monger would find Athens too hot for him and take to the hills with a price on his head. Then since the ' patrols ' were also the police of Attica, there would be a leisurely pursuit, picnics by the roadside and eager speculations about some figure on the skyline. It was perhaps a relief when he was discovered to be a shepherd after all.

Rare visits to the capital occurred, generally for special festivals in which the ephebes were given a leading rôle to play. They escorted the mystery-march to Eleusis ; and they were prominent in the great procession at the Panathenaea. It was thought that by these ' Church parades ' the instincts of patriotism and religion were fostered and combined.

Finally, though this was rare, they might be called upon active service outside Attica. As when Demosthenes was planning one of his character-istically venturesome raids on Megara, he embarked some ephebe-patrols along with a few light-armed Plataeans, and stealing across the bay of Eleusis concealed them near to a temple of Ares—over against the gates of the city. These gates com-manded the entrance to the Long Walls that joined Megara to its port. Some Megarian citizens, who were in the plot, had for some time made a nightly habit of going out upon what—with the benign and unsuspecting approval of the town authorities— they gave out to be privateering expeditions. On the particular night when Demosthenes and his ephebes arrived, they were bringing back their boat up the fosse (for they kept it within the walls), and when the gates were opened to receive them, and the ephebes at that very instant charged down upon the gates—they contrived to get the boat most conveniently jammed half in and half out. The result was that the Athenian ephebes captured the walls. Of the final issue of the matter, in what perplexity the Megarians were next morning, and how the ingenious 'privateering' party made themselves oily all over that their Athenian friends, should they capture the city, might not mistake their identity, all this can be read in the history of Thukydides—but with the ephebes it has little concern, and with Alkibiades still less; for long before this his two years of probation were over, he had grown his beard and passed into the ranks of the citizen army.

DELPHI

DELPHI

In the foreground is the Sacred Close and the great Temple of Apollo.

The cliffs rise upon the left, and the great chasm down which flows the Kastalian Spring. Mt. Parnassos is hidden by the cliffs. Up the valley runs the road to the interior by which Oedipus came to Delphi.

IV. DELPHI

Thus then will God to wise men riddling show
Such hidden lore as not the wise can know;
Fools in a moment deem his meaning plain,
His lessons lightly learn, and learn in vain.

SOPHOKLES.

(Translation by F. W. H. Myers.)

THE dogs which the shepherds breed among the wild hills of Phokis have at all times been a lively terror to the traveller.[1] Savage and hungry as the very wolves, they never fail to scent a stranger across the whole width of a valley, nor to entertain withal an amiable fancy to devour him raw. There was small likelihood, therefore, that a solitary Athenian traveller, adventuring himself on the hills below Delphi about the fall of dusk, would escape from their attack. No prey could be more inviting than such a stranger, plump, tender and white-skinned. That stranger he was, there could be no shadow of doubt, for he wore the traveller's cloak and high strapped boots, and the broad-brimmed hat of felt such as pilgrims wear in mediaeval pictures. But perhaps it was his air of complacent Attic urbanity that most betrayed him, a complacency destined to be rudely shocked when at a turn of the track three monsters at once came at him with a murderous rush.

Poor fellow, everything seemed against him.

[1] 'Man kann gelegentlich durch die Hünde der Hirten etwas in Verlegenheit kommen.'—Baedeker's *Griechenland.*

Clearly it was not, after all, Apollo's wish that he should ever set foot in Delphi. Such an Odyssey of misadventures had beset him since he left Peiraieus. At Corinth in some thievish den he had been robbed of half his ready cash.[1] But he pressed on notwithstanding, and all that day he had sat in the stern of a Sicilian trader, watching the interminable nakedness of the grey shores and the snows of Parnassos mocking him from the distant clouds, and more than once he had wished himself at home again. At the port of Krisa where pilgrims for Delphi disembark, his slave had insulted the collector of tolls and had been clapped in the stocks. So that he himself was left alone to the tender mercies of the muleteers that drive the hardest of bargains and the stubbornest of beasts. Sixteen tedious furlongs covered on mule back threading through the olive yards of the plain ; then level ground had ended, and the ascent up the foot-hills of Parnassos began. His guide turned him out of the saddle— and he was left to follow on foot as best he could : this was ill enough, and presently he lost sight of both mule and driver round a bend of the road. Here was a sad plight for a man who in Athens, if he took a walk, had a slave at his heels with a folding stool. Twilight was falling ; the track grew steeper and wilder. He thought with a qualm how guides had before now been leagued with bandits. As such vague terrors grew, his superstitious fancy began to conjure out of the darkness all the fearful hobgoblins of fable and belief, Will-o'-the-wisp Empusas, fiends with snaky locks, dead men's spirits

---

[1] The wealthy and vicious town of Corinth was a notorious haunt of thieves.

that called for blood, and all the pale horrors of the
under-world—Charon and his ferry, Kokytos and
Styx. And now on a sudden at his back came a
threefold barking as of Kerberos himself.

Face to face with his triple foe, with nothing in
his hands but a staff and a large parasol, he was in
a helpless plight. Were he to sit down and feign
death, as did Odysseus in a similar predicament,
there was no Eumaios at hand for the rescue. Yet
sons of Kekrops have a ready wit : it was not for
nothing that he had fought and run at Koronea.
He faced promptly about, shouted a war-cry, waved
his staff like a brandished spear and lowered his
parasol shield-wise full in the enemy's face. Then
slowly he began to beat a cautious retreat back
foremost up the road. With a howl the baffled
enemy fled, leaving the traveller to pursue his way
unmolested. Just here the lonely track climbed
round the shoulder of the hill. As he looked back
he could see far below him the shining waters of the
creek and lights of the little port. Then as he
turned again to round the shoulder of the hill,
he felt on his cheeks a breath of mountain snows,
and the moment after a great sight opened to his
wondering gaze. Directly ahead of him and overwhelming in their black mass, a sheer wall of cliffs
shut out the sky. From the cliff's base a rocky
slope fell sharp away, till its roots were lost to view
in the remote blackness of a wooded gorge below.
Upon this slope lay that which made him pause.
For, climbing steeply up it, tier upon tier, terrace
upon terrace, rose a mass of low buildings, very white
under the rising moon, and out of the centre of these
loomed the monster pillars of a temple. Phoebos

Apollo was still, it seems, at hand to save his votary in hour of need. And never did pilgrim offer him a more grateful prayer. Yet more cheering still to the traveller's ear was the murmur of human voices, the friendly rattle of the bolts as they unbarred the Hostel door. And he entered for the night.

When next he emerged, it was to see the Sacred Close under a full blaze of morning sun. Picture a broad paved way running steeply aslant the slope, line it with buildings, in style of a uniform severity, in detail of infinite variety, shrines of regal offerings, treasure-houses of cities across the sea, shelters for pilgrims from the four ends of heaven; people well each alcove and colonnade with Princes wrought in stone and Pugilists of bronze. On the roof corners above set carved palmettes or floating 'Victories,' and under the gables, marble conflicts of heroic forms. Trace meanders of purple and azure to outline and emphasise each moulding, hang ornaments of brass and silver to decorate the spaces, and over the whole scene, if you would grasp it well, let there be thrown a burning sunlight, that makes the marbles glitter like crystals and sets the gilded victories flaming up towards heaven. You may close your eyes on the dazzling street, but the image of it seems to burn still behind the very eyelids, clear cut and fresh as the outline of sunlit snows against the blue of a Southern sky. And such is the vision of the Sacred Way at Delphi.

Overhead are the cliffs hiding from sight the snow-fields of Parnassos; below, the still valley sleeps in the sun; there is no wind to ruffle the olives, but all around the air stirs with small sounds in the grass and the busy murmur of far waters.

A hundred yards up the slope the Sacred Way bends at a sharp angle, and immediately above it rises Apollo's Temple: at this bend our pilgrim lingered before a shrine to pray: and now it is high time we discovered who the man is and what business brings him to Delphi. To that question the Hostel priest could perhaps supply some answer: or was it from pure politeness that he was careful to mix the drinks at supper with his own hand? And did he pry upstairs at midnight simply to see that his guests slept sound?

Alkibiades, when his father fell at Koronea, became the ward of two guardians: one was his uncle Perikles, and Ariphron was the name of the other. It was this Ariphron who now stood at the bend of the Sacred Way. Between them the guardians had a charge of some difficulty to perform: and the mission which had brought the one of them to Delphi concerned their ward's career. The problem what to do with boys is about as modern as man, it is certainly as old as Greece. For a Greek the choice was, it is true, somewhat circumscribed. Military service, for instance, was more of an interlude in his career than a career in itself. Politics was every man's pastime and no man's profession —indeed, for that matter, if a man wished to cut a popular figure on the Bema, he might well be engaged in some such lowly trade as leather-work and still be in the fashion.[1] For all this Alkibiades had a wide choice before him; he might turn merchant or manufacturer, he might be 'prenticed to a physician or an artist. Priesthoods were in the main hereditary: but in Alkibiades' case (one trembles for those

[1] Kleon, for instance, was a leather-worker and a popular demagogue.

august bodies) family influence was strong. He might even be trained professionally to run or box. The parents of one famous writer, in reliance on an oracular response, did actually train their son for the foot-race; but, as the event showed his genius not to lie in his feet, the victories of which the prophet spoke must have been the triumphs of the pen. So Ariphron being in doubt, like this innocent couple, concerning his ward's future, had like them thought it best to withhold his judgment till he knew what Delphi had to say.

There seems no stranger business in the ancient world than this innocent and firm belief in oracles. Why in that age of growing scepticism could a man not be content to forgo a visit to Delphi or Dodona, and simply spin with a drachma piece instead? There would, after all, have been two main advantages in that method. First, it would have been conclusive: this the oracle seldom was, as in the case of that man who was left in ' distressing uncertainty whether or no he should take the emetic.' Secondly, when the verdict lay simply between ' Athena ' and ' her owl,' [1] the odds on a right decision were at least even, a proportion which Apollo could hardly hope to emulate. Yet the Greeks now, as later, were an all too superstitious race, and on this occasion Ariphron was only one of many applicants for ghostly counsel. By an inherited privilege which gave him precedence of the vulgar herd, he should have been the first to consult the god, but that a Spartan who put in a similar claim forestalled him on a cast of lots. Ariphron

[1] The 'obverse' and 'reverse' of an Athenian coin were stamped in this manner.

therefore concealed his impatience and turned to inspect the monuments of the Close. He admired the great tripod set up after the battle of Plataea : he chuckled over that erasure which blotted out the self-laudatory dedication of Pausanias, the Spartan general : this he promised himself the pleasure of pointing out later to his Spartan rival afore-mentioned, throwing in perhaps a reference to the great Temple gable which would add something of a sting to the compliment. For the marble group erected therein, and representing Pallas doing battle with the Giants, had been given by members of his own family out of their private purse. High up on the temple wall he could read the famous inscription ' Know Thyself ' and the mystical letter E. But as he pondered over the wisdom of those sages who added as much to their own reputation by this inscrutable conundrum, as they advanced man's moral progress by the motto, his survey was suddenly cut short.

The time had come to pay his fee and choose his victim ; so selecting a sheep that seemed likely to accept its fate without undue commotion, he went up to the high altar below the Temple steps. Here a priest was awaiting him, not the grave immaculate figure that a priest should be, but a snuffling old fellow in dirty white robes, with a crown of shrivelled bay leaf on his shiny bald head, and an odour about him of unmistakable garlic. As he was ready to officiate, the sheep selected for its passive demeanour was urged gently to the spot, giving, as luck would have it, no ill-omened sign of resentment. A torch was taken from the altar-embers, and plunged in holy water. With it an acolyte then hastily bespattered

the whole party, calling loudly on them as he did
so to ' hold their peace.'   A piper struck a note, and
the priest, throwing his palms ostentatiously upwards, rattled off the ritual prayer in a high-pitched,
nasal sing-song.   Then, just as the victim was
quietly licking up some barley-corns which the busy
acolyte had been scattering over its head, the priest
sprang upon it with a knife, seized a tuft of hair on
its forehead and, severing it at a touch, threw it upon
the altar fire.   The blaze had barely time to die
away before the attendants had caught the animal ;
they stunned it ; then forcing its head up skywards, and holding a bowl to catch the blood,
they drew the knife across its throat.   With equal
speed it was skinned, the thigh bones wrapped in
raw fat, and laid among the embers.   The priest
now checked the flow of his prayers that he might
peer into the organs of the carcase—and presently,
without so much as extricating his nose, he pro-
nounced all to be propitious.   Apollo was, so to
speak, at home, and Ariphron might put his question
to the god.

He was accordingly ushered up the Temple steps,
while the priest departed on his way rejoicing.   For
was not roast mutton in prospect for his evening
meal ?

If any one enters a cathedral of the Greek Church,
and listens for a while to the dreary and perfunctory
performance of the office, he will soon turn for relief
to the pomp and solemnity of the building itself.
Something of the same contrast, one fancies, must
have been felt, however dimly, by the good Ariphron,
as he left the altar of sacrifice, and passing under
those massive pillars, entered the mysterious twi-

light and still presence of the god. A marble group of the Fates stood by the door, and he kissed his hand in reverence, half afraid that they might open their mouths and pronounce his doom upon the spot. The tablet containing the question which he wished to put was here taken from him and carried behind a tapestry that covered the end of the hall. This veil screened from profane eyes a group of priests and with them the woman that in a few moments was to be the mouthpiece of the god. To this end she had duly bathed in the Kastalian spring—a stream which descends in a thin cascade between those two halves of the great cliffs which they have named the Twin Tors; water trickles still in that rift or chasm, but if the homeless Muses ever revisit their favourite haunt in these prosaic days, they will now find a water-trough rudely cut into their grotto, and their pool fouled with the rinsing and scouring of the village washerwomen.

The Pythian maiden climbed on to a high stool supported on three bronze legs, and sat there inhaling the smoke from some laurel leaves which smouldered on a brazier, and chewing some more in her mouth. Half suffocated she swooned away,[1] and the fumes working in her brain fermented there a kind of epileptic frenzy which vented itself in loud hysterical cries. Of these the priests, hitherto indifferent, took careful note, and the fit dying away, they conferred together while the prophetess was coming to. The purport of her utterance, if purport there can have been, was written down, and then by an allowed tribute (though a doubtful com-

[1] There is not really enough literary (there is no geological) evidence to justify the theory of a mephitic chasm.

pliment) to Apollo's literary powers, was converted
into obscure and somewhat pedantic hexameter
verse.

The tablet of bay leaf on which it was written
was sealed and sent out by the usher who attended
at the curtain. On the further side Ariphron was
waiting in great impatience. He had approached
as near to the curtain as was proper : but so little
could he hear of what was passing that his eyes
soon wandered round the building, and discovered
through the gloom a curious object. It was a large
egg-shaped stone, wreathed with garlands,[1] and he
recognised it at once as the famous Navel or centre
of the earth. The spot had been fixed, so it was
said, by Zeus, who it appears had made this quaint
geographical discovery by loosing two eagles from
either rim of the world. It was here at Delphi that
they met. Ariphron was speculating whether the
new science that certain wiseacres were just then
propounding at Athens, would upset this comfortable theory when the tablet arrived. Wrapping
it in the fold of his cloak, he emerged into daylight,
and refusing the services of a self-styled Expounder
he carried it apart to read : it contained a single
line :—

CONQUEROR OVER THE SEAS, SO HE SHAME NOT THE
SONG OF THE MYSTAE.

The Immortal Doctor had given his prescription ;
the homeward journey gave ample period to digest
its meaning. Yet truth to tell the divine pronounce-
ment called for some more human interpretation.
In his perplexity Ariphron went round to consult

[1] This stone may have been in the Inner Sanctum. It is a doubtful
point.

his friends. Nikias, whom he stopped in the market, answered impatiently that he should obey the voice of heaven and, with a hint of pressing business with the priests, bustled off to the Metroun. Ariphron next called on the High Warden of the Mysteries, who held forth on the advantages of vegetable diet. Chancing on Sokrates by the Nine Fountains, he was bullied into giving two distinct and highly inconsistent definitions of Shame and Shamelessness. Sophokles was no better, wandering off on to the relation of dance and song in the cult of Dionysos. Perikles, who was mildly sceptical, gravely lectured him on the dangers of foreign conquest. Herodotos by ill-fortune had lately migrated to the West, or he would, for aught I know, have retailed some miraculous fustian imparted to him in a personal interview by a priest in Pekin. In a word, everybody gave him much good advice, scanty sympathy, and of light on the oracle none. 'What *that* meant,' the despairing Ariphron said, 'nobody knows but a bird in the air.'

TRIREME

TRIREME

The view is taken looking north across the Corinthian Gulf, a few miles west of Patras. A galley with close-reefed sail is being rowed near the shore. Note the oars arranged in triplets, the decked poop, and the 'eye' at the prow painted there as a charm against evil. The bronze beak may be seen more clearly on the galley beached upon the left.

V. A BATTLE AT SEA

'Safety lies in the *wooden walls*.'
(DELPHIC ORACLE.)

IF the grave old historiographers of Greece could
live again, how they would smile at our modern
theorists with their fragments of pottery or stone,
and their papyrus and statistics, and endless vilifica-
tion of German tracts. Thukydides having an inscription to quote, as often as not quoted it wrong.
To his idea the only source worth the name was
the living speech of Agora, Pnyx and Peiraieus, but
especially Peiraieus, for here the news was fresh at the
spring, and not as yet fouled by passing many mouths.

One morning in late autumn when the gales
begin, and such men in ships as are able to do so
get quickly home to port, Thukydides left his house
and turned down towards the Peiraieus. Athens was
just then a dreadful place : for the plague was rife ;
and it was good to come out upon the quay, and
better still to find a cock-fight there, and a handful
of young men in a gay mood. The sport was so
keen that even his eye never noticed a galley put in,
nor yet a little man passing by, as he presently did,
with a twelve-foot oar over his shoulder. Alkibiades, however, who had also joined the ring, had
quicker eyesight, and turned to grasp the stranger
by the hand. Now at Athens one does not so accost
a casual acquaintance in the street : there was even
something solemn about the handshake : for it was

the only symbol of final parting which the sculptors allowed themselves in those little scenes of farewell on tombstones. At any rate it was thus that one bade God-speed to a traveller or welcomed one returned from distant lands. Therefore Thukydides scented news. ' By the gods of Olympos,' he heard Alkibiades say, ' if it be not Kleigenes' brother, the barber, may I never be shaved again. What, my little fellow ? Home from playing watch-dog on the Straits with Phormio ?[1] Covered with glory, sir—and blisters ? God be praised that they have spared you yet awhile from the Banquets of the Blest. Zeus 'a' mercy ! but that look of yours will turn us all to stone. Relent, Odysseus, and spin us a wanderer's tale. Come now, we 're just ourselves : the battle at the Straits.'

A member of the new-comer's profession, for barber he was, could not even in antiquity resist so golden an opportunity for talking, and he took up his tale forthwith. ' One night—I have lost count of the moons long since—we were all of us ashore on the beach at Naupaktos, and very miserable we were. Zeus, but I never spent a night more pitifully. Such storms, such bursts of thunder, that by sunrise we were all wishing ourselves in Egypt, that we might never smell rain again. It was this same rain, I make no doubt, saved them in Plataea,[2] quenching, as they tell me, a big fire. But no matter,

---

[1] See Introduction. Phormio's squadron were blockading the Gulf of Corinth, thus cutting off all traffic between the Peloponnese and the West. A Spartan army was attempting to secure a land route across Aetolia and Acarnania.

[2] The Plataeans were besieged by the Spartans ; and an attempt was made to set fire to their barricades. A timely storm quenched the fire, as Thukydides relates.

for our part we were barely dry, and still busy draining the water from the holds, when a native longboat came clattering into port, at top speed with sail and oar, and sung out peremptorily for Phormio.

'To cut the story short, our score of galleys were soon run out, and we were pulling up the gulf, till our look-out at the bows sighted some twenty sail to the south of us and near in shore : undeniably Corinthians, and clearly on mischief bound. We fetched about to take stock of them. They were making little way, being clumsy barrel-bottomed craft, with a contraband cargo of military gentlemen, and a crew more at home, I dare wager, with short sword or pike than with thole-pin and halyard. Not wishing to oversail them, we took in a double reef and hung upon their rear as a Spartan hound follows at the tail of a sow's litter. Poseidon's Temple at the Naze should at our own pace have been cleared by noon ; but by Zeus, sir, it was after dusk ere we had made open water. Just then under cover of dark they made as if to anchor on the sly— but with such a clatter and ado that it would have needed the very cap of Hades to have effectually concealed them. We for our part were soon ware of it ; and lay off the northern shore to watch. A night at sea ! Oh, what is there to liken to it ? By the Dog, my masters, Salamis was a cheap victory in comparison with ours : they at least spent the previous night ashore. It was the better side of midnight when a marine on deck roused us all by shouting that the enemy were already half across the gulf. So we are in for a battle, thought I to myself, and remembered my hands and back

were sore, and strange to say the latter consideration, the soreness I should say, troubled me by far
the more.

'There was not long to wait: a snatch of dithy-
rambs [1] was chanted to the god and a pint of the
best Pramnian [2] spilled on the deck for luck; and
we weighed anchor without more ceremony. In
the grey of morning I could just see them from my
bench dumping the anchor stones on deck, lowering
the main mast in its crutch, and making ready the
battle sails against need. Then they drew the
canvas awning over, and left us ten score shivering
souls in the hold as black as Charon's ferry. I was
on a trireme,[3] you must know, and so had two
partners to my bench. One was that starveling poet
Kinesias, a melancholy fellow who had never before
been to sea. The other was a ferryman from
Salamis, he was as brawny as Milo—and had a ready
turn of wit, for he set us a riddle to hearten us.
" King, Satrap, and slave," it ran, " ploughing one
furrow." " The King," says he, without staying for
an answer, " that 's me on my throne up here: the
Satrap is Kinesias upon my step, and the slave is the
fellow there down on the floor," meaning me. For,
as you must know, each bench in a trireme arises in
three levels, as it were three steps towards the middle
of the ship. But the oar of the top step and the oar
of the middle step and the oar of the lowest step all
pass through one rowlock-port, and all strike the
sea even, ploughing, as a man might say, one furrow.
It 's well enough if the sea is calm and you keep

---

[1] A popular metre of a swinging unrestrained type.
[2] Pramnian wine was a special favourite.
[3] See Note at end of chapter.

good time : but in a heavy swell it 's long odds you will bark your knuckles on your partner's oar.

'As our Salaminian expounded his riddle the ship's master thought fit to leave his cabin aft, and strut up the middle gangway to give us a lecture. At home he keeps a vegetable store and has made a fortune in garlic since the supply from Megara was stopped,[1] a close man of business if you will, but no soldier nor sailor either. And though primed for the nonce with much second-hand eloquence, he had a tell-tale yellowness about the gills. With the hold as black as night and him chattering like any cricket, I put my head to the porthole that I might pull down the leather flap and make all water-tight. As I did so, I saw Phormio's ship go by, smooth as an eel and as black as pitch. All but the great scarlet eye, painted under the prow, and the gilded figure of Pallas shining above the beak. I could see the teeth of the beak, too, and the Admiral's purple ensign at the mast ; but it was only a glimpse, for the boat-swain was crying "Ready," and I must pull in my head. Another word and we were rattling away like a race, to the time of the flute, and the boatswain's call of "R-r-rhý-pa-paí-pa-paí!"

'Kinesias, who was blue with fright and sickness, kept asking nervously if all aboard had been baptized into the Holy Mysteries ; and presently when one of the marines on deck shouted that the enemy were within hail, he fell to muttering prayers, till the boatswain called him to silence. At our approach, so I heard from a marine, the enemy formed a ring, prows outward. Have you seen a hound

---

[1] One of Perikles' first acts of offence against Sparta was to declare a blockade against all exports from her ally Megara.

move in circles about a crouching hare ? just so we circled round them for a while. And at dawn, when a fresh breeze sprung up which set them jostling one another like pilchards in a net, the trumpet from Phormio's ship gave us the sign to charge. The boatswain quickened the time ; we rowed for very life : one long, long moment and then came "ship your oars," just as we grazed a hand-breadth from a Corinthian hulk. Their marines on deck dropped the grappling hooks to catch us : but they fell late and missed the ship. Their men were ready on the deck too, meaning if possible to board us ; one mad fellow caught at our rigging with a sort of scythe and came dancing along at the end of it, hopping like a flea in a blanket, all down his deck.

'But our ship shaved past and, as it did so, every oar of them from prow to poop was snapped clean off at the rowlock-ports, clean as the hairs fall, sir, under my razor's blade. Then the helmsman put our steering paddle hard to port ; we swung round, and before you could cry "cuckoo" we had charged again, crashing into their stern. Our whole boat shivered at the shock, till you would have sworn the girding ropes would burst, but not a plank started : while as for them, our beak ripped their timbers with its bronze teeth, and there they lay water-logged and helpless.

'We secured such of the crew as had not swum away and then took the hulk in tow. As we made for port we raised the song of victory—and we must have waked old Archilochos down in Hades with his "Ri-fol-di-ray for the hero of the day." [1] As we

---

[1] The 'Tenella Kallinikos'—the first word is merely an imitation of the trills of a pipe or flute.

swung up the narrows, we could see the folk in Patrae scuttling up into their keep, in a desperate hurry and alarm at the turn things had taken. Once on shore we set to work and hacked the figure-heads from the captured ships, and with them we raised a trophy out on the Naze cliffs. So it was, sir, that we handled their precious fleet, and we balked the Spartan schemes into the bargain, for not so much as one skilly-fed Helot ever reached General Knemos in Aetolia ; and he, for the matter of that, suffered defeat at the very self-same hour, so men told us who came from the inland parts. Aye, Corinth, "son of Zeus," [1] as they call you, it was a bonny harvest that you reaped that day ! '

Then Thukydides went home and set to work upon the third roll of his history, which we term the eighty-second chapter of his second book.

NOTE ON THE ARRANGEMENT OF OARS IN A TRIREME

The arrangement of oars in a trireme is still a much debated point. On the commonly accepted theory, the oars were in three banks, one above the other : this would give three tiers of rowers, the top tier sitting over the heads of the second, the second over the heads of the third. At this rate, however, the man on the top bench would be required to pull an oar double or treble the length of that of the man nearest the water—which is absurd. Time-keeping would be a farce.

Let us turn to the alternative suggestion. Suppose (as is but reasonable) that all oars be rigged on the same level, so that all the blades strike the water at an even distance

---

[1] An expression of somewhat obscure origin, to which allusion is often made in the Classics.

from the ship. Then arises the question, what means the number 3 implied in the name *tri*-reme?

Now we are expressly told that the oars were not all equal, but of different lengths, 'like the fingers of the hand.' Suppose therefore that they be grouped in threes, No. 1 of each triplet being a little longer than No. 2, and No. 2 a little longer than No. 3; all three passing out of one oblong slit or porthole, and pivoting upon thole-pins placed six or nine inches apart. How will our rowers sit now? Not one above the other, but *side by side*. No. 3 with the short oar will sit nearest to the ship's bulwarks. No. 2 will sit elbow to elbow with him, but, as the more advanced position and the greater length of his oar demand, his thwart will be slightly to the front of No. 3 and on a slightly higher level. In the same way No. 1 will sit at the side of No. 2, but slightly in advance and at a slightly higher level. Thus we find our rowers still ranged in three tiers—and the only question is whether it will work in practice.

Some difficulty there might still be in keeping time: but no more than accurate training might overcome. The position of the thole-pins could easily be adjusted somewhat aslant, in such a way that each oar should pivot on the proper point of its shaft. There is one curious fact in confirmation. During the Middle Ages, it seems, galleys were actually built at Venice which were propelled by oars thus grouped in triplets. Not so long ago, under the direction of Admiral Fincati of the Italian navy, experiments were made with a boat rigged in this fashion. The model achieved remarkable success, and gave a speed of some nine miles per hour. The illustrations show a trireme rowed on this system. The theory is explained more fully by Mr. A. B. Cook in the *Classical Review* of 1905.

THE INTERIOR OF A TRIREME

For explanation of the arrangement of the rowers in triplets, see Note at end of the chapter.

A piper is giving the time to the oarsmen, his pipes held in place by a sort of muzzle or head-strap. On deck is a marine.

INTERIOR OF A TRIREME

VI. A LAND BATTLE

These that their country might continue free
    From sorrowfullest slavery,
Wear the wan livery of dusty death,
    But whosoever reckoneth
The prize of their endeavour, let him stand
    And bravely die for fatherland.

(GREEK EPITAPH.)

ON a day when men in Athens were already growing
weary of the war, Trygaios the vine-dresser [1] came
up from sentry-go on the Long Walls. Strolling
over the Pnyx hill and down into the hollow beneath
the Areopagos rocks, he passed hard by the open
space where the ten Tribal Patron Saints stand in
effigy, and saw there a great crowd gathering. He
turned aside somewhat wearily (for his watch had
kept him up all night) to see what this new thing
might be. Some one was reading aloud. Indeed
several persons were reading aloud with great vigour,
all at once (for in Athens no one ever reads silently
and to himself). That which they were reading
was written in charcoal upon the whitened boards
suspended on the pedestals of the effigies aforesaid.
Alkibiades and other young dandies, fresh from
cavalry drill at the Lykeion, outside the walls, tossed
their long hair [2] as they passed, clinked their spurs
upon the stones and gave a loud cheer for the

---

[1] Trygaios is the name of the hero of Aristophanes' *Peace*. He
represents the agriculturalist's point of view.

[2] The cavalry by a special privilege wore their hair long.

generals. Trygaios wondered at their impudence, seeing what was the popular feeling at the time : but he soon ceased to wonder any more when the news, passing rapidly from mouth to mouth, reached his ears ; it was marching orders for all Athens—every male that could bear arms, from the raw recruit of eighteen to the veteran of threescore and ten. Well might Alkibiades and his friends, the young fire-eaters, look pleased, but for Trygaios it was very different : he had not even the heart to search for his own name on the list ; he thought instead of the long-promised peace and the old farm at the head of the plain and the seeds he had meant to sow when autumn came, and very heartily he cursed the generals and all that deal in war.

Like Trygaios the vine-dresser, every one grumbled, and like him every one acquiesced ; and the evening was spent in much wild conjecture over the campaign, in abuse of Hippokrates the general, and in diligent polishing of arms. But that is, after all, the true spirit of Democracy. Trygaios unhooked his second shield from the ingle-nook and brightened its leather face with oil. His wife made up a bundle of onions and garlic in a knapsack and put in three days' rations of salted fish. Then after a farewell to his children, and a cheery word to his wife, Trygaios was ready to go at early dawn to the rendezvous at Kolonos. Those were his orders, and what the next move might be, neither he nor any one else could tell.

Organised secrecy was scarcely suggested by the babel and confusion of that meeting. As each squad [1] fell in with its tribal company, the orderly

---

[1] λόχος = squad.   τάξις = tribal company.

screamed out the muster-roll. Some names passed
unanswered. At Ameipsias' name none spoke : he
was dead of the plague. But when Meidias did
not reply, there was a buzz of comment. 'At
home with sore eyes,' said his friends : 'an excuse
as old as Thermopylae,' said others, and hinted at
a trial for desertion. Gaps, however, were few
enough—all Athens was out ; striplings with only
half a training, veterans that had not held a spear
since Oenophyta, twenty years back; the very
rabble of the poorest class were there, useful as
skirmishers at a pinch—even the 'outlanders' had
been pressed into service in the ranks. Yet for all
that it was a very exceptional muster there was
never a hint of whither they were bound. Some
wiseacres nodded their heads very sagely, but they
knew no more than the rest. Soon, however, the
word of command was given, the squads filed past,
the cooks packed up their saucepans, the muleteers
whipped up their beasts, hoplites' bodyservants
shouldered their masters' shields ; slowly, with some
confusion and with a great undisciplined crowd of
hawkers, slaves and sutlers straggling in its rear, the
great line got fairly under way. When finally the
van set its face for the mountains to the north all
doubts vanished, and they knew that Boeotia was
their goal. There is a pass over these northern hills
called Dekelea, which afterwards became famous as
a stronghold of the Spartan enemy. To this dip,
which can be clearly seen from Athens, the cavalry
now galloped on ahead. Alkibiades led the way,
seated on a mettlesome charger and carrying a new
and gorgeous shield on which the device of a golden
Cupid was blazoned. He was the envy of the corps,

and no wonder : he might well have stepped down straight from the Parthenon Frieze.

' Will it be an army ? ' the sleepy Boeotian shepherds vaguely wondered as the next day dawned and their panic-stricken flocks came scampering up the slopes. They were not left long in doubt, for they could soon see great clouds of dust rolling down the valleys through which the road runs to the plain. Their dull wits were still slowly waking to the truth, when the first Athenian files struck level soil. A messenger was then dispatched in a hurry to Thebes, but before he was well on his way these same ominous dust clouds were steadily creeping across the plain and moving along the shore of that blue lane of water which men called Euripos or the Fair Current,[1] because it is very subject to tides. On the farther side of the water the wall of Euboean mountains rises and falls, in swelling outlines, and up the strait westwards ; where it begins to narrow in, there is a low hill lying back some distance from the shore. On it, conspicuous above a cluster of low red-tiled roofs, there stands a temple. It is Delion : and they are at their goal at last.

The place was empty when they reached it. The servants of Apollo had not awaited their arrival : only the huge ungainly idol was there to receive them, ' with a smile on his face like any silly Theban,' as Alkibiades irreverently put it. The image[2] was certainly not beautiful ; but the precinct offered

---

[1] Doubtless a euphemism for the Foul Current. Cp. Euxine Sea, Eumenides, etc.

[2] The statues of an early date always wore an idiotic simper which the artists seem to have considered a lifelike expression. Boeotian art was always a little backward, and the Boeotian character was always a laughing-stock in Athens.

excellent shelter to a tired army. They soon made themselves at home, dipped with their helmets in the rock-cut cistern of the god, smirched his marble columns with the smoke of their camp fire, finally spread their sheepskins under his cloister walls, and, one by one, went impiously to sleep. Soon all that could be heard was the sentries going on their rounds and passing the bell along from post to post.

Overnight, General Hippokrates had viewed the place carefully, and judged it to have the makings of a first-class fort. Accordingly when the sun was up, it was all hands to the work. Walls were heightened, doorways blocked, timber towers were knocked together from rafters and beams, and mounted at the weakest points. An outer palisade and fosse were part of the scheme ; and here it was lay the chief business of the day. The earth which was thrown up from the ditch was packed together between a framework of wattle-fencing, and vines cut from the neighbouring fields were thrown in to make it bind. Here and there rough facings of stone were added, formed from boulders out of the stream bed or blocks from the ruined cloister. As may well be imagined, this work continued all that day, and most of the next. It was past the hour of the midday meal before all was complete. Then Hippokrates, feeling secure of the strength of his position, and keeping only some few picked troops with which to garrison the new-made fort, gave orders for the march. Having accomplished his purpose, he was ready, like the king of Spain in the song, to lead his army home again. The men were naturally in good spirits, and, as they armed, they joked. Years afterwards, forgetting the disasters

that followed, men talked of the incidents of that
arming: how Kleonymos, 'that huge hill of flesh,'
needed two men's help to strap him into his breast-
plate, and how when the trumpet sounded, Sokrates
was still stamping up and down with his helmet on,
and with the plume in his hand, blindly fumbling
for the socket on his crown.

Scarcely ten furlongs had been covered, and the
Attic frontier barely crossed, when the heavy infantry halted and let the light troops go by. They
laid their shields on the ground where each man
stood, and composed themselves for the midday
siesta, ever jealous, as Greeks were, of the appointed
times and habits of their daily round, and sadly
inattentive to the principles of strategy.

At this very moment, an hour's march away
behind the hills, Pagondas was already haranguing
the levies hastily raised from Thebes. This, indeed,
seems a foolish and unnecessary delay when all turned
upon speed. But it is one of the axioms of Greek
warfare that though you may bring your men to
the battlefield, yet unless you have first assured
him that the gods are with him, that the omens are
good, and (if possible) that his cause is good also,
unless, in short, you have well persuaded him that
he has every reasonable prospect of victory, he will
make a poor fight of it. This delay gave time for
news of their danger to reach the Athenians.
Warning was sent back to Hippokrates, who immediately hurried up from Delion. He found the
heavy column on the road again; they were marching as usual, in squads eight deep and four abreast;
and squad followed squad, marshalled, as it were, like
a long line of dominoes, end on end. Hippokrates

gave the command to form battle order at once, and the men passed it down by word of mouth from rank to rank. It was a somewhat lengthy manœuvre, and not easy over the rough ground. The front squad halted, and the other squads moved up and formed upon its left, so that the squads were now placed like dominoes side by side, and the line therefore stood eight deep. In this manner the leaders in each squad came to the front, and that (as will be seen from the character of the fight) was an important matter. But of all the front-rank men none were more important than our friend Trygaios. For he was posted at the point of danger, Number One on the right. Hitherto he had stood his ground watching the shield wall lengthen and lengthen till it reached the shore far away to his left. Then came the order, 'Turn upon the spear,' and wheeling upon Trygaios as pivot-man, the whole army swung round right-handed till they came into position along the line of the road. Here they rested. There was indeed no call to go out to meet the enemy, for the fight must take place down on the plain or not at all. This was a necessity imposed by the nature of the country. Above the point where the ploughland ceases, the hill-sides are clothed knee-deep in spiky moorland scrub, under which lies a loose litter of stony rock such as would rejoice the heart of a cony, but is sheer despair to a top-heavy hoplite with a twenty-pound shield on his arm, not to mention the greaves and breast-plate that encumbered his person. An agile man unarmed might leap lightly from boulder to boulder, but the hoplite would flounder after the first step on such treacherous foothold. Now since this is the

E

character of all Greek mountains, the Greeks, holding that an honest battle should be fought between
two lines of men both armed to the teeth, accepted
the plain, by a sort of etiquette, as the only proper
place for a fight. In their position on the plain the
Athenians therefore stood their ground, waiting
for the enemy and shading their eyes under the
westering sun for the gleam of shields descending.
These moments Hippokrates turned to ready use :
the critical moment called for speech, and on the
instant the general became the orator, ' his eyes
flashing fire, his frame all quivering with emotion,
wielding his every limb, he poured forth the eloquent
torrent of his commands and prayers.' The customary appeals came aptly to his mouth—Temples
of the Gods, homes and country, wives and children,
the memory of past victories, the horrors of defeat
—not half the commonplaces of battlefield rhetoric
had rolled off his tongue when Pagondas' shields
were sighted on the skyline. His last words were
drowned in a clatter of arms, as every man by instinct drew nearer under the cover of his neighbour's
shield. Even the wheezy ill-conditioned baker
from Peiraieus could feel a borrowed confidence in
the shelter of the burly woodman at his elbow.
Only for Trygaios, Number One on the right, there
remained still a doubt and a fear. His, as has been
said above, was the post of danger. For, though
the hoplite's shield is large and covers him from
chin to knee, and though above the rim of the shield
there is solid bronze helmet, and below the rim of
the shield solid bronze greaves, and though thus it
is true that he presents *from the front* an armour as
impenetrable as a tortoise's shell, yet take him upon

the flank and you may pass his guard as easily as you scotch a tortoise on its back. A light cuirass and a kilt of leather is all that protects his vitals. This is the reason why Trygaios hardly heard the trumpet call and took no part in the trolling of the War-hymn, for he was thinking with exceeding anxiety how he might swerve just so little to the right as to clear the extreme shield of the Boeotian left and avoid attack on his unguarded side. A little manœuvring, thought Trygaios to himself, and he at any rate should not be the one to be outflanked. Oddly enough, Number One on the enemy's right was all the while thinking the self-same thoughts.

A last order down the line : the standards were hoisted and spears rattled to the shoulder. A few long springing steps and they fell to the couch. Then, with a kind of exultant jodel, ' Elleleleu, Elleleleu,' the armies sprang to the shock of col-lision. The extreme left, as it so happened, found itself checked by some stream beds that had fur-rowed the plain with miniature ravines, but the rest of the line closed, like two bulls that struggle with heads down and horns locked. It was a critical moment. The two armies pushed and heaved, swaying this way and that in the breathless grapple.[1] Panting, shouting, thrusting and fending thrusts, they strained and heaved and strained again ; then a thing happened. On the left centre, where Pagondas had purposely massed his men twenty-five deep to the enemy's eight, the weight of the Theban line began to tell. The Athenian host wavered, broke,

[1] The whole business must have borne a strong resemblance to a football scrum—(although of course the fighters did not put their heads down)—and naturally a scrum that is twenty-eight deep would get the better of a scrum of eight.

and took to its heels. Even their right wing, which was on the point of routing the Thespians opposite, took alarm and followed the rest. The disaster was complete.

So long as the ranks still held their ground not a man had flinched, and even the wounded, if here and there the shield wall were pierced, had been stayed up in the press. Now all was changed; no longer was heard the sound of labouring fighters breathing deep, nor the slow grinding of shield on shield, but instead the sharp cries of the hunted hoplites, and the rattle of shields flung desperately behind them, and (with yet more ominous a note) the ring of bronze helmets as they met the stones, and a moment after the thud of the hard ground beaten by the heels of men, but that (as in Homer's grim saying) 'not for very long.'

As the rout swept by, the cavalry hung upon the wings ; least of all was Alkibiades in a hurry to retire : he lingered upon the outskirts watching what he might see or do. Across his path lay a wide, steep-banked gully, a waterless river-bed carved out by winter rains, and very difficult for a horse to cross. Now as he was picking his way from stone to stone and leading his horse, he caught sight among a clump of junipers of a shield and under the shield a man, or such portions of his person as were grudgingly exposed to view. Under this cover the man appeared to be scrambling to a place of safety ; but at Alkibiades' approach he peered nervously out, jumped upon his feet, flung away the shield, and without so much as a look behind, fled away roaring and bellowing with all his lungs. In an instant Alkibiades had recognised his stout

countryman Kleonymos ; he never knew the fellow
run so fast, and it was worth the day's defeat, he said,
to see the fat monster leaving the field, not like your
wounded hero *on* his shield, but *under* it. That
lost shield was the joke of the whole town and the
butt of comedy writers for years to come. The very
urchins shouted ' Delion ' after the fat glutton in
the streets, till his name became a household word
for cowardice.

When Alkibiades had crossed the gully and the
rout had passed him in a whirl, a solitary figure
came in sight, far behind the rest. It was no other
than his friend Sokrates moving along without fuss
or flurry, at a long swinging stride, the same pace,
no faster and no slower, as he used in Athens—at
home it was thought a trifle vulgar to walk fast,
and whenever he passed through the market he set
all the loungers laughing : but Sokrates would not
bate his pace for their mockery, neither would he
quicken it now for all the regiments of Thebes.
His head was cocked in the air in a comical style, and
from time to time, if an enemy approached, he threw
over his shoulder a cautionary glare as if to say ' Who
dares to meddle with me ? ' Unhappily in crossing
the gully he missed his footing on a loose stone, and
would have been run through there and then as he
lay, had not Alkibiades jumped to his side. He kept
off the enemy, till Sokrates had picked himself up,
which done, he resumed his retreat with the same
imperturbable demeanour. Alkibiades for his part
now vaulted on to his horse's back, and made off after
the rest to the border town of Oropos.

Here the beaten army was at least safe, for the
pursuit stopped at the approach to the town—but

behind them (and here lay the sting of the defeat)
hundreds upon hundreds of friends and kinsmen lay
on the field, dead and, worse still, unburied.[1] Now
it was part of the etiquette of warfare that a truce
should follow the battle for the purpose of burial ;
and the Athenians having come off second best,
sent a herald with the customary request. Upon
the way their enemy met a Theban messenger coming to demand on his part that the occupants of
Delion who had profaned Apollo's precinct should
quit Boeotian soil. The Athenians, arch-casuists
as they were, prevaricated, declaring that Delion
was no longer Boeotian soil, since they themselves
had captured it. The Thebans sent back the curt
reply, 'Quit Boeotia, and then bury what you will.'
So the quibbling argument went on : it was like
some sophist fencing with a country clown. The
Theban envoys were refuted but unconvinced.
They wagged their forefingers in protest and stuck
to the point ; neither side would give way. And
all the while that the heralds passed and repassed
between the camps, the corpses lay naked and
festering in the furrows, and the siege of Delion
went on. Then one day the Thebans invented an
ingenious kind of fire hose, set the palisade alight,
and carried the fort by storm ; thus the knot was
cut, and a discreditable squabble ended, the corpses
were buried, and Phoebos Apollo came by his own
again.

[1] The defeated army from the nature of the case lost out of all proportion more than the victors. One battle is recorded in which the
losers had three thousand killed, and the Spartans, who kept their ranks,
no more than eight.

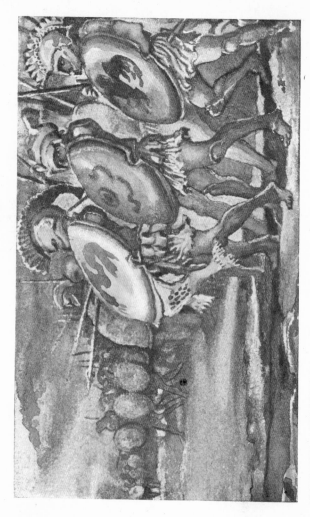

HOPLITES ADVANCING TO BATTLE

HOPLITES ADVANCING TO BATTLE

The hoplite's panoply consisted of a helmet with horse-hair plumes, cuirass of metal or studded leather, leather kilt over linen shirt, short sword at waist, bronze greaves, spear six feet long, and a shield generally of hide, and often provided with a leather flap to protect the legs.

VII. THE MYSTERIES OF ELEUSIS

Thrice happy he, who, ere he dies, that vision gains; he knows
The heavenly source of life and what its close.

K. J. FREEMAN.

'COME, give me an answer, Sokrates, and let there be no evasions. How comes it, pray, that you, who in other matters of religion are the most scrupulous of men, have never yet enrolled yourself among the number of the Initiate?'

'Softly! my dear Alkibiades, softly! I cannot answer you yet. For lies it not with you rather to act teacher to me and to convince me first, that, by so doing, I should be the gainer? Do you therefore answer my question and tell me the truth. If you became the apprentice to a cobbler, would it not be in the hope of learning something new about boots and shoes?'

'I could indeed have no other reason under the sun.'

'Do you then submit yourself to the discipline of the priests and those who profess knowledge in such matters, with any other hope than to ascertain something new about Life and Death and things Divine?'

'That, Sokrates, is just such a method of argument as I have learnt to expect from you. Nevertheless I will yield you the point, and admit that I have this hope, and not this merely, but that I shall learn many things greatly to my profit con-

cerning the life after death and concerning many
other holy things, which to reveal, however, would
not be proper, seeing that I am to be initiated and
you are not.'

'That would certainly be neither proper nor
desirable, Alkibiades. But answer me again. Have
you not read what Homer has to say upon this topic,
both in other portions of his poem, and where he
conjures up before Odysseus the " souls of many
heroes dead " ? '

' And if I have, Sokrates, what follows then ? '

' Are you content with the assurances which the
poet gives us that men do live after death ? or, let
me put it thus : would it be true to say that a life
such as Homer describes and in such a place,
"shadowy and grim," where the souls of the departed
go fluttering and gibbering like bats, is it true, I say,
that such a life appears to you no more worth having
than in the vulgar phrase, " a donkey's shadow " ?
What do you say ? '

' By Zeus, that is just my feeling ! Indeed, I
would answer in Homer's own words, " Better to live
the serf of a liege lord than to reign king among
the dead." '

' And, O Alkibiades, have you so soon forgotten
our words of yesterday, and do you not recall how
you admitted, though loath you were to do so, that
of what lies beyond the grave we can have no cer-
tainty whatsoever, but only hope and expectation ?
Yet now you reject the testimony of Homer and
cheerfully embrace the promises of the priests,
knowing full well that neither they nor he, nor you,
nor I have seen (nor can see, before the day of death)
the facts and realities of Hades, and that no man,

except in fables, has ever visited and brought back news of those regions, concerning which these priests of yours so confidently affirm such and such things ? '

' When, Sokrates, I have returned from Eleusis, maybe I will answer your question—and maybe I will not.'

And with that, leaving the imperturbable old free-thinker to the happy contemplation of his own self-taught creed, Alkibiades departed.

Now just as great a danger (though it escaped the notice of that shallow fellow, the maker of proverbs) lies in too great a fund of knowledge as in too little. The philosopher sifting the problems of the religious truth is repelled by the husk and misses the core. The cheerful fool may swallow both, and the Mysteries, half savage survival of a seed - time ritual, half the vague imaginings of a profound mystical instinct, contained beyond all doubt a core of truth concerning the immortal soul. That the pagan world, reading a simple parable in the passing and recurrence of the seasons, should have plunged, year by year, at autumn, into a brief ecstasy of im- pulsive adoration towards the great Earth-Mother, and out of all the hocus-pocus of her Mysteries caught wistfully the shadow of a hope, and a dark hint, if no more, of the tremendous secret, may seem strangely foreign to our modern minds, but it is no more than the truth. For the hearts of the people craved for something which the orthodox religion of the day could never give. The national theology appealed to intellect, literary imagination and patriotic ardour, rather than to the more elemental feelings. The lofty instinct of their

poets had purged it of grosser and merely popular
elements ; the subtle philosophy of their thinkers
had ennobled it, raising it clear above the level of
vague superstitious emotions ; the state, too, with
its love for the clear-cut and definite, had moulded
it by strict canons and empty formalities. And
yet in this process of refinement something had
been lost. Zeus, Apollo, Hermes and Athena were
well enough for pompous ceremonials ; but little
might they reck, sitting aloft on their Olympian
pedestals, of the innermost conflict and passionate
yearnings of simple human souls. To such, these
high abstractions of Wisdom, Justice, Poetry and
Art must have seemed at best cold and condescending
divinities ; as well seek private consolation from the
Sphinx herself. So, just as the faltering faith of the
mediaeval peasant had recourse to the magical
virtues of the Boxford Crucifix or Our Lady of
This or That, the Greek in his sorrows or perplexities
would turn perhaps to the homely image of some
rustic shrine, dignified maybe by the high-sound-
ing title of Athena, Zeus or Aphrodite, but in
reality taking its origin from some local superstition
infinitely old, and linked, as often as not, with
strange barbaric rites. But more and more did
they turn, as time went on, to the more mysterious
attraction of those wild ecstatic cults of Sabazios,
Dionysos, the prophet Orpheus and the rest, which
came to Greece nobody knows how, and sent men
and women revelling and hymn-singing through
the woods and countryside. Worshipped at first
in private by select and privileged bands, these
new gods became gradually linked with the more
orthodox beliefs ; and thus regularised, their rites

took a place among the other ceremonials of the public calendar, offering at due seasons a useful outlet to pent-up emotions, and easing the burdened soul of its half-felt consciousness of sin.[1]

In short, it was the fashion of all cultured Athenians at least to make the journey to Eleusis. So it was that Alkibiades with a conventional complaisance and in a keenly inquisitive frame of mind, became a candidate for initiation. Shortly after, as his custom was, he turned the whole thing to ridicule.

There would not be space here to describe at length (even from our most imperfect knowledge) the wearisome preliminaries. They were long, for initiation was a solemn matter and not lightly to be undertaken. It cost more than a twelve-mile tramp to Eleusis. For many months previous the candidate must undergo an arduous probation, pass tedious hours listening to ghostly admonition and submit to humiliating scrutiny. For many days he must curb his appetites and regulate his diet with all the scruple of a Jew. The flesh of domestic animals was by a strict rule denied him ; he might touch neither pomegranate nor bean. This and much else there was to puzzle and perhaps disgust a man, before he might enter upon the full state of blessedness, and in crowning revelation know the joys of the Elect. During spring a foretaste came in the local celebrations at Agrae close to the city,

[1] True, the purity demanded of the Initiated was a ceremonial rather than a moral purity. But it is not fanciful to trace in these mystic rites (particularly in those introduced from the East at a later date, I mean, the rites of Isis and Mithras) the presence of a self-dissatisfaction which is wholly foreign to normal Greek religion, and which seems to prepare the way for the coming of Christianity itself.

and in autumn, about the month of September, the great Days arrived. On the first of those days and early in the morning, there was held a solemn assembly in the market-place. A proclamation was read banning all but those of the clean hand and the pure heart from participation in the festival. Secrecy was very rigorously enjoined on all, under penalty of death.[1] Then they dispersed until the morrow, when the opening ceremony took place. This was a quaint and even laughable affair. Each man took himself a small black pig (great care must be given that the pig shall show no blemish and, in particular, shall not be wanting a tail). With the pigs, or may we say, the scape-pigs under their arms, the whole body of devotees passed with a cry of ' Sea-wards ! Sea-wards ! ' down to the neighbour-ing shore, where they dipped, themselves and their animals, under the cleansing waters, and rose with their bodies purged of the pollutions of the flesh and their spirits divested of the slough of this mortality. Next day the pigs lost their lives ; and when the sun rose a second time it found a busy scene in the market square.

Once more they were gathering, clothed now in short white tunics, crowned with myrtle, and carry-ing in the hand an unlighted torch. When all was ready, ranks were formed and they filed down, men and women, a long and silent column, towards the Double gate. Ahead went the image of the infant Bacchos, at its side walked the Bacchos Warden, the High Priest, the Chief Torch-bearer, while others of more or less honourable degree carried

[1] So well was the secret kept that, like the mystery of the masonic brotherhood, it has never been fully revealed.

close in the rear the emblems of the god, his cradle, his childish toys, and, in token of their harvest hopes, a winnowing fan of monstrous size. Outside the gate they formed up again, and then directly they set foot upon the Sacred Way, they burst out, with a capering of legs and a swaying of arms and bodies in the air, into their first ecstatic chorus :[1]

> ' O Iacchos, power excelling,
> Here in stately temples dwelling,
> O Iacchos !   O Iacchos !
> Come to tread this verdant level,
> Come to dance in mystic revel,
> Come whilst round thy forehead hurtles
> Many a wreath of fruitful myrtles,
> Come with wild and saucy paces
> Mingling in our joyous dance,
> > Pure and holy, which embraces
> > All the charms of all the graces
> When the mystic choirs advance.
>
> Come, arise, from sleep awaking,
> Come the fiery torches shaking,
> O Iacchos !   O Iacchos !
> Morning Star that shinest rightly,
> Lo, the mead is shining brightly,
> Age forgets its years and sadness,
> Aged knees curvet for gladness,
> Lift thy flashing torches o'er us,
> Marshal all thy blameless train,
> > Lead, O lead thy way before us,
> > Lead the lovely youthful chorus
> To the marshy flowery plain.'

Thus singing they departed in a whirl of dust. The first stage of the journey lay direct and level

---

[1] The Hymn, which Aristophanes in the *Frogs* puts into the mouth of his chorus of Mystae, must serve to reproduce the spirit of the song. Translation by Rogers.

across the plain, the white road plunging almost immediately under the shadow and hoary shimmer of the olives. On either side of the road the trees stood back, rank behind rank, a well-ordered army of wrinkled, distorted veterans. From the banks and open spaces beneath the branching trunks, wherever the plough had not yet passed, there shone a sprinkling of wild flowers, not in a great profusion, but singly or in rare clusters like stars ; the autumn crocus and tall spiky sprays of withered asphodel. Mile after mile they threaded their way through this pale, mysterious orchard-land, only stopping here and there for some ceremony at a roadside shrine. So frequent were these halts, however, that, though the distance covered was a bare six miles, it was dusk when they left the plain behind, and struck up the mountain side. Aigaleos—to give the hill its name—thrusts its ridge between Athens and Eleusis, parting plain from plain. And as the procession wound slowly up its side and the torches were lit, down in the city they could see answering lights spring up, one by one, out of the twilight ; for those who remained behind made it a custom to set up torches outside their own street doors ; others indeed, being more inquisitive (and these were in general strangers come purposely to see the sight) had followed in the wake of the procession, some in carriages, some on foot. But the citizens for the most part were content to mount to their roof-tops and watch the line of lights as it went flickering and dancing up the distant mountain like a swarm of fire-flies, and to catch the sound of the singing, as chorus after chorus rolled faintly back.

At the top of Aigaleos, in a lonely pass among the pines, another halt was called. Here stood a chapel sacred to Aphrodite, and prayers were duly addressed and libations offered to the goddess, before the descent began. They dropped down now towards the narrow frith of water which divides the mainland from the hills of Salamis. The descent was short, and once they reached the barren and marish shore, the road swung sharply to the right and skirted the rippling margin of the wide bay. Here by some salt lagoons that lie between shore and mountain, they were met by a band of priests, the ancient Order of Krokon, whose part it was by immemorial custom to welcome the procession on the borders of Eleusinian soil, and decorate the pilgrims, binding a yellow riband about the right wrist and right ankle of each. Eleusis was still some three miles distant, but its lights were now to be seen burning steadily across the bay, and as the line was once more set in motion, the song was taken up again. The step of the dance grew wilder at the sight; hearts beat quicker; for the pilgrims were close upon their goal. The spell of circumstance was working; the influence of the long day's march, the exhaustion of a continued fast, the wild music and the still magic of the autumn night, came strongly over them, till as they thronged through the gateway into the blaze of the temple court, there came into their hearts a strange excitement, a blind exultant worship of they knew not what.

It was upon the second evening, after a day's interval of sacrifice and preparation, that the great Rites fell. At sundown they wandered with loud

lamentations up and down the shore, the very spot,
as legend said, where Demeter herself had once so
wandered, lamenting her lost child.   And then at
the appointed hour they forgathered, fennel-wand
in hand, within the great Hall of the Mysteries.
To the mass of them it was no new adventure.
Many and many a time in years gone by they
had witnessed the ritual drama, or scenic mystery,
which presented and enforced (whether by the
sanctity of legend, or symbolically, from the fertile
energies of nature) a pale metaphor, as it were, of
the future life.   Yet it was hard for them to shake
off the fear of doubtful things, and that terror of
the outer darkness that weighed heavy on the pagan
spirit.   They came again, therefore, craving a fresh
lease of certitude.   But to the novice, such as was
Alkibiades, it was something altogether new and
deeply stirring.   He had already received, so to
say, his baptism (when and where we do not know).
He had sat upon a stool, his head and figure enveloped in a white shroud.   He had heard a priest
behind him muttering incantations in odd, unfamiliar phrases ; [1] he had felt the holy flour poured
by an unseen hand over his head, and had been led
out to do sacrifice at the altar.   Thus perfected,
it was his privilege now to enter with the rest the
great illuminated hall.   It must have been a man
of sluggish temper who would not at such a moment
be moved to an almost insupportable emotion.
Many indeed gave vent to their distress by groaning dismally like tortured souls at a revival
meeting.   The novice had been told to expect

[1] Among the mysterious sayings attributed to the liturgy were the
two unintelligible words 'Konx, Ompax.'

F

here the fullest of revelations, and to await the drawing of the veil. That veil was now to be drawn back.

Scarcely had they eaten of the 'Sacred Cake,' breaking their fast for the first time that day, and drinking with it the blessed elixir (known as Kykeios), when on a sudden all the lights were simultaneously extinguished. A voice out of the darkness began to chant in musical tones a queer liturgical jargon ; the form of this the novice had already got by heart. He was able, therefore, when the responses were made, to add his voice to the rest, and to repeat with proud conviction, 'I have fed from the timbrel ; I have drunk from the cymbal.'

No sooner was this said than a flash of light from the roof illuminated a species of stage at the extremity of the hall. The apparition of a figure, in stature greater than man, seated upon a winged chariot and surrounded by writhing serpents, showed for an instant and then was gone. The spectre was clearly seen and recognised by all. It was Triptolemos, a divine being closely linked with the worship of the great Mother. Then in the darkness there were more voices, words of exhortation and texts interpreting the vision, and then again another tableau, a presentation of the Sacred Marriage, which came and was gone in a flash as the first had done. This procedure continued for some while, till at last after a series of such visions of the under-world the High Priest appeared clad in a robe of great magnificence, all patterns and embroideries, and the crowd witnessed with breathless wonder the monstrance of the Sacred Wheat

Ear, symbol of the life which 'is not quickened except we die.' That was the closing scene and all was over.

Next day the procession was led home in a sober and chastened mood. They were met at the Kephisos bridge by a party of their friends who had remained behind in Athens, and who now came out with masks over their heads to see the Mystery Marchers home. There was an ancient custom (and, since these three days of tense sustained emotion called for some such antidote, a sane and healthy custom) by which the pilgrims were welcomed back with all manner of rough humour and boisterous merriment. Coarse jokes were bandied. A favourite butt was the 'Mystery moke,' on the back of which the sacred properties were carried. It was also a never-failing jest to sniff the air and affect to discover a strong smell of roasted pork. In the tired pilgrim this cheerful nonsense worked a quick and salutary reaction, such as is felt when in the theatre a comic piece succeeds the gloomy sequence of tragedies. The relief was welcome, and they entered gladly into the spirit of the fun. Outside the Double gate a last ceremony was enacted. Two jars of water were solemnly poured upon the ground, the whole company dancing wildly round and shouting

'Rain flow,
Crop grow.'

In this manner the procession, which had set out so solemn and serious, was returning to the city as gay and giddy as a carnival, and Alkibiades was departing to repair his long deficiencies of diet by a convivial evening when in the road he encountered Sokrates.

' I am on my way,' the philosopher explained, ' to visit a friend who is mortally stricken with a plague. Will you not bear me company ? '

' Surely you are mad,' replied the young man with some impatience, ' or do you speak in jest ?   I set some value upon that paltry thing my life.'

' To be sure,' said the sage, ' and yet is it not strange, my friend, that I who have no knowledge and pretend to none, concerning this mystery of death, will yet make bold to meet it, whensoever the God wills, without flinching and without regret ; while you who boast yourselves to have such knowledge, and that not by way of guesswork or of pious speculation, but with the certitude of full conviction, you are not ashamed to play the coward in the face of danger, nor to stand guilty of confessed hypocrisy ?   When I wonder at this, as in truth I do wonder, there comes to my mind an old saying, which I think is not ill said, " Many bear the fennel,[1] but few find the truth." '

.   .   .   .   .

Before the year was out, Alkibiades had by a deliberate act insulted and profaned the Mysteries by engaging at a friend's house in an irreverent and outrageous parody.   It cost him dear, for it was on this account, if not wholly, at least in part, that he was banished.   Yet by an ironical trick of fate, it fell to his lot at a later time to turn the tables once more, and to restore to Athens the just celebration of the ceremony.   The city was hard pressed at the time ; the Spartans had built and occupied a fort

[1] The fennel-wand was carried by all the pilgrims.

on the neighbouring hills, for fear of which the annual procession was abandoned, and the pilgrims went by sea. Alkibiades, upon his return, set his face against such a humiliation, and under a strong escort of armed men, he led out the band of Mystae once again by the appointed route along the Sacred Way.

THE SACRED WAY

The Sacred Way is here descending the western slope of Mt. Aigaleos. Over the pine-woods is Salamis, and across the bay to the right, Eleusis. The ruins of Aphrodite's Chapel lie in the foreground.

THE SACRED WAY

VIII. A DINNER-PARTY

How came I hither? whence? and why?
  Came but to be going—
Yet, if my wisdom's sum is naught,
  Can aught be worth knowing?
For all mortality is less
Than nothing is or nothingness.

Born of nothing, back to naught
  I must turn hereafter—
So up and fill me Bacchos' cup,
  True friend to honest laughter.
For cares within and cares without
Wine 's the sovran'st antidote.

(FROM AN UNKNOWN GREEK AUTHOR.)

KINESIAS, the dancing-master, was pacing up and down in the Painted Colonnade. It was the time of full market : and it was fashionable to stroll there at that hour. Now if Kinesias had a foible, it was a desire to be seen in company with men of fashion. So he often walked in this place of a morning, and though he had but one slave in the world, that slave always attended him. To-day he had not taken above twenty turns this way and that, when Pulytion came up behind and, plucking him by the cloak, invited him to dinner. The dancing-master was vastly flattered by his courtesy (for was not Pulytion a man of society and a friend of Alkibiades to boot?). But in the embarrassment of the moment he lost his wits and quite forgot his manners. ' The best of health, sir ! ' he began in a flurry, and the instant after could have bitten out his tongue for shame.

For though this was the fashionable formula for bidding a friend adieu, as a greeting it was ludicrously out of place.[1] The poor fellow's distress was pitiful. But Pulytion took no advantage of the gaucherie, and passing it off with a laugh, left Kinesias quite at his ease, and as proud as Punch at this prospect of dining with the great.

Yet see how a pleasure may be marred, above all for a petty nature, by some mean consideration of economy. It was the mode just then, as Kinesias recollected, to appear at supper in canary-coloured slippers. Such slippers he did not possess, and being poor he had no thought of buying. So he began to be very miserable ; and from that moment a doubt obsessed his mind, whether, after all, Pulytion were not quizzing him.

The dancing-master was indeed not ill-designed for ridicule, being a small sort of man, with narrow beady eyes that squinted, and a short black beard with a prominent point that poked out under an equally sharp little nose. In figure he was underfed and insignificant, yet so vain that he suffered great distress on account of his skinny arms and kept them, whenever possible, under the folds of the cloak, which he also wore very long purposely to hide his legs. It was popular gossip that he would never undress except when the wrestling-ground was empty. In short, he was notoriously of a furtive and ungenerous disposition, and he now sent off his slave with some plausible tale, and borrowed the canary-coloured slippers from a neighbour.

Pulytion's house lay near the Double gate, and

---

[1] ὑγίαινε : cp. 'Look after yourself.' Theophrastos mentions an awkward man who made a habit of this error.

Kinesias' way thither took him down a dark and ill-kept alley, full of holes and pitfalls. Down this he went at the hour of sunset, picking his way delicately in fear for his borrowed shoes. As he had just bathed, he was well oiled and smelt abominably of cheap oriental perfume. His cloak, which was his best, had a purple border, and since he was exceedingly proud of this, and since there was nobody about, he carried it tucked up to the level of his knees. It was well he did so, for as he passed under the walls of a disreputable tavern there came out of the doorway, quite suddenly and without warning, a whole bucketful of foul, slimy water, and there were his new slippers drenched with filth. This was past endurance, and Kinesias stopped to take the wench to task for her carelessness and scold her for never crying out the customary 'gardy-loo.'[1] But as he bent down to examine his shoes he caught sight of Alkibiades coming up the street behind him. And not wishing to appear before the great man in so undignified a posture, he hurried on and passed out into the Kerameikos and so to Pulytion's door.

He was late. The other guests had one by one entered the room where seven long low couches were set out. As they entered there came with them a fragrance of rich unguent, which mingled there with the smell of earthenware oil lamps spluttering fitfully in the niches round the wall. The illumination was not brilliant; and it was thanks to this deficiency of light that when Kinesias took his place and a slave removed his slippers, no

[1] The old English corruption for 'gardez l'eau.' The Greek phrase meant 'stand aside.'

notice was taken of their soiled condition. He felt some small satisfaction at this, but it was brief, and his fall was of his own bringing.

When he had arrived, the other guests had already paired off each with a partner (they were all men : for no lady appeared at these dinners), and had lain down two by two upon the couches, so that no choice was left for the late-comer but to take the worst couch—that farthest from his host—and, since one of the invited guests had failed, he was without a partner to share it. His nearest neighbour, it so happened, was one Philippos, a professional jester brought in by a friend to fill a vacant place and entertain the company with his witty sayings. When water basins were brought round for the diners to wash their hands, this wag seized the opportunity and asked the company in his humorous way, ‘ What is the favourite water with the hungry man ? ’ Now though this was a trite enough riddle, and though one declared that he had heard it but yesterday, and another vowed it was as old as Iapetos, yet nobody, as is usual on these occasions, could recollect the answer, till Kinesias, thinking to score a point, cried out, ‘ I have it— the wash-hand water which precedes a meal.’ At these words there came an answering peal of laughter from the farther end of the room, and there was Alkibiades standing in the doorway, scarcely able to speak for merriment. He took the vacant seat beside Kinesias and, as he did so, he gave him a knowing nod and said, ‘ Aye, wash-hand water, sir, got where you will—but *not at an inn*, my friend, *not at an inn*! ’ And the whole story came out, the miserable little man sitting by and laughing nervously in ill-concealed discomfort. His evening's pleasure was spoiled.

Nor for that matter was the master of the house more manifestly at his ease. Alkibiades' presence was not an honour he had counted on. The meal provided was no more than second-rate. There was barley broth, Phaleric pilchards, and as a make-weight a black pudding. Had he only known Alkibiades' intention, his steward should have gone to market for a dish of eels; his country bailiff should have sent in some fieldfares or a leveret from the farm; he might even have engaged a Sicilian chef for the evening. As it was, he called the butler to his side and whispered to him to keep the Euboean wine back—for that is a sour brand which, owing to an evil habit they have of preserving it with resin, leaves a wry taste in the mouth—and bade him to serve instead a jar of fragrant Thasian or, better still, to borrow a little Chian from next door. All this Alkibiades was not slow to perceive, and rising from the couch he began to apologise for his ill-timed visit. 'Never ask pardon, dear friend,' Pulytion replied, 'thou art more than welcome, though it is simple fare. There is a place set and we'll see thee fill it, and count ourselves the gainers. Besides, 'tis an old saw and truly said, "To the feasts of the lesser the good go unbid."' Alkibiades laughingly kissed his hand to the flatterer and climbed back on to the couch.

The viands were now coming in. They were set out upon tables, which the slaves brought in at the door. These were about the size of a stool, and since no Greek ever sat to eat with his knees under

a table, they were put down at the side of the couch,
one apiece for each of the guests who now set to
with ladles modelled from dough to swallow the
barley broth. The meal was not large, the Greeks
never being other than small eaters, and regarding
with horror the athlete who dined upon a joint.
The fare, simple as it might be, was eked out with
plenty of cheerful talk ; and besides, to do honour
to the new guest, the cook had devised a special
dish, and a savoury was brought in compounded of
cheese, goats' milk and eggs, sweetened with honey
—for sugar was then unknown—and served up in
a fig-leaf wrapper. When this was finished, the
fingers, which during the meal had done duty for
both knife and fork, were carefully wiped upon a lump
of bread, which was then politely thrown upon the
floor. This was a signal for the host to call in the
slaves once more. Pardokas—queer names these
foreign slaves rejoice in !—was told off to bear the
washing-basin round with a napkin and some soap,
Skablyas carried off the tables ; while a third arrived
with a fresh set on which olives and nuts were laid.
At the same time a flute girl entered and handed
to each guest a wreath of myrtle for his head. Then
a tune was struck up. Pulytion took a great bumper
of neat wine in his hands, and calling upon the God
of Good Chance, he tipped it up with a ceremonious
gesture and spilled a few drops upon the floor. The
rest chanted a verse by way of grace after meat ;
and the great bowl passed from hand to hand, each
taking a sip from the ' Cup of Kindness,' and the fun
of the night began.

The slaves, who had meanwhile made haste to
serve out cups, now placed before Pulytion a huge

mixing bowl. This bowl was a lovely piece of painted ware. It stood a full foot from base to rim and a rout of satyrs chase white-faced maidens round the ample frieze of it. The cups, too, were of earthenware, wide and shallow as saucers, and in the centre of each some figure was delicately picked out with black lustre upon the tawny ground.

Before, however, these cups were to be filled, the dice were brought and each guest made his throw. Alkibiades, in merit of throwing two sixes and a three, was declared winner and took command as Lord of the Feast. 'Two and one' was his first order, and at the word the butler poured in water chilled with snow, until the bowl was two parts full; he then broached a jar and emptied in a rich syrup of sticky red wine. Lastly, taking a ladle he dealt out the mixture into the cups. Alkibiades gave a toast, the cups were emptied, and all praised the vintage. Only Philoxenos, glutton as he was, shook his head ruefully at the shortness of the draught. And when some one remarked upon the wine's ripe age, he affected great surprise. 'Mercy on us,' he interjected, 'but it is mighty small for its years.' Alkibiades laughed at his impatience and declared he should not have long to wait. They soon filled up again, and time after time the toast was given and the wine went down. Yet, taking it diluted as it was—and the water always beat the wine—not a man seemed a drop the worse. The night was still young—and they would take their time—to hurry matters would be a pleasure spoiled. Therefore the Greeks counted it folly to take good liquor neat, and left that, as the men in our own island do, to

the mighty topers of the North—abhorring the
bibulous habits of the Scythian. The hotter and
closer grew the air, the deeper and more recklessly
they drank. Yet there was to be observed a sort of
rhythm and method in their drinking. They never
emptied their cups but at the call ; thereupon up
shot a dozen arms together, a dozen cups were
brandished for an instant in the air, a dozen voices
pledged the toast in boisterous unison, and then, as
they threw back their heads, and took the wine at
a gulp, there fell a short silence that seemed to
punctuate, from time to time, the tumult of the
merriment, only the music of the flute sounding or
perhaps the muffled echo of some distant shout, as
a band of roysterers went by in the street. Outside,
the moon had risen in the sky, shining down into
the little court, and casting through the open doorway pale beams across the floor. The summer
night was sultry, and when a breath of wind stirred
in the heat of the low stifling chamber, those who
sat there welcomed it, thrusting back the garlands
from their melting brows, and even letting their
cloaks drop about their waists, glad to bare their
body to the night air. They sank back, after the
toast was drunk, sprawling in graceful languor on the
pillows and the drapings of their couch. And all
the while the slaves went in and forth, trimming
the lamp wicks, bringing the full wine jars and
bearing the empty out.

They drank in no sodden or deliberate fashion,
but with infinite talk and jest and laughter, which,
as the evening wore on, grew into a very fury of
merriment. Each guest at the Feast Master's call
had to play his part and entertain the company with

this or that, now some play of words or rhymed
conundrum, now a discourse in praise of love or wine.
Philippos was often called upon, and he delighted
them with his resourcefulness, and first he would
puzzle them with a riddle:

> ' I wot of a thing which low must lie
> In the blossom of youth, but by and by
> Unwinged it floateth at liberty
> In a fairy flight to the viewless sky.'

Then, when no one could guess what this might
be, he had the answer ready in a second verse:

> ' Flower of the thistle 's an earth-bound thing
> With a cumbersome burden of seed in spring,
> But at summer's coming it taketh wing,
> And the children follow its wantoning.'

Then songs were sung; in particular they in-
stituted a round of catches, each singing in turn
and taking the cue from his neighbour. Alkibiades
himself refused, saying it was not his habit to sing.
But he had the loving-cup filled and passed to
Theodoros. There was a branch of myrtle en-
twined, as was the custom, around its two handles,
and the singer led off appropriately enough with the
brave old ballad of Harmodios and Aristogeiton: [1]

> ' In branches of myrtle my sword I 'll enfold,
> Like Harmodios and Aristogeiton of old;
> By whose daggers the tyrant oppressor was slain,
> And Athens had freedom and justice again.
>
> Belovèd Harmodios, thou canst not be dead;
> In the Isles of the Blest, thou art living, 'tis said.
> Where with fleet-foot Achilles thy place thou hast won,
> And with stout-hearted Diomed, Tydeus' bold son.

---

[1] Translation by Mr. H. Rackham.

In branches of myrtle my sword I'll enfold,
Like Harmodios and Aristogeiton of old,
Who once on Athena's high festival day,
With daggers the tyrant Hipparchos did slay.

Your glory immortal in Attica's land,
Harmodios and Aristogeiton, shall stand,
By your daggers the tyrant oppressor was slain
And Athens had justice and freedom again.'

When he had ended, he passed the bowl and it fell
on Philippos to follow suit. Theodoros' song had
been of liberty, so it was Philippos' duty to cap
that sentiment and to see that his verses chimed in
somehow or other with its conclusion. So the
song of his choice was a praise of liberty also, though
of a different sort. This is what he sang:

' My wealth's a burly spear and brand,
And a right good shield of hides untanned,
Which on my arm I buckle;
With these I plough, I reap, I sow,
With these I make the sweet vintage flow,
And all around me truckle.

But your wights that take no pride to wield
A massy spear and well-made shield,
Nor joy to draw the sword:
Oh! I bring those heartless, hapless drones
Down in a trice on their marrow-bones,
To call me King and Lord.' [1]

That was apt enough; all were well content and
applauded loudly. It was now Kinesias' turn;
but, being somewhat of a novice at the game, he

[1] 'The Song of Hybreas the Cretan.' Translated by Thomas
Campbell.

made an absurdly irrelevant choice. For the catch
he sang was as follows :—

> ' "'Tis foolish to wriggle when in the law's grip,"
> Said the crab to the viper and gave him a nip.'

This broke the rules of catch sequence in a ridiculous manner, and called forth a roar of derisive
laughter. Alkibiades declared that he must pay
a forfeit ; and had a bowl filled for him with salt
water, which, after much protestation and spluttering, he was forced to swallow down.

It was now that Chaerephon, who was an un-
conscionable prig, and who had listened with scorn
to these frivolities, announced that for his part he
preferred the pursuit of wisdom to paltry nonsense
such as this. Without waiting to be asked he embarked upon that well-worn theme, a notorious
puzzle to philosophers, the Owl and the Egg.
Most men, he was inclined to think, allowed the egg
priority of existence. That was not his belief. In
a rambling and maudlin discourse—for by now he
was well in his cups—he probed the dark problems
of the origin of life, and was about to vindicate in
triumph the superiority of the bird's claim, when
his audience lost patience and shouted him down.
' Philosophy,' Alkibiades decided, ' was, like the
ladies, no proper company at table.' ' So out with
the jack, sir, and give us a game of the Kottabos,'
he added, turning to the host.

At this the slaves fetched a tall pole which they
fixed up in the centre of the room, setting round its
base a circular metal tray. On the tip of the pole
they balanced a saucer. Pulytion, by general
consent, was given the first throw. He drained his

cup of all but a few drops, and then calling out loudly ' Here's to my love,' he flung the dregs in the direction of the saucer. He missed, and spitting on the floor, he sat down again disgusted. It was now Alkibiades' turn, and he fared no better. So the game went on till a lucky throw from Kinesias brought the saucer clattering on to the tray beneath. Kinesias was highly flattered; and they all voted him a special drink in honour of his luck. Now there stood upon the side dresser a gigantic vessel, used for cooling wine and holding half a gallon at the least. This Alkibiades ordered the slaves to place in the victor's hands and to fill it to the brim. ' It must be drunk at a draught,' said he, ' and no heel-taps,[1] mind.' Kinesias was aghast; his head was none too clear, for since the goblet of brine he had been drinking freely; if he accepted the challenge he would be downright tipsy, and he was of no mind to cut a ridiculous figure in such company. He therefore begged them to excuse him.

Alkibiades, much tickled by the poor man's perplexity, but hiding his amusement under a mock air of indignation, called out that this was rank blasphemy against Bacchos himself. ' Name of the Dog,' cried he, ' but who is this pestilent spoil-sport, to spurn at the god's good gifts so? Such cant is past all patience. I'll none of it. What, my lads, shall we not learn the lean rogue a lesson? O the infidel! O the unregenerate water-bibber! Shall he not do penance? Shall he not sing sacred hymns? Shall he not turn to the truth and become as one of the Blessed? Shall he not bathe in the milk? Shall he not carry the wand? By Demeter,

---

[1] ἄμυστις is the Greek word, signifying a draught taken at one gulp.

but he shall learn Dionysos' high mysteries before to-morrow's morn.' The company hailed this proposition as an excellent jest. They were in a mood for mischief, and took Alkibiades at his word ; and nothing would content them but to initiate Kinesias in mock-serious make-believe. All was settled on the instant. The ringleaders took embroidered tapestries from the couches and draped them over their shoulders to mimic the robes of the priests. Alkibiades was to be High Pontiff, Pulytion his torch-bearer, Theodoros acted as herald.

While all this was arranging, the slaves had brought in a little pig, the destined victim for the morrow's sacrifice. This completed the preparations for the parody. They set the unhappy Kinesias in the middle of the room and muffled his head up with a blanket. Alkibiades began with muttered incantations sung in a high falsetto voice. The rest snatched the torches which had been placed about the court, and danced wildly round. Finally they discharged half a bushel of bran over the wretch's head, half smothering him. This was too much for the pig, which, scenting food, struggled free from Pulytion's embrace, and then bolted out of the door. There was a hue and cry after the animal all round the court ; and Kinesias, left for the moment to himself, escaped by the street door and made away home. So horrified was he at the impiety that had been done, that even he forgot the risks he ran going through the streets at night and unattended, without even so much as a stick to beat off robbers with. However, as luck would have it, no cutpurse or gown-snatcher came his way. He reached home with a whole skin and with the loss of nothing but his breath. Nor was it until he was safe in bed that he recollected how he had left the canary-coloured shoes, the property of a neighbour, reposing beneath his dining couch. But though he had to buy the owner a brand-new pair, he never breathed a word to Pulytion, and never again did he walk of a morning in the Painted Colonnade.

DRINKING-BOUT

A DRINKING-BOUT

A slave-boy enters with a mixing-bowl (Krater).

The drinkers hold shallow cups (Kylix); one of them is flipping the dregs at the Kottabos 'jack.'

Small tables are placed before the couches.

IX. THE MARKET-PLACE

'Αγοράζειν : ' To be in good agora form.'
                                A. E. ZIMMERN.

HE sleeps a heavy sleep who sups on Chian wine, and
when Theodoros awoke on the morrow of his
carouse, it was full day and the sun was shining into
his chamber between the pillars of the court. The
door-curtain had by his neglect been left undrawn
overnight and he could see out into the sky. But,
though the sun was well on his way, it was early
hours yet, and there was a new freshness in the
morning air as though it had been rinsed in cold
spring water, and purged of the stale dregs of
yesterday's heat by the coolness of the night, as
happens every day in Greece.

Rolling out of his sheepskin rug, Theodoros slid
either foot into a shoe and picked up the ample
woollen wrap that lay where he had tossed it in a
corner. Scanty as was the Greek costume, its
arrangement was no such simple matter ; taste told
here, and a smart gentleman was always to be recognised by the accurate hang of his cloak. Passing it
across his chest, Theodoros looped it under his left
armpit, round the back, and over the right shoulder
(for this was the style then in vogue), and finally
shook out its loose end like a plaid so that the folds
hung free down his right side and leg. Thus
covering his naked body without over-burdening
it with complicated clothes (it was now a regular

mode with many Athenians to ape the Spartan simplicity of dress), he stepped from his room into the court and from the court into the street. Here he fell in with young Archedemos bound for the grammar-master's school, with his luckless slave-tutor in tow. Theodoros walked with the boy as far as the Nine Fountains, which lay in a hollow between the Akropolis and Pnyx ; the women were busy filling their pitchers for the day, and as he passed, the last of them was shouldering her vessel, which dripped a wet trail behind her in the thick dust. Theodoros left the boy to go his way and stepped down into the cool rock cavern of the well-house—not that he had any idea of a morning wash (such cant superstition was no habit of his, and if he took a wash at all, it was just before his supper)—but his mouth was sour and dry and the water was cold, and clearing to the head. After his draught he struck down the road that branched to the market-place.

As he sauntered through the narrow streets, the still morning air was filled with the sounds of merry workers, men and women, freemen and slaves, weavers and cobblers, dyers, tanners, tinkers, car-penters, smiths and wheelwrights, all setting about the business of the day. In one workshop which he passed he saw a sculptor engaged in shaping out a group of the Three Graces, while his slave was grinding the tools on a stone. Theodoros knew the man well, and gave him a hail in passing. No need to catch a glimpse of the snub nose and bulg-ing sockets to recognise that sturdy figure. It was Sokrates, throwing the same simple-hearted zest that he gave to conversation into the earning of his daily bread ; for neither he nor any true son of Athens

thought shame to labour for his livelihood.   Not that
he would let out his labour for day-hire ; that was
worse, if anything, than to take a fee for a lecture as
his rival sophists did.   But free, independent crafts-
manship was another matter.   Offer him a contract
for a statue, a herm or an epitaph, and he will make no
demur.   For upon those conditions he may remain his
own master, free to work or idle as he chooses, and not
like the day-labourer or the poor menial grinding at
the stone in the corner.   No chance for the slave to
knock off work at noon if he wishes, and have a friendly
chat at the barber's, nor to stroll down of an evening
to Peiraieus and watch the boys running in the torch-
race.   For, though he works with a will and earns as
good a wage as many a freeman, yet he is bound to
his task body, soul and spirit, the slave of his master's
pleasure, as Aristotle says, a 'living tool.'

Theodoros saw that Sokrates was in no mood for
conversation and left him at his carving.   Round
the corner he came upon a smithy, then another and
another ; the street was full of them (for this was the
quarter of the metal-workers' 'gild') ; and in each
a score or two of slaves were busy at the forges,
blowing up the embers, hammering out the metal,
burnishing the breastplates and shields and panni-
kins, which shone out of the dim recesses under the
light of the flickering fires.

Theodoros stopped his ears and hurried out of the
clatter.   On past the Temple of Hephaistos,[1] down
a steep winding alley, under the pillars of a lofty
colonnade, and he was standing in the open market-
square.

[1] Now misnamed the Temple of Theseus.   It is the most perfect
specimen of a Greek temple which survives.

Here a busy scene was already in progress; the peasants and hucksters had spread their wares, and the flies had assembled in thick swarms to devour them before even the buyers could arrive. Theodoros himself had not come a-marketing, so he did not linger here, but crossed the square and turned down a side-alley where a knot of men were lounging round an open door. It was the entrance of a barber's shop, and the barber was within, intent upon a customer's hair and beard. A perfume of almonds and sesame spread out into the street, and along with it came the plaintive tones of a young man's voice. Its owner, who was seated on the barber's stool, was making loud lament over his love troubles, and his friends outside the door were rallying him in reply. 'What,' cried one of these in a mocking tone, 'jealous, lad, and in love? Lord, thou couldst break a staff on some one's back, couldst thou? And Kleinias had a son, had he? Patience, dear Kleisthenes, and bide thy time, bide thy time!' And he went through an odd pantomime of gesture; throwing his head back, he gulped down an imaginary draught, shivered in his legs and closed his eyes, all with so perfect a mimicry of a death by poison that it raised a loud laugh. 'That for Alkibiades, son of Kleinias,' he added. 'Wait, little Kleisthenes, wait!'—'Waiting is well enough,' replied the doleful voice, 'but dost thou mind the old saying, "Wait for the swallow and it never comes"?'

By this time Theodoros had come up behind the jester and laid a hand upon his back. Feeling his cloak plucked, the man turned round. Theodoros knew the fellow well. It was Panaetios, an arch buffoon whose extravagant antics had won him some reputation as a wit, and the appropriate nickname of the Ape. When asked what he meant by the foolery just ended, Panaetios wagged his finger knowingly, ' Nobody could tell better than thou, Theodoros, I 'll be sworn. But, mark my words, my man, if once your last night's doings come to light they will serve our friend with a dose of hemlock yet, or never trust me for an oracle.'—' A pox on thy idle gossip and thy false prophecies both. There was some mad work, I grant thee, but would the people pass a decree of death on Alkibiades, think ye, for a mere drunken frolic ? Why, he is their very darling and their hero, now that Kleon is cold meat ; they call him their " watch-dog " already; and it 's " Alkibiades' horses," and " Alkibiades' hounds," and " Alkibiades' boots," and " who 's our man but Alkibiades ? " morning, noon and night. They will not hear a word from Nikias, and small wonder, he is as timid as any turtle-dove. He has not the heart to say " gru," no, not to our poor Chaerephon here.' He pointed at a pale-faced, weak-eyed fellow known to posterity as one of Sokrates' favourite pupils and to his intimates as the Bat. ' Puff out your cheeks,' said the barber as he ended by shaving his customer. ' No,' continued Theodoros, ' Alkibiades is much in the people's mouth.'—' Aye, a deal too much,' drawled Kleisthenes, appearing at the door, ' a devil*ish* deal,' he added, using a termination which, like many young coxcombs of the day, he much affected in his talk.[1]

' O Ekbatana, what a sight,' cried Panaetios, turn-

---

[1] Kos in the Greek. It was the fashion of the day to use adjectives with this termination. Oxford slang can give many counterparts.

ing round to stare at the new-comer and smacking his thigh in his vulgar fashion. 'O Kleisthenes, my pretty fellow, costly as King Xerxes on his ivory throne!' and Panaetios made mock obeisance to the young dandy. He was indeed an exquisite sight: his cheeks rouged, his long hair anointed, combed and (his enemies said) dyed. He wore an enormous onyx ring on his hand, which he carried in a lacka-daisical fashion upon his bosom. He turned out the toes of his high-laced boots with the mincing elegance of a female dancer, and his cloak, which was elaborately embroidered, was allowed to trail behind him as he walked. Chaerephon, who stood by the door, looked sneeringly at the brilliant hues. 'It is most men's habit, as the Master said in his debate with Antiphon, to change their clothes according to the sun's heat—but, in sooth, our friend here resembles nothing so much as the chameleon, for he matches his clothes with the colour of his cheeks.' Chaerephon's own homespun was of the texture and colour of sackcloth, and greasy with wear, for it had not seen the inside of a fuller's shop for a twelvemonth past. And Kleisthenes could afford to ignore the sneer. 'Smart*ish*, I grant you, friends,' he said, turning to his friends. 'Let the town judge now between Kleisthenes and the son of Kleinias.' —'O men of Athens,' cried Panaetios, 'the cock-sparrow, being jealous of the eagle, has stuck a peacock's feather in his tail!'—'Hark to him!' cried Theodoros in the same breath; 'why, man, Alkibiades has more grace in his manner and more matter in his wit than thou hast vermilion on thy two daubed cheeks!'—'Aye, talk wagg*ish* and welcome,' replied the fop, 'thou 'lt not gammon me.

Now that thou speakest of birds, I call to mind a scheme I have to get the better of my foe; there is a fighting cock of mine I 'll match with his, and I 'll back it to win for a talent of gold—a toughish bird, I 'll warrant you.'—' It seems to me,' said Chaerephon, ' that those who consider themselves to be somebody, but are not, are the most ridiculous of all mankind,' with which sententious utterance the young philosopher walked into the shop, there to have his eyes treated with a queer compound of ashes, fig juice, and spurge. For, like many who frequented those foul and dusty streets, he was much troubled by an inflammation of the eyes.

Not twenty paces from the barber's shop the close and shadowed alley led out into the sunny square. And here, while the young dandies lounged and gossiped, all was bustle and confusion. It was the hour of full market, and business was in full swing. Heavens, what a babel! Hark to the salesmen shrieking their falsetto sing-song, ' Buy my charcoal,' ' Buy my myrtle,' ' Fresh rolls for sale,' and a score of other such cries. Now and then, as a variety of discord, came the high-pitched tones of some eager pair in the heat of a hard-driven bargain. The business seemed most brisk at the fruit and greenery stalls—for the Athenians are vegetarians by taste, and are most particular about their salad. They may take their choice from an ample store— onions, leeks, lettuce, radish, vast bundles of garlic. Fruit lies round in heaps upon the ground : grapes, ripe figs and pomegranates, huge pumpkins and cucumbers; but for all this plenty a man must be wary and take time over his bargain, or he will get the worst of it. Not so at the bread stalls, however :

there his stay will be short ; the women that preside over them have short tempers and sharp tongues ; besides, bread is a necessity and it is no use to haggle here. The pastry-cooks are in a different case, they must puff their wares ; so there is a tempting look about those sesame cakes sweetened with honey and flavoured with wine. If you have a dinner-party in view, you will purchase one or two and pass on in search of conger-eels, fieldfares and other delicacies. You need not search long, for there is everything here that money can buy, and time would fail to run through half the list. Such a miscellany of wares gave a strange and pungent odour to an air already laden with dust and heat ; here an acrid savour of pickles and sour wine, there a sturdy whiff of garlic, a stale stench of rancid cheese, or a nauseous vapour of tripe and entrails roasting on charcoal embers round the corner ; and, permeating all these, the sickly reek of the ubiquitous olive-oil—smells, every one of them, dear to the nostrils of a Greek, who likes his flavours strong. And besides all this, fruit rinds and butcher's offal lie rotting in the dust and black with swarming flies. Thus the pleasures of shopping are not of the most refined, and many prefer to send their slaves a-marketing ; others come themselves, but bring a slave to carry the parcels. The women do the shopping only in the poorer families, and even then the husband is often sent on errands. The market is conveniently arranged, for the trades are massed together in groups or rings : some under wicker booths, others beneath rude awnings, which serve as a shield against the sun : each bazaar has its appointed place. Slightly apart sits the money-lender at his table, with seals, bags, tablets and counting-board before him, waiting like a spider for his prey. Here comes a customer, some young Pheidippides, with an expensive taste for horseflesh. The thirtieth of the month is drawing near, when all debts are due. A loan of two minae? That is easily done! Out comes the tablet and the loan is entered at the interest of two per cent., paid monthly, and the luckless fly is in the toils. Outside, beyond the Agora proper, the market spreads into the neighbouring spaces. The scent bazaar is near at hand: here, if you still lack a guest for your dinner, you may be sure to find the smartest beaux. And, as luck would have it, the myrtle market lies next door, where you can buy each of your guests a tasteful garland. Pass down the other way and you will come on a score of cobblers seated behind rows of shoes. One fellow has obtained an order and he is upon his feet; his customer is stood upon the table while he himself, half naked, with cloak tucked round his waist, traces the foot's outline on the leather. Meanwhile his rivals redouble their noisy chorus: 'Chian shoes,' 'Ambraciot shoes,' 'Spartans or Argives,' 'Sandals and Saffrons,' 'Red shoes,' 'Hemp shoes,' 'Scarlet shoes,' till you are nearly deafened. Are you wanting a new slave, there is a dealer near by; he too puffs his wares like an auctioneer, now pinching a naked Phrygian to display his muscle, now setting the crowd in a roar over a negro's short black curls.

Everywhere are many who have not come to buy. The market wardens pass in and out among the crowd, settling disputes, regulating prices and seeing that the fishmongers do not water their stale fish. As a symbol of office they carry whips.

On the fringe of all this bustle, where the space is clear, saunter groups of merry idlers and indefatigable talkers. In the Painted Colonnade a dozen grave and bearded men are in hot dispute. It may be only a rumour from Peiraieus or a point of politics that has aroused discussion, but all are in deadly earnest; all talk at once; and when you hear the words rapped out and see the tremulous play of fingers in the air, the whirligig of gestures and the shaken fists, you could swear it was a serious quarrel and half expect a Scythian constable posted at the corner to step up and interfere. At the other end of the building some lewd young bachelors are playing at dice or whispering the latest scandal : here reputations are destroyed by a pointed finger or a nod. Well-known figures come and go. As Nikias crosses the square, avoiding as well as he may the observation of the vulgar crowd, a common fellow sees him and pursues him with abusive criticisms of the speech he delivered yesterday up on the Pnyx. In a shady corner a loud-mouthed sophist is engaged upon a discourse, questioning the beliefs of centuries and turning even the tale of Troy to ridicule. A crowd has gathered to listen, when suddenly comes the clatter of a bell. A catch of fish has just come in from Phaleron; and in a twinkling the sophist's audience has melted away—all but one old man, and he, deaf as a post, as all the town well knows. ' Thank you kindly,' said the grateful sophist (who is a stranger and does not grasp the situation), ' you at least scorn the pleasures of the body : you have a soul above the sale of fish.'—' Bless me, did the fish bell ring ? ' cries the old man, and off he stumps away after the rest. Hippias, Prodikos, nay even

Pythagoras himself, might talk in vain just now; for when fresh fish is selling at the price of salted sprats, even Athens herself, for all her love of learning, cares for none of these things.

So the morning wears on. The day's purchases are made and the market empties. That way goes a six-foot knight-at-arms with a dish of fried eggs in his helmet. Here is a fine gentleman who has been sent to market by his wife, packing his slave off home with the morning's purchase—leeks, a large pike, sesame cakes and a bundle of wool. ' A load fit to break an Egyptian's back,' groans the slave as he passes the barber's door. After him come two workmen casting up their simple accounts.

' What did I get of Archedemos yesterday, think 'ee, for setting a new bar to his door and an oak one at that ? One drachma and a half. A long day's work and a poor day's wage, say I.'

' Nine silver obols,[1] neighbour ; but that 's a fine sum. Look 'ee, what did I get for sitting all day judging cases in a jury-court, aye, and voting " guilty " like a man each blessed time ? Curse me if I got but three.'

' Nine silver obols,' said the first, pursuing his own thoughts, ' and what is left of them now ? ' and opening his mouth he produced three plump diminutive coins from between the cheek and the gums.

---

[1] 6 obols = 1 drachma, the equivalent of 1 franc. Menial labour brought a man only 3 obols a day (viz. about 2s. 6d. per week); an ordinary workman's pay was 1 drachma per diem, equivalent to 5s. weekly. A highly skilled labourer earned as much as 2½ drachmas per diem (=about 13s. weekly). Money had perhaps four or five times its present power of purchase. So that with the simple tastes of the vegetarian Greek, it would be just possible to support a family even at the lowest rate.

'Lend me thy pin, neighbour, to scratch the count on this sherd.'

He totted up his expenses :—

'Garlic and a bunch of radish, ½ obol.
Bottle of oil, ½ obol.
Firing, ½ obol.
Two loaves and a pint of barley meal, ½ obol.
Salt fish for a relish to the same, 1 obol.

'Total, three obols in all, and three more did I pay to that false thief of a fuller who cleaned my cloak for me against the Lenaea feast-day, and swore, so help him, it should cost me but two.'

'Have the law of him, neighbour,' cried the aged juror, 'and I'll vote him guilty too. Yet, I am thinking, it would pay thee well to spend but a half-obol and hire a cloak, as I do. Did I fare the worse for that ? Not I, I sat in the front seats and hissed old Agathon's plays with the best of you.'

'Taste and economy combined, as old Perikles said,' laughed Theodoros to his friends, as the old men went past the door. 'Why, I could not have done better myself, for all that I am paying my professor, like a king, thirty minae if you please, and slaving all day at a course on the theory of composing Tragedy.'

'And practising the art of Comedy at nights, eh ?' broke in Panaetios, 'but here comes your high pontiff, sir, your counterfeit bacchanal ! here's your mock-mystery ! Watch him coming past the Hermae ; see the sour looks men give him now.'

True enough, Alkibiades was crossing the square, and all eyes were turned his way. It was not at him, however, they were looking. At his heels trotted a hound of unusual size, but (no wonder men stared in amazement) with not even the ghost of a stump to wag at his tail.

'Well,' said Alkibiades, when he reached his friends, 'your stare would make a Scythian bowman blush. Zeus in heaven, what ails you all that you have lost your tongues? Has the wolf been and seen you before you saw him? [1] Is it felony, pray, or high treason, to cut the tail off a dog? I understand my own business best, I think, and I know this giddy populace; they must needs have some scandal to occupy their filthy mouths: so I pay my score by proxy. The more they talk of the maiming of the dog, the less they will comment, sirs, upon his master's morals. You take my point?'

Panaetios laid a finger on his crown and shook his head with the air of a grave physician. 'I was wrong, by Asklepios,' he said. 'I spoke but now of hemlock, the dose I should prescribe is hellebore.[2]

'Friends must share and share alike, says the proverb; and thou shalt make that good at dinner, my man,' cried Alkibiades laughing; and when in his courteous way he had extended the same invitation to the others, they all parted to their several homes for the hour of the midday meal.

For by now the shadow on the public dial measured noon. At such an hour, even Greeks will seek shelter, when the sun beats down so fiercely that the very stones are scorching to the touch. The dealers packed up the unsold remnants of their

---

[1] It was a country superstition that a person seen by a wolf before he saw it was struck dumb.

[2] A supposed cure for madness. Hemlock was the poison used in putting criminals to death.

wares ; the policemen returned to their huts ; the loungers departed ; even the philosophers bethought them of lunch—and very soon the place was empty. By and by the shy green lizards, one after another, poked a nose out of the crevices and crept from under the statue bases, to bask at peace in the deserted square.

THE MARKET-PLACE

The 'Painted Stoa' faces us; the round building on the right is the Tholos, where the Prytaneis lived. Between these two buildings a glimpse may be had of the northern cliff of the Akropolis.

Among the figures may be noted a gentleman driving a bargain with a dealer, his negro slave-boy in attendance; in the foreground a peasant with his rough cloak tucked up in a typically bucolic fashion. Alkibiades and his dog advance in the centre, his richly embroidered cloak trailing behind him. On the right a banker sits at his table, folding-tablets in hand. Behind him enters a stranger in travelling hat and cloak.

THE MARKET-PLACE

X. A FUNERAL

Life's voyagers sail a treacherous sea,
Where many founder piteously.
With Fortune at the helm, we keep
A wavering course across the deep,
Blow fair, blow foul, we all must come
To one last anchorage, the Tomb.

GREEK ANTHOLOGY.
(Translation by Mr. H. Rackham.)

KING DAVID, as we are told, knew better than to nurse a foolish pride before the grim alternative of pestilence or a wasting war. But Athens, beset by both plague and war at once in terrible partnership, did not learn her lesson, and held on her course with an ever-hardening heart. For under this calamity her spirit, though not broken, was, which is far worse, seared and embittered, so that she lost all faith in what might have been her truer self. And in the later pages of Thukydides the air is full of mean suspicions, frantic audacities, savage recriminations and cynical revenges. Athens, in more senses than one, never recovered of the Plague.

It had come to her with the spring, and as the heat of summer grew, so the sickness spread. Nor was there any escape. To leave the walls was madness, when the Spartans were on the Boeotian border planning no one knew what sudden raid. There was therefore nothing for it but to sit and wait within the walls, some dicing and drinking, some staking their property or part of it in desperate vows to the god of Medicine,[1] some abusing Perikles, some Fate, and one and all playing at hazards with Death, who took his pick, we are told, of rich and poor, godless and devout, with a fine impartiality. He would pass up from Peiraieus through that narrow strip of unwholesome land between the two Long Walls, and the country-folk encamped there perished by scores. So fast did they die that there was often nobody to bury the bodies, and these lay, as they fell, round the pools and cisterns, to which in their last agony the fevered wretches had dragged themselves to drink. Next he would turn to the low hills around the Pnyx, where in their filthy hovels the poor of Athens were awaiting in despair. Down in the city he would catch some wretch rifling a stricken house, and would kill him at his sorry work. Nor did he spare the homes of the rich. And one day Perikles' last surviving son was fatally seized.

It so happened that Alkibiades was passing the house, and seeing a water-stoup hanging outside the porch, knew it for a token of death. It was an old custom to set water at the door, that visitors who came to see the dead might on departure cleanse themselves of pollution. Men were by this time careless of infection, and Alkibiades entered. In the court the bier stood out under the open sky, the feet towards the door, vine branches were laid against its sides, and a slave stood by driving off the flies with a spray of myrtle; round the bier crouched women who crooned a weird, unceasing dirge. More horrible still than the sounds they made was

---

[1] Asklepeios or Aesculapius, to whom in her need Athens now turned and built her a new precinct on the slope of the Akropolis Hill.

the sight of their scarred cheeks, their torn hair,
and battered breasts. Perikles himself, who would
have restrained these ugly excesses of grief, was not
within but in a shady corner of the court, a group
of relatives were unsealing the dead man's will.
Alkibiades spoke with them briefly and then departed that he might, in quality of a kinsman and
mourner, prepare himself for the funeral by having
his hair cropped to the scalp.

Next morning, and, true to custom, before the
sun was up, the train of black-robed mourners set
forth from the house followed by the bier. The
corpse was swathed in bands of linen, and covered
with a pall. The face was chalked and painted very
garishly. With those who wheeled the bier, came
hired mourners who wailed in hideous accompaniment to the thin scream of the pipes. Women
brought up the rear, but only such as had blood
kinship with the deceased. No female stranger
might follow the bier unless she had passed sixty
years of age.

Outside the walls they came to an open space
where were the charred remains of numberless fires,
now mere heaps of wood ash. One band of
mourners had just set light to their pyre, when a
second party approached hurriedly, and hurling a
body upon the half-burnt logs, fled back to the city
—to such shifts were men driven for means to do their
duty by their dead. And never surely did Hermes
ply his trade more busily between Styx and Kerameikos.[1] For it was in this quarter that the more
respectable conducted their funerals ; of the poor

[1] The suburb outside the Dipylon gate was known as the Outer
Kerameikos or Potters' Quarter.

who could not afford a decent cremation, he could hardly have had the time to take account.

Not far from here was a field which was the property of Perikles and in which many of his family were already interred, his sister and his other two sons having lately died from the same scourge. And in this field the pyre had been constructed. When the body had been placed upon it, and the final dispositions made, Perikles came forward to perform a last honour to the dead. His stoicism was sorely shaken by this last bereavement, the loss of his other sons he had borne with remarkable fortitude, and had hitherto refused to assist in the funeral rites or to join in the procession to the grave. But at the death of this last son his proud spirit was subdued, and though he endeavoured even now to maintain his calm behaviour and serenity of mind, yet when the moment came for him to place a garland on the brow of the deceased, his courage forsook him at the sad sight, and, says Plutarch, he 'broke out into loud lamentations and shed a torrent of tears.'

The friends now gathered round the pyre, and as the torch was set beneath the timber, and the flames shot up, they threw into the blaze a few small offerings modelled from bronze or clay, miniature dolls, birds, dogs, and other trifling tokens of farewell. So they sped him as a traveller is sped upon his journey, neglecting no provision which might make that journey easy or agreeable. In his hand had been placed the honey-cake with which to appease the appetite of Kerberos, and in his mouth (the mouth was the poor man's purse) he carried small change for the Stygian ferry. For the Greeks faced the thought of the undiscovered country with a strange mixture of emotions, hovering between two opinions, on the one hand the well-defined certitude of a superstitious creed, on the other a hopeless doubt. At best, they held the dead to have seen his happiest days : he would never enjoy more the scene of vivid and wholesome sunlight flooding the Attic plain, nor feel in his bones its cheerful warmth. Instead, the wan light of a filmy shadowland would feebly illuminate the aimless flittings of his unsubstantial soul. The single luxury of Hades was to remember Earth.

As the flames died presently down, the human ashes were collected out of the smouldering heap, well soaked in wine, and placed in a vase or coffer. This was finally placed beneath the earth and covered up. When time served, a slab of white marble would be set to mark the place, and on it carved the figure of the dead, not, as was the way of mediaeval sculptors, in the likeness of a wasted corpse, nor even as a sleeping effigy, but rather as he had been in the full vigour of manhood, stripped for wrestling-bout, or making ready for a chase, as if to perpetuate in death the happiest moments of his life. At this tomb it was the duty of the next of kin to make frequent offerings, on the third and ninth day after the burial, and again at the termination of the month's mourning. Year by year, too, on the anniversaries of his death and birthday, they must pay visits to the place. They were very scrupulous in this observance, hanging garlands of leaves [1] and coloured streamers on the stone, pouring from long-necked jars a libation of honey, milk and wine. They would even lay out and ceremoniously

---

[1] Sometimes, as in modern cemeteries, these were made of wax.

burn a mimic banquet, under the pious fancy that
the soul in Hades would somehow benefit thereby.
There was also (as there is even now in Catholic
countries) an All Souls' day, set specially apart for
universal mourning and celebration of the dead.
Indeed, the memory of a brother or parent was to
a Greek the most sacred thing on earth, and he
treated with respect even the tomb of an enemy.

Meanwhile the funeral party, having fulfilled
their task, turned back to the city, repairing to the
house of Perikles, where a repast was ready. The
mourners were not sorry to break their prolonged
fast, and a certain revulsion of feeling was not
unnatural. Before the company dispersed, Perikles
himself delivered the customary speech in his dead
son's honour—then perhaps he recalled with bitter-
ness the words he used to other mourners in days
not so long ago, when he had better hopes of Athens :
' . . . Though it be a hard matter to dissuade you
from sorrow for the loss of that, which the happiness
of others, wherein you also, when time was, rejoiced
yourselves, shall so often bring into your remem-
brance (for sorrow is not for want of a Good never
tasted, but for the privation of a Good we have been
used to), yet such of you as are of an age to have
children, may bear the loss of these, in the hope of
more. . . . As for you who are past the age of
having children, you are to put the former and
greater part of your life to the account of your gain,
and supposing the remainder of it will be but short,
you shall have the glory of these for a consolation
of the same. For the love of glory never groweth
old, nor doth that unprofitable part of our life take
delight (as some have said) in the gathering of wealth,

so much as it doth in being honoured.' [1] Something, no doubt, he had to say of the dead man's life and of his achievements : of his death he would say little, and of what followed after death (now, as in his great oration) not a word ; and if he smiled when they poured a libation to the spirit of the dead, it was the smile of a philosopher, not the sneer of a cynic.

> ' Squander for me no scent of myrrh !
>   Spread on my tomb no myrtle !
> Kindle me no burning pyre !
>   What purpose in such waste ?
> My dust will turn to merest mire,
>   For all thy wine flow purple.
> Give the living his desire !
>   Dead men cannot taste.' [2]

---

[1] Translation by Hobbes.
[2] Epigram by an unknown Greek.

XI. OLYMPIA

Sunt quos curriculo pulverem Olympicum
Collegisse juvat, metaque fervidis
Evitata rotis, palmaque nobilis
Terrarum dominos evehit ad deos.
HORACE, *Odes*.

DOWN the road from Elis there had hung all day long a cloud of dust, astir with voices and the sound of trampling feet. It arose from a host of Greeks, miles upon miles of them, straggling along, on foot or in saddle, shuffling through the deep white sand and joking and jostling and gesticulating as they went, as merrily as ever did a Derby crowd or a Canterbury pilgrimage. Like the proselytes at Pentecost they were drawn from every nation under heaven. All the world ' from Caria to Carthage ' was there : no wonder the country-folk of Pisa and of Elis stared to see their country invaded by strangers from the Nile or grandees from the court of the Great King. But many and various as the pilgrims were, all were bound alike for the same goal, and as day wore on, even the peasants ceased from staring and set off in the wake of the rest. Up a broad valley they went, leaving the sea at their back, and following the course of the Alpheus, as it wound this way and that, in its wide stony bed. There were hills on either hand, but these sparsely wooded and rising to no great height. Among them the pilgrims will presently catch sight of a landmark that arrests the eye, a bare conical knoll standing up in the middle of the valley, and a furlong or so distant from the river bank. At the foot of it something flashes in the sun, and presently through the haze and the dust there comes a glimpse of gilded statues on a gable point : it is the Great Temple of Olympian Zeus.

A few steps more and they are in the centre of a giant world's-fair : the road is already well lined with beggars squatting on their haunches with hands outstretched, with mountebanks hawking charms for the evil-eye, or, it may be, pennyroyal for the cholic, with fortune-tellers offering the oracles of Bakis scrawled on papyrus slips ; pedlars with brooches, scents and oil ; boys selling long strings of dried figs spitted on a reed. Here the wine-vender does a lively trade, and hard by a crowd has gathered to watch a boy acrobat turning somersaults through a hoop. A conjurer is busy producing pebbles from an astonished rustic's mouth. A few paces farther on a pale-faced ' professor ' is mounted up on a three-legged stool, in which precarious posture he is spouting samples of his own bombastic essays. His audience is somewhat distracted by a pair of muscular northerners, who are giving a performance of step-dancing near by ; up and down they go, now pirouetting on one foot with odd excited cries, now swaying monotonously to and fro to the drone of a Theban bagpipe. In short, there is every kind of diversion and every type of man. One thing alone seems wanting : there is not a woman to be seen. For the female sex is forbidden by law to be present at the Festival.

In an open space at the side of the road there is a great activity, much hammering of tent-pegs, and much quarrelling and discussion over the pitching of camp ; no one, however, is so busy but he has the leisure to stop and jeer as the official represen- tatives of Megara [1] jog in upon their mules, or stare at Alkibiades as he is carried past lolling in his sedan chair. The arrival of the well-known boxer Auto- lykos brings untold gratification to this crowd. He has come in search of some kinsmen ; and as he moves through the encampment a group of admirers follow him about, eager to pick up such athletic gossip as he deigns to dispense to them. They listen with growing interest to each fresh recital of the story which he has to tell of his friend the boxer from Sikyon, who was ruled out of the Games on the ground that he was a half-breed. 'Name of the Dog,' he is saying for the twentieth time ; 'what may a man pretend to know if he knows not his own parentage ! And a pretty pass, surely, for a man's word to be called in question by these meddle- some stewards of the Games ! They were a public nuisance with their plaguey rules and regulations. Why, he himself, honest man as ever wore the glove, could not enter for the Games unless he should pre- sent himself at Elis a full month's space in advance and endure thirty mortal days under the eye of these almighty stewards, pommelling a pigskin full of sand, gnawing raw steaks, and never getting so much as a sniff at a pasty all the time ! Name of Herakles, but they laid it on over thick ! '

Athletes are notorious grumblers—and having delivered this outburst to the prodigious edification of the company, he led away his Athenian friends to view the wonders of the place.

[1] The Megarians were a byword of folly in Greece.

Within the Altis or Precinct, they admired the Great Temple of Zeus, where sat the God's famous statue whose face and hands were of ivory and whose mantle was of beaten gold. His head, seated as he was upon his throne, touched the coffering of the roof, and such was the splendour of his presence and the majesty of his brow that the very sight of him was counted a liberal religious education. Round the Temple in the crowded precinct there was much else to see. Here stood that floating figure of Victory raised upon a high column, which had been newly set up by Athens' allies of Naupaktos at the close of the war.[1] Here was also the very ancient shrine of Hera, which men said was well worth a visit. What its antiquity might be none could tell ; but there was this curious fact about it that one or more of its columns were cut out of wood, a relic of the original structure, harking back to the remote times when men had not yet learnt to build in stone. Within its walls stood the Chest of Kypselos, famous throughout all Greece, and, as Homer would have said, ' a very great wonder to behold,' but the marvellous legends told in the cunning carving of its sides it was by this time too dark to see, and it is certainly too tedious to describe.

In the dog-days, when, as travellers say, Greece is one great oven, Olympia burns at a white-heat. It has been no trifling hardship for our friends to take the road at such a season, and, as spectators in the stadion, they will suffer little less. It is therefore a welcome respite to the weary travellers, that the day following upon their arrival is spent in mere

[1] At the time of Nikias' Peace. The monument commemorated the Athenian victory at Pylos.

preliminaries—Public Sacrifice, to wit, and the draw for heats. The vast crowd thronged the Altis for the ceremony. The victims were slain, the smoke rolled up from the great altar-slab, and public prayers were offered in the name of Greece. Here, for one brief interval, the citizens of all Greek cities forgot their feuds and rivalries, and felt themselves, in the bond of a common faith, to be one people. For it was not a love of sport merely that had brought them from their homes, but reverence for a festival of high antiquity and deep national significance.[1] Yet all this is soon forgotten when in due course the draw begins. Friends and backers of the rival athletes crowd eagerly round to watch the judges at their work. For when heats and finals fall both on one day (as at Olympia they invariably do) victory itself may hang upon the lucky drawing of a bye. So when Autolykos has drawn the letter ' Pi,' there is an anxious moment's waiting till it is understood that the Spartan has drawn its fellow ; and then the evening is spent in forecasting the issue of the fight.

Youth before age is at Olympia the order of precedence, therefore the Second Day is given up to events for boys. The programme for them is the same as for men (the Pankration alone, on account of its severity, being excepted), and a victory is so highly prized that when Gnathon [2] has won the Junior Boxing, his Arkadian supporters vow they do not care a fig who wins the senior event next day.

[1] Connection between games and religion is somewhat obscure. Probably these trials of strength were a ceremony substituted at an early date for the older practice of human sacrifice.

[2] Most of the names which are here given to the victors of this year's games have actually come down to us in written records.

Of this they think better, no doubt, during the
night ; for when the Stadion fills again next day
they are in their places with the rest and no one
more excited. The crowd is as thick as flies along
the earthen banks that surround the course, and
late-comers must take back seats on the knoll known
as Kronos' Hillock. The stewards in purple robes,
with branches in their hands, proceed to the end of
the Stadion, and there seat themselves beneath a
gaily coloured awning, and thereupon the Men's
Games begin.

First Event : the sprint (200 yards). This is the
blue ribbon of the Games and the winner gives his
name to the year.[1] In the fresh air of the morning
six of the runners strip, and take their places between
posts set in a long stone sill that runs across the
course. They stand there, like naked swimmers
ready for the dive. Their feet are planted close
together in two grooves channelled in the stone.
One of the stewards stretches a cord in front of
them. They bend forward their hands upon the
ground.

' Away,' shouts the steward, dropping the cord.
They leap forward swinging their arms stiffly like
joints of a semaphore, and what is curious to remark,
advancing right leg and right arm *together* : their
progress is thus a series not of steps, but springs,[2]
and as they run, they lash their energies and waste
their breath by shouting themselves hoarse. The
winner, so a poet declared in a laudatory ode, was

---

[1] Some say this was merely because it came first on the list.
[2] This if we are to trust the vases. Mr. E. Gardner does not. The
case then is like this : of two things one, either the Greeks did not
know how to draw or they did not know how to run.

scarcely visible between the start and finish, so swift had been his transit.

The poet's words bore perhaps a more literal truth than he intended, for the runners, running as they did in a bed of sand, ankle-deep, raised such a cloud of dust, that the spectators could see little of the race, and as heat follows heat the nuisance only becomes worse. But so it goes on till the Final is reached, and the victor's name, Exainetos of Akragas in Sicily, is proclaimed by the public crier.

Then follows the Double Course—that is, to the stone sill at the farther end and back again.

The Long Race next : It measures four-and-twenty furlongs at the very least, an excellent test of a man's wind and useful for the training of good soldiers if they are to emulate the famous charge of Marathon. Plato in later days thought it far too short ; his ideal test would have taken them over ten miles of ground, and that the roughest available : in full armour, too, if he could have had his way.[1] But even in these days men must train for a good six months beforehand, submitting to massage for their muscles and enjoying a diet which consists almost wholly of beef, so that the appetite of an athlete is proverbial.[2] The style in the long race differs widely from the sprint. They keep a long, steady stride, with elbows well into the ribs. This suits the longer distance : for even Pheidippides himself could never have reached Sparta had he progressed by bounding like a kangaroo.

---

[1] There was in point of fact a Hoplite race at Olympia too, run with shield and helmet on.

[2] The Greeks disliked meat, and an army which was reduced to such a diet considered itself in a bad way.

Before midday the running is over. And presently some men enter with pickaxes and proceed to break up the hard ground in the centre of the course. This preparation seems to indicate the wrestling match, and sure enough the wrestlers enter in due course, naked and oiled like sardines from head to foot. The rest of the crowd will sit the whole performance out, trial rounds and all ; but as it is some hours now since early morning, let us buy from the boy who is crying fresh rolls for sale, and retire to eat them in the shade. We will return for the final bout. In this Eumolpos of Megara is to meet Kallias of Corinth. Had we been here a short while back, we should have seen Kallias hard put to it in beating Eukrates of Athens : this has given a breathing space to Eumolpos, his present rival, who had merely to wait standing near ' at attention,' the conventional attitude of the ' bye.' Little wonder, then, that Kallias, being tired, is on his guard and hangs back when the signal is given, manœuvring for a hold ; as they stoop forward, walking on their toes, the two give sharp grunts and cries, as Japanese wrestlers do. These dilatory tactics last some while, and when at last they close, both fall simultaneously to their knees, and the bout is declared drawn. The second and the third bouts go to Eumolpos ; and in the fourth, Kallias is more than ever loath to close. Presently, however, Eumolpos catches his wrist, then rapidly turns his back upon him and in a trice draws the other's arm over his shoulder. Another instant, and by bending sharply forward he shoots the whole man clean over his head, as a labourer might throw a sack of potatoes from his back. As a result the other is sent sprawling in the sand.   This dexterous throw wins the prize and much applause into the bargain. A master-potter went home and put it on a vase— where, if you visit the British Museum, you may see it to this day.   Modern wrestlers also use the throw, calling it the Flying Mare.

The day is now at its hottest; but Greeks do not repine : on the contrary, they warm to their work. Sport was for them something more than a mere pastime, and if it was a pleasure, it was at least a grim one.   Boxing, according to their notions, was meant as a test of endurance rather than of skill. Therefore when they arranged the programme at Olympia, and fixed the boxing not for the cool of the evening, but for the heat of noon, they did it of set purpose.   It is the toughest man who wins ; and often men would die rather than consent to raise a finger and thereby admit defeat.   All is designed to make the combat as severe as possible. These leather strips, known whimsically enough as ' soothers,' are twisted round hands and forearm, merely with the purpose of saving the knuckles, and with no idea of softening the blow.   It is true that the thongs were not at this period studded with metal knobs : for the Greeks were not brutal, though they were austere.   The caps, however, which in the gymnasium are worn to protect the ears, are now discarded.   As the champions face each other, there is something very like murder in their eyes ; there is nothing soft or friendly about the sportsmanship of Greeks, and there is no pre- liminary shaking of hands.   Two seconds stand by to see fair play.   It is well that they carry forked staves in their hands.

Tactics have altered little since Odysseus boxed with the beggar Iros in the courtyard of his palace. There is some manœuvring to get the sunlight in the other's eyes ; but apart from that, foot work is hardly used. They stand somewhat astraddle, the left foot slightly advanced. Instead of rapid sparring or lunging straight from the shoulder, they deal long swinging blows, sideways and directed down upon their opponent's head. Their arms are held at full stretch, and the fists half clenched. It is a veritable ' mill ' ; compared with modern boxing the tactics are as the sabre to the foil. The blows are aimed almost entirely at the head ; there is little body work. Indeed a prominent stomach is counted an advantage, since by so much the more is it difficult to reach the owner's face. We need not wait for the finish ; it will take some time and it is not a lovely sight. Besides, if such scenes are to our mind, we shall have our fill presently at the rough-and-tumble fight known as the Pankration.

This is a barbaric form of sport. A learned preacher, who ought to have known better, once entered upon a description of the game of Rugby football : that was played, as he averred, between four boundary lines, within which limits *everything was fair*. There is only one game which might properly be so described : and that is the Greek Pankration. Short of biting or gouging out his eyes, a man may assail his opponent as best he can, break his fingers, squeeze his windpipe, twist his arm, or kick his stomach until he admits defeat by the raising of his hand. The Pankratist differs from the boxer in physical development. He needs to be tough and short. One champion was known as the

Dumb-bell on account of his proportions. But it was a bad training for the purposes of ordinary life, and some cities forbade the practice of it, at any rate to boys. When one champion faces another, his first object is to get him down to the ground. Some would seize him by the heel, but Andros-thenes, who was winner in the last Games of four years ago, has another stratagem to-day. As they come to grips, he deliberately falls backwards—as he does so he plants one foot firmly in his opponent's stomach—then, while he sinks to the ground him-self, he lifts the man clean off the ground, giving him a somersault right over his head, and whereas Androsthenes rolls gently over on the sand, the other lands head foremost with a fearful crash.

Then follows a long and panting struggle on the ground. The shadows of Mount Kronos lengthen ; twilight comes on ; and still they are rolling in the dust. At length Autolykos, who has the other's head in chancery, and seems to be throttling him, sud-denly gives in to the agony of a broken toe, and raises his finger. He rises defeated ; the victor still lies on the sand. The umpire prods him with his stick, but he does not move. They turn him over. Androsthenes has been dead already some minutes since.

Next day the only event which takes place in the stadion is the Pentathlon or championship in five events. 'The Quoit, the Sprint, the Wrestling Match, the Javelin and the Leap,' as a poet once put it.

The leap, to take the last first, is of course the Long Jump. There is no high jumping in Greece. The competitors take only a step or two by way of run ; in either hand they hold large oval stones pierced in the centre like a primitive axe-head ; these they call *halteres* or ' jumpers.' Just before the leap a man swings his arms violently back, slightly bending the legs at the knee. Then, as the arms swing forward, he makes the spring. While he is still in mid-air and just on the point of alighting, he once more brings his arms into play, jerking them back so as to give a last impetus to his flight through the air. This time he allows the jumpers to leave his hand. They have helped him materially by aid of this twofold swing. The stewards now measure with their rod the length of the jump. The soil has been prepared with a pick, and the dent made by the heels is easily visible.

The quoit is a flat disc of metal. The method of throwing it is intricate and is also worth describing. Holding the quoit in the right hand the thrower swings it backwards till his hand is almost on a level with his shoulder. His right foot is at the same moment advanced.[1] Then the quoit arm descends with a sweeping swing underhand and his whole weight is thrown forward on to the left leg, which is now in its turn advanced. As the hurl is made a great lift is gained by suddenly straightening the body, thrusting from the thigh off the advanced left foot. Distance is all that matters ; direction is of no importance. Quoit-throwing must indeed have been a serious danger to bystanders.

In javelin-throwing, on the other hand, direction was the chief object : even greater accuracy was attained by winding a strap round the shaft : a

---

[1] This is the position depicted in Myron's ' Diskobolos '—really a pose of momentary rest.

rotatory motion was thus imparted, similar to that which the rifling of the barrel gives a bullet. Even so, spectators were sometimes killed. The quoit, one would think, must have done still greater execution.[1]

Whoever wins most events in this Five Tests Championship is declared victor. In the case of a tie there must be further trials. There was once a young man called Phayllos who jumped fifty-five feet, landing beyond the pit and breaking his leg ! As he had already put the diskos ninety-five feet, he deserved to win on those two events alone : for he must have been an altogether remarkable young man.

In the Stadion the race is to the swift and the battle to the strong, but in the Hippodrome victory goes to the rich. While the charioteer is risking life and limb round those perilous turning points, the owner lolls at his ease on a purple tapestry, lays odds with his neighbour that his ' Koppa-brand ' can last the course, and then, when all is over, steps in and claims the honour. The more he spends on his horses the better his chance of victory. Alkibiades, for instance, at this very moment can lay claim to no less than seven out of the teams that are now chafing in the starting-boxes, impatient for the dropping of the rope. The crowd have left the Stadion and gathered in the race-course. Soon they see a slave set up a bronze dolphin on a central pillar, and at that signal the drivers shake out their reins, and they are off. Their long robes that fall about their feet soon

---

[1] Instances of accidents to spectators from quoits occur even among the legends of heroic times.

flutter out behind, and the dust is whirling from the wheels. They crane out over their four-in-hand, leaning forward from the flimsy rail of their bounding chariots. Eleven times they round the two turning-posts, and then a trumpet sounds the last lap, and an eagle takes the dolphin's place on the column.

A chariot race is largely decided by the survival of the fittest. Before the last lap is begun five of the chariots have fallen victims to some accident at one or other of the twenty turns already accomplished. As the survivors gallop past the winning-post, three of Alkibiades' teams are among the first four. The Athenians are half mad with joy. The young Athenian made his compatriots a feast that night.[1] It was a memorable and sumptuous banquet : not least because Alkibiades had borrowed of the representatives of Athens large quantities of the official plate. There was good cheer for all, and Alkibiades sat at the head on a very conspicuous couch, drinking with his friends and boasting of his victory. He vowed that Euripides himself should write an ode in honour of it : as came to pass. Indeed the young man's head was somewhat turned, but the height of his infatuation was reached when the official plate was needed for the Grand Procession of the following day, and he firmly refused to give it up.

For the morrow is the last day of the great festival, in the course of which each victor will come to be crowned by the Stewards of the Games. Then

---

[1] There were other horse-races for pairs, etc., which it would be tedious to enumerate. There also was a prize for trumpeting ; one is reminded of the piping at Highland games, in many ways so like the Olympian.

he will depart to his own city, and there it is that he will enter upon the full fruits of his success. There he will he hailed more as a god than a man. The whole city will turn out to greet him and hang garlands on his neck. He will receive large sums of money and enjoy free meals at the City Hall for the rest of his life—and possibly the post of honour on the battlefield. Sculptors will perpetuate the perfection of his muscular development. Poets in their panegyrics will devise for him some fabulous descent from the heroes of olden time.

Meanwhile in the Stadion at Olympia he is to be crowned. There are first processions and strewing of rose-petals and banquets. But the supreme moment comes when he stands upon a tripod before the stewards, ribands trailing from his neck and arms, his head modestly inclined, and his limbs glistening in the sun. It is a fine sight ; one could almost fancy that the statue which after his last victory Polykleitos made of him and set up in the Altis, had positively come to life and stepped down from its pedestal. The herald pronounces his name, adding his father and his country ; the stewards place on his head a crown gathered with a golden sickle from the wild olive-tree that stands by Aphrodite's shrine. He has reached the limits of this world's ambitions. ' Die, Diagoras ! Life has nothing more to give.'

So the festival ends—the ninety-first since the institution of the Games. The Sacred Truce, under which Spartan and Athenian had sat cheek by jowl in perfect amity for four whole days, is now declared closed. At the last festival from which the Spartans had been excluded, threats and fears of hostilities hung over the whole affair like a cloud : this time all had passed off as peaceably as could be—yet before another four years are over and the festival comes round again, Greece will be racked once more from end to end by the old unforgotten feud.

THE DIONYSIAC THEATRE

On the right rise the sheer cliffs of the southern side of the Akropolis. The Parthenon would be almost directly overhead. Below the auditorium may be seen the *orchestra* or dancing-ring, with its smoking altar, the stage buildings, and the Temple and sacred Close of Dionysos. Beyond these are the Museum Hill, the Long Walls running to Peiraieus, Salamis and Mount Aigaleos stretching across the horizon.

THE DIONYSIAC THEATRE

XII. THE GREAT DIONYSIA

'This may be very well; but for my part I prefer the smell of a flambeau at the play-house.'—BOSWELL.

To keep a School of Wrestling was at Athens no unprofitable business : therefore Taureas was rich. Yet for all that Taureas was a miser. So stingy had he grown that he grudged even the poor grammar teacher his pittance, and would keep his sons at home for the whole month of Anthesterion because, as he said, it was more than half holy-days. And when the month following the Dionysia came round, rather than pay two obols to see the plays, he would stand a whole forenoon in the sweating crowd to secure a free ticket.[1] Public duties were an abomination to him ; and whereas poorer men than he had often paid the cost of producing a tragedy, he had somehow shirked it with unfailing regularity. In fact, had an oracle from Apollo himself announced that Taureas was about to undertake that costly function, not a soul in Athens would have believed it, and least of all Taureas himself. Yet such was indeed the case.

How he came to accept it, nobody knew. For when first the archon selected his name from the list of the wealthier citizens, his indignation knew

[1] These were provided out of a public fund called the Theoric Fund : the richer citizen preferred to pay for his ticket. Compare the cheap or gratuitous performances that are given from time to time in Parisian theatres.

no limit.   He declared that he would exercise his
legal privilege and challenge his wealthy neighbour
Nausikydes either to undertake the function in his
stead, or else to exchange properties with him outright.   Under the circumstances it was long odds,
thought he, that Nausikydes would accept the former
alternative and he himself be rid of all responsibility.
But suddenly, and without apparent reason, Taureas
altered his tune.   Maybe he was so advised by the
wizard who sat at the Dipylon gate and told men's
fortunes by the aid of geometrical diagrams and
dreams—for Taureas habitually consulted him, being,
like most misers, superstitious beyond measure—or
maybe again he had schemes of revenge upon
Alkibiades, who, it transpired, was also to finance a
tragedy—for between him and Taureas there was no
love lost—whatever, in short, was the true motive of
his determination, it remained a fact that Taureas was
to act choregos (as the phrase went) with Alkibiades
and one other at the Great Festival in the spring.

It came about in due course that the archon,
having selected three playwrights also, summoned
the three producers to take their pick of them.
And Taureas drawing the first lot, was mightily
pleased to secure Agathon.[1] Not that he knew much
about Agathon's verse, but he held that his name
was a great omen of success, and the battle was
therefore half won at the start.   When however it
came to drawing for actors (which the State provided, leaving the producer to look after the chorus)
it was a very different story, and difficulties at once
began.   For when the actors were assigned their

---

[1] 'Agathos,' signifying good, was naturally counted a propitious omen
by a race which attached great importance to such trifling superstitions.

parts the fellow who was cast for Phoebos Apollo in the prologue gave himself airs, and declined to reappear in the great 'Recognition Scene' as the Baby's Nurse,[1] so that the whole play seemed likely to be wrecked.

While this difficulty was being settled, the preparation of dresses and scenery went forward. Cloth from Cyprus, embroideries from Susa, purple from Sidon, golden ornaments from Thrace: Taureas' extravagance was the wonderment of Athens. The masks were being painted by the hand of the master-painter Apollodoros himself. As for the composition of the choir, such a superior set of voices had not been known for years. It was said, too, that they knew their dance figures to perfection : for had not Kinesias himself been hired to train them ? He was a choir-master and minor poet to boot, and had composed, it was said, a sword dance of his own. In short, Taureas had good reason to be proud of his chorus of 'Theban elders' (for it was in that rôle they were to appear), and boasted so insufferably of their perfection that Panaetios the Ape started a rumour in the barber's shop that to cultivate the true Boeotian mellowness of voice they were being dieted exclusively upon eels from a Boeotian lake. And though it was manifestly absurd, since in war time no such eels could come from those parts, the Theban voice moreover being far from mellow, yet it was true enough that Taureas grudged them no delicacy and stinted no expense. First and last it would cost him, he said, a mint of

[1] The number of actors employed in a play being fixed by law, it was often necessary for each actor to perform in more than one character. This rule may have been made to equalise the chances of the competitors and give no undue advantage to a rich choregos.

money—thirty minae, or half a year's income at the least.[1]

Then came the great rehearsal. It took place in a building which they called the Hall of Song or Odeion. All the chief officials were there, and Taureas marked their satisfaction with unconcealed delight. Agathon had written, Heaven be praised! no tedious Aeschylean trilogy with a continuous plot, but three distinct and separate tragedies, and there was a short 'tragedy-comedy' following to round them off, as the Bergamask dance followed on Bottom's tragedy of *Pyramus and Thisbe*.[2] Each of the tragedies dealt with a popular myth, and Taureas was more than satisfied with each. He would indeed have had the poet change a prologue and shorten a messenger's speech ; but the fellow was as proud as Perikles since he had won a prize at the local festival at Peiraieus. But no matter, the final speech in praise of Theseus atoned for all minor imperfections : there was a fine patriotic ring in those last lines. If that speech were fresh in the judges' minds when they came to cast their votes, all would yet be well. Taureas offered up a secret prayer to Dionysos that his own plays might come on the third day and last of the three competitors. And when the eve of the festival came and the image

---

[1] 30 minae = 3000 drachmae (3000 francs or £120). The professional class at Athens (teachers of music, grammar, gymnastics, etc.) earned at lowest about £70 per annum. A capitalist or landowner would do better. A rich banker like Pasion, with a capital of 40 or 50 talents (1 talent = 60 minae = £240), must have reaped an income of well over £1000 per annum, the current rate of interest being one drachma on a mina, or 1 per cent. *monthly* (= 12 per cent. per annum). Money had of course four or five times its present power of purchase.

[2] Of the Satyric drama, which was an integral part of the coarser elements of Bacchic worship, no fuller account need here be given.

of the god was taken from his shrine and borne into
the adjacent theatre with torches and merriment
and dancing, Taureas in the thrill of the moment
vowed to Dionysos a pair of yearling goats, as a
backing to that prayer.

Nor was this vow in vain. It was duly announced
that the plays of Agathon should be presented on
the third and final day. For two days, therefore,
Taureas must sit idly by, spectator of the gay
familiar scene, the citizens thronging in at dawn,
the bright colours of holiday dresses, saffron-yellows,
brick-reds, and brown of every shade, the vine-leaf
crown on every head, the eager scramble for seats, the
pompous entry of the archons and the priests, the
train of envoys bearing Tribute from all the cities
of the League, the cheers that greeted Alkibiades,
the coarse jokes and the careless laughter—and then
the Herald's call for silence and the sacrifice to
Bacchos. In a twinkling the jovial crowd was as
solemn as the dead. When the ritual was finished
various proclamations were made, of the price set
upon some criminal's head, or special honour voted
to some benefactor of the state, or of privileges
conferred on some fallen soldier's sons. Then at
last the competitions could begin. First the choirs
of boys that danced and sang ; then choirs of men
that sang and danced. But for these Taureas cared
little and never gave a thought which tribe should
win. He was waiting for the moment when the
Herald rose and cried, ' Let Alkibiades lead his
chorus on.' Then indeed he listened with all his
might, weighing the merit of his rival's plays and
calculating his chances against Alkibiades. The
plays were long, and as gloomy as tragedies could

be ; the audience was sad and silent, and sat with puckered brows.   Then at length followed a comedy, this by Aristophanes, and every one was merry again, and cheered, and so departed.   And so once more the second day.   The plays this time were bad ; every one acknowledged as much, and Taureas, thinking of the morrow, heeded them as little as the great clouds which March winds were sweeping down the sky.

He rose betimes on this morning ; his toilette was lengthy and punctilious.   Yet when he reached the Green Room at the back of the stage, day had not yet dawned.   The great hollow semicircle of seats stood empty but for a single figure in the second tier.   The early-comer was free of every seat, since none but the front row were reserved, so any man gifted with the patience of our enter-prising friend might occupy the bench next to the marshals for his pains.   Soon, however, others begin to pour in from the openings to right and left into the Dancing Ring, and the space before the stage is soon choked with figures that hurry and spread, clambering up the narrow gangways, which radiate out like the spokes in a wheel.   Little by little the tiers begin to be peopled, up and back, seventy— eighty—ninety yards from the stage.   Thousands are there and still they come ; it is a strange, ill-assorted crowd—there are wits from the market-place, yokels from Hymettos ; there are athletes from Sicily, merchants from Pontus, professors from Rhodes; there are dandies be-ringed and be-scented; there are mangy jail-birds on holiday ticket-of-leave ; there are nabobs from the East with em-broidered cushions to sit on and carpets for their feet; and there is the thrifty Ktesias squatting in his shirt for fear the stone should fray his cloak; there are generals, magistrates and poets, and politicians and philosophers. Not a few there bear immortal names. Was there ever such a gathering of genius in the history of the world ?

> ' Art, science, wit,
>   Soldiers like Caesar,
>   Statesmen like Pitt,
>   Sculptors like Pheidias,
>   Raphaels in shoals,
>   Poets like Shakespeare,
>   Beautiful souls.'

Now Alkibiades too has entered; to-day in his insolence he wears a brilliant purple robe—and last of all, when the rest are seated, panting up the steps, and gently urged from behind by the usher's white wand, comes the ' mighty bulk of Kleonymos.' He thrusts his huge carcase into the topmost tier where the seats are carved from the rock of the Akropolis cliff, and places his cushion without more ceremony between a staid old gentleman and a disappointed dramatist. Panaetios the buffoon was sitting near : the coming of the fat man was a godsend to the wit. ' There 's your greedy glutton,' he jeered, ' even a-playgoing down he must sit where the priests throw the offal down the rocks, if so be a lucky tit-bit may light upon his lap.' This sally was lost amid the protests from both dramatist and farmer between whom Kleonymos had just sat down. ' Save us,' cried the latter, ' how many roods here-abouts have thy two obols bought thee ? '

' Are we to sit in close order, sir, like kilted men-at-arms ? '

'Aye, closer order than at Delion, I 'll be bound,'
put in Panaetios, harping on the old familiar joke.

'Give me my due, master, give me my cubit,'
cried the farmer, panting for air, 'or, by Zeus, I 'll
have the law of thee.'

A blear-eyed sophist sitting below here saw his
chance: 'Shall I prove for thee that thou art
wronged of thy right, and show how thou mayst
be righted of thy wrong ?   For a trifling fee,' he
added, but seeing his offer wasted, yet wishing to
display his skill, the fellow went on : 'The measure
of all, you will grant me, is the Man.   Now the
measure of the playgoer is the measure of his . . .'

'O Dionysos,' groaned the unhappy farmer,
'bring this babble to an end and hasten on the play.
If this be death by inches, I had rather die by . . .'

'By feet,' put in Panaetios, 'by feet, I say, if
Agathon's iambs scan half as ill as did Philokles'
yester-morn.'

'Nay,' said the sophist, taking up the challenge.
'If his muse went limping, yet, Phoebos Apollo,
how his thought was winged !   I can, an it please
you, set forth the heads of that argument whereby
Elektra showed that she must needs make an end of
her mother.   Now in prime, she setteth forth that
Klytemnestra is her mother, being her father's
wife ; good !   Secondly, that her mother did
commit murder ; good also !   Thirdly, that she
being her mother's daughter could do no less ; like
parent, like child.   Killing was in the family.   A
most excellent argument.   But God help us the while,
here 's old Tithonos looking mere mustard !'   At
this the farmer's patience was indeed exhausted.

'Gall, sir, as I live, to me every word of it was

gall. Oh that I should have hearkened to such knavery, and with my youngsters sitting by. Nice notions they've learnt at the play. Last night if I should scold them for this or that it was, " Who filched the tripe-ends when father was a boy ? " " Who did not like the slipper when father was a boy ? It's in the family," till I could fair hang myself. Oh, that sacrilegious pagan of a poet.'

' Nay, thou mistakest, my friend,' rejoined the sophist, ' in letting these opinions to the poet's count. He did but put the words in Elektra's mouth.' As a downright quarrel seemed likely to rise upon the point, Panaetios intervened with a suggestion.

' Now friends, let's lay a wager on it : the stakes to be that parcel of comfits, and,' pointing to Kleonymos who was nodding off to sleep, ' let pot-belly decide. The point at issue, Sir Oracle, is this : Did the poet declare the murder just, and not Elektra ? Down goes his head for " aye." Nay, up it comes for " no." [1] He gives the award beyond cavil to . . .'

' To Kleonymos,' said the fat man waking up from his nap and taking the comfits from his knee.

' Hold ye your peace,' shouted the Herald. And the play began.

There was here no pompous raising of the curtain, no borrowed glamour of mimic forests and pasteboard castles, no unearthly stare of the limelight. The bare stage stood empty under the plain and wholesome daylight. The wall behind the stage was hung simply enough with the painted semblance of a palace front ; to either side of this was a crude

---

[1] The Greek method then, as now, of signifying dissent is to throw the head up and back, of assent to nod down.

likeness upon a narrow strip of canvas of some landscape or other : so much of make-believe there was,
but no more ; the frame, as it were, to the picture
was the wide familiar view, the level plain stretching down to the shore, the little rocky hillocks dotted
over it, and beyond them the sea.   As the mist
hanging round the Phaleron Bay went up like smoke
under a scorching sun—(there had been a fall of snow
not many days before and there was moisture in the
earth)—Salamis stood up on the right, a line of
rambling hills ; Aegina rose out of the open gulf,
and far away on the sea-line were the faint blue hills
of Argolis.   How shall we see horrors and not despise
them under this friendly sky ?

Suddenly at the palace door stood a figure clad
in sweeping robes, fantastic, super-human, vast,
much as one pictures the Genie of the *Arabian
Nights*.   It wore a face mask that was one terrible
grimace, more forbidding (since it was less grotesque)
than our own Gothic gargoyles.[1]   Above the forehead rose a towering frontlet of black hair.   Out of
those bulging eye-sockets peered human eyes : if
the figure speaks it should surely be in some
strange exalted tongue, the high grandiloquence
of Olympos.   Yet when the slit of the mouth gave
utterance it was with a man's voice.   It came a
long-drawn recitative of chanted speech.   And as
he stood mouthing the words, he was all the while
swaying his whole tall figure to the rhythm of them.
As he moved forward to the edge of the stage (he
seemed to glide rather than walk), the trailing robe
of rich embroidery swept aside, disclosing great

---

[1] At the first appearance of a tragic actor at Sparta several women
fainted.

club-soled 'buskins,' half boot, half stilt. He used his padded arms and gloved hands in apt and measured gesture, quickening as his speech quickened, and pointing the periods as the voice rose in a shrill torrent of passionate rhetoric and then slowly again, as it sank at the close to a smooth monotone. Then ceasing at last, he stood stock-still: and standing there thus magnificently posed, he became part, as it were, of the painted scene behind him, as the figure of some god appears planted on the rich field of a coloured tapestry.

Those that sat and watched had held their breath during some thirty lines or so, and now emitted it all at once in a raucous cheer. They knew the tale well enough, having seen it figured in plays, I know not how often: therefore they considered in their minds what the knot of the tragedy would be and how it all might end. And as they considered this, they were aware of a second mythological figure that entered and stood by the first: then the two held heroic colloquy in iambic verse, until the sound of dancing feet and chanting voices broke in upon their talk, and from the opening to the right, fifteen white-bearded elders entered the ring. They came stepping and singing to the time of a flute: the air which they sang was of a melancholy and altogether outlandish sort, and full of those strange untempered harmonies which, when the world was young, men held for music. Of these something still lingers in the chants which we set, I know not why, to the account of St. Gregory, but their full secret is still hidden even from the wise. They ranged themselves, these fifteen elders, still treading a measure the while, round the altar of Dionysos that stood in the centre of the ring.   Then their leader stepped towards the stage and addressed the two mythological personages.   There was a brilliant clash of wits in the argument that followed, and all through the thrust and parry of the logic the critics nodded their heads with an approving and judicial air.   The sophist delighted in the well-turned epigrams, rattling his heels against the stone bench and clucking at times with his tongue ; this behaviour was a source of great discomfort to the dramatist aforementioned, who made it a point of honour to hold his tongue when others chose to applaud and to applaud when they were silent.   Kleonymos sat meanwhile munching the comfits with great complacency.

As the play moved on, the audience poked their heads forward and warmed to their work.   They would pounce upon a misplaced emphasis, and even treat the actor to a shower of nuts.   They were quick to catch some veiled allusion to the new alliance with Argos, and cheered it loudly.   One choice song specially took their fancy, wherein the beauties of Athens were catalogued, and the old tag dragged in about her ' crown of violet hills.'   There were cries of αὖθις, or encore, but the song and dance swept on, the choir threading an intricate figure in and out and back and forth, moving round the altar like the morris-dancers of mediaeval England.

The stage was now empty and the audience were half aware of catastrophe to come, when the melody changed suddenly into a quavering minor key.   The choir, parting in two bands, took their place on this side and that of the palace steps.   Their swaying figures seemed alternately to lunge and cower as if in prophetic mimicry of some murderous struggle.

At the last burst of song there came a hush. Then a cry rang from within the palace, and at the same moment the walls were seen to part asunder, and swinging round on hidden hinges they revealed a horrible tableau : the murderer was standing with his victim at his feet, and a bloody sword in his hand. Then the walls rolled back again.

As the chorus wailed a dirge, a woman entered, mourning. But there was no flinging of arms, no frantic grief, no agitated sobbing. Her hands were held out stiffly and appealingly to the sky, and the plaintive long-drawn lament of φεῦ φεῦ was all the cry that she uttered. Then came a calm and dignified soliloquy, and so the tension imperceptibly decreased, and the interest flagged—until it was presently revived in a strange fashion. A platform or balcony above the stage suddenly rattled down with not a little creaking of chains and winches, and landed upon the boards the helmeted figure of Pallas Athena. With a thrill the assembled people listened as she cut the tangle of the plot, and watched her depart as she had come, turning to bestow her final blessing on the chorus. The latter attempted to explain their supreme conviction of the unreality of human fortunes and their unfeigned surprise that things had turned out like this after all ; but their last words were drowned in a burst of cheering.[1]

As they filed out of the ring, Taureas went forward ostentatiously to praise and to criticise—but he did neither, for Alkibiades stepped out before him and seized one of the choirmen by the arm.

---

[1] Many plays end with this identical tag, whether from pure convention or whether, as some have thought, it marked the finish of the play, and it mattered little whether its fatuity was lost to the audience.

As he did so he demanded in a loud voice his exclusion from the choir. ' I inform against him,' he cried, ' before the people of Athens as an impostor and no true citizen. It " needs no lamp " to see he is a branded slave.' Purple rage and green fear chased one another over Taureas' cheeks, and as Alkibiades led his victim off, the little man took courage and seized his persecutor by the cloak. Alkibiades turned on the funny bald little old man, and said, ' Off to the crows with thee,' and smacked him over the ear with the flat of his hand.

There was a hush of dismay : assault had been committed in the sight of all Athens : it was sheer sacrilege, no less, at the God's Festival with the Priest of Bacchos sitting by. Then Taureas began loudly to call his friends to bear him witness of the affront which he had received, and this set all tongues furiously wagging. Night itself would have fallen and found them still debating this new scandal but that the performance was only half through.

The ' scene ' was changed : a simple matter, for each of those two little side-scenes that flanked the palace front were in reality canvases stretched on a sort of triangular prism, which prism had two other landscapes on its two other faces. One of these other faces was now switched round so that your knowing Athenian said to himself, ' Ah, now we are in Delphi, and the rock can be none other than Parnassos, for it has a tripod under it,' or ' that wavy line with a dolphin beneath clearly indicates the sea,' and with that he was perfectly content.[1] So

---

[1] Localisation of a similar sort was effected in the Shakesperian theatre by the interior ' scenes '—or still more crudely by the notices in writing hung up to give the cue to the audience.

the two succeeding tragedies were gone through
in a dreary fashion with a crestfallen and diminished
chorus. The audience did not listen to them
nor to the comedy that followed, but when the
music was loud enough, they whispered furtively to
their neighbours, debating whether Alkibiades' action
would cost him the prize.

Every one had therefore framed his own opinion
long before the time for judging came. The ten
judges to whom it fell to award the prize, had been
chosen by lot at the beginning of the Festival.
They now came forward into the ring, each bearing
in his hand a tablet upon which he had written the
names of the poets in order of merit. The tablets
were placed together in a bowl; then the archon,
dipping his hand at random, drew forth five out of
the ten [1] and ascertained the result. He then made
it known to the crier, who bawled it to the crowd;
and behold! neither Taureas nor yet Alkibiades
was the winner, but their third despised rival. This
verdict was ill received by the partisans of Alkibiades,
especially by the young aristocrat faction who sat
in a bunch upon the left. But in spite of their cries
of derision and protest the choregos and the poet
were both summoned to the stage; there the sacred
tripod was put into their hands and carried off by
them in triumph. A final offering blazed upon the
Wine-god's altar, and so all departed—the populace
to revel in his honour, the victor and his friends to
celebrate their success in a banquet—Alkibiades to
drink both late and deep—and Taureas to consult

[1] This is only another instance of the precautions taken by the
framer of Athenian institutions to lessen the risks of favour or
corruption.

a friend upon a point of law. Kleonymos was left in undisputed possession of the theatre, comfortably snoring on his cushion. The stale quips about his shield, as he declared afterwards at supper, had sent him off to sleep.

It was a merry party at which Kleonymos sat down, and towards the end of the evening boisterous. All Athens was in a mood of misrule. The plays of the morning had deeply stirred their souls, opening the springs of honest laughter and the strong current of wholesome passion. Yet there was mischief untamed in them still. It was the hour of that mysterious spirit which, in the very early days of spring, moves in the sprouting furrows and the growing trees, and bidding men to shake off sluggish winter, breeds in them a riotous impulse and a lust for life, and sends through their veins a gush of happy animal spirits. Now for this life-giving god the Northern nations, little conscious of such influences, have found no peculiar name, but the Greeks called him Dionysos. And it was he who this night in Athens was to lead the rout. As the city grew dark and quieter, there rose great bursts of song and laughter, fitfully at first and in scattered homes, but by and by the revellers burst out of their street doors and carried the flare of torches through the public ways, mingling in a riot of mischief and high ecstasy under the stars. So they danced far into the night, and so presently they sank towards dawn into an exhausted slumber, to wake again in full morning with heavy heads, but saner hearts, exorcised and cleansed, as it were, of the wild spirit of spring.

NOTE ON THE GREEK ART OF ACTING

It is strangely difficult to conjure before the mind any clear vision of the Greek play as done 'in action' before an Athenian audience. It is a task which calls for a strong effort of the imagination; and for that task small help is to be got from those amateur revivals which may from time to time be witnessed upon our academic stage. It is not merely that we miss in these the old face-mask and the tragic-boot: something far more vital fails us, something which is the very core and centre of tragic action—I mean the influence of a live emotion. The dead hand of Classicism follows us from the lecture-hall to the playhouse. Now and again perhaps some individual part is played with deep feeling and evident sympathy, but these are as single and scattered sparks struggling in an ill-lit fire, there is no sustained or steady glow, no true emotional atmosphere.

Like all peoples of Southern Europe, the Greeks were excitable, high-strung folk. They are not less so to-day. Listen to the talk of half a dozen peasants in a railway train. Set out in cold print it would perhaps appear as stale and flat as the sedate gossip of six Northerners, but heard and witnessed, it is immediately alive with incident and meaning. Two things chiefly make it so: first the rapid play of gesture, the darting fingers and waving arms; secondly the eager modulations of the tones as the voices rise and fall in varied and rapid cadences: these are the two elements of emotional expression which stamp these people as a race of actors born.

The first thing needful to an orator, said Demosthenes, is action; the second too is action, and the third again action. What he said as orator other Athenians might well have said as players. Gesture was indeed to them a second nature, gesture not in the narrow sense alone, not the mere employment of the two hands, but the power of giving expression to every thought, word, by a suited pose, a co-ordinated movement of the whole body. Gesture of this kind is a language of itself, and independent of the tongue. The conversation of the railway carriage becomes intelligible by virtue of it, and needs no better interpreter.

In Tragedy, no doubt, gesture was limited and controlled, not merely by the material hindrances of heavy cloaks and clumsy buskins, but also by a strict convention and well-understood restraint. But even so it must play a vastly important rôle; when the features are covered by a mask the actor is deprived at the start of means of interpretation which our modern actors rate perhaps over-high. Gesture stood for the Greek in the place of this facial expression. Indeed an accurate and sympathetic pose is at once more artistic and more deeply moving than mere grimace can ever be. Jocasta, when first she learns the terrible truth concerning Oedipus, might in the modern style express her horror by agitated and nervous hand-play and painful contortions of the mouth. But were she to stand quite motionless with a fixed gaze, body erect, head bent, and hand upon her cheek, she would convey to us the sentiment of grief much as it is conveyed by a statue of the Mater Dolorosa. And it is the statuesque, not the passing movement, that counts in art.[1]

I seem to see the Greek actor then as master of a whole code of calculated gesture, able to suit the action to the word, not according to his own momentary whim, but according to a well-formed tradition.[2] But still more strictly must we believe tradition to have ruled the movements of the chorus. Their dance figures were, we know, closely united with the spirit of their songs.[3]

[1] Some approach to the old ideal has lately been made in the acting of the Savoy. The posing and gesture of the Fairy King and Queen in the *Midsummer Night's Dream*, a difficult pose being often sustained through a dozen lines of soliloquy, were most effective and, I believe, most truly Greek.

[2] What the traditional and favourite gestures and poses were, the vases would to some extent reveal.

[3] Greek dancing, like that of Pavlova and others, aimed at expressing a particular idea or incident—an excellent illustration of this fact is the epigram upon a stiff-jointed performer, 'Snub-nosed Memphis danced Daphne and Niobe; Daphne like a stock, and Niobe like a stone.'

But the concerted dance must to be effective contain something more than an ingenious adaptation of panto-mimic gesture. New 'motives' were, no doubt, readily and constantly supplied, but the whole bias of Greek art makes it all but certain that the origin of these dances was rooted in an old and well-sustained tradition of country-side festivities. The Greeks learned to dance in the natural course as girls and boys; they practised it through life. Only by such an established and universal habit can the dance become a spontaneous and expressive art.

With us the tradition has lapsed, and only in recent years has enjoyed an artificial resuscitation. Neverthe-less, when in the recent production of a Greek comedy, a morris figure was adapted to the purpose of the play, there seemed to be struck a note of freshness and suit-ability seldom felt in the rigid and unmeaning gambols which usually are made to serve our turn. The Greek dance was, of course, incomparably more elegant, and as a method of expression incomparably more facile. It varied according to the moment's need, from the slow step and sinuous sway and swing of dignified composure to the riotous reeling scamper of a Bacchic rout.[1] Yet, every-where it was instinct with art, and must have been at least as satisfying to the eye as were the poetry and music to the ear.

And with the mention of the ear, we come to the second element of expressed emotion, the use of the vocal instrument. Here again we know the Greeks to have possessed a fine habit of elocution. Not else could their actors have been for a moment audible to those vast assemblies who were, as we are told, keenly critical over any lapse in pronunciation or a misplaced accent. Yet the actors did more, we may be sure, than simply make themselves heard. In all great actors the voice is a subtle and powerful instrument. But here again, I imagine, the Greeks did not leave so much as we do to the interpreter

---

[1] Here again dancing is to-day coming by its own again, though, as hinted above, nothing can take the place of a national tradition when once lost.

of a passage, to the fancy of an individual actor. I should conceive them to have been ruled in this matter also by some sort of tradition and convention. In the first place, it is not amiss to observe that among all peoples, and especially among the Latin races, there are certain fixed cadences appropriated to special moods and sentiments. A Frenchman, for example, will at once upon embarking on a narration fall into an animated sing-song with an even stress and fall. I have heard the same cadence come from many different lips. In comparing the tones used by various Italians engaged upon a quarrel, one may discover a similar identity of rhythm. So, in all likelihood, the Greeks employed a variety of cadences, one for the heated dialogue, another for the long-winded even rhetoric of the inevitable 'messenger,'[1] a third for passionate soliloquy.

But they seem to have gone further yet, and to have suited the actual metre closely to the dramatic mood of the verse. The lyrical passages in a play are more than mere interludes designed to break the regularity of the iambic verse. Take, for instance, the *Alkestis.* Whatever may have been the inner motives of Euripides in writing the play, it is hard to believe that he does not intend Admetos' feelings to undergo a radical transformation after the burial of his wife. Before the departure of the funeral train the bereaved husband uses none but the coldest and most unconvincing protestations of sorrow, spoken, be it observed, in the conventional iambic and standing in vivid contrast to the lyrical lamentations of his son. Upon his return from the grave-side he speaks in quite a different way. Apart from the moaning and groaning (the ἒ ἒ and φεῦ φεῦ of the written texts), it is impossible to overlook the fact that he breaks out into the appropriate language of passionate remorse and utters some threescore lines of lyric poetry.

This can hardly be accident. No doubt much of the

---

[1] The monotonous elocution of a somewhat 'churchy' type which prevails at modern productions makes one feel the want of some variety.

lyrical part of a play, notably the choric odes, was a conventional necessity, and originated in the early history of the dramas. Nevertheless, in Euripides at least, there could probably be traced a close connection between the variation of the metre and the mood or temper of the character.[1] In a word, the Greeks studied far more closely than we allow for the resources of the human instrument, upon which in other ways they set restrictions so harsh and so insistent that anything which we should call an individual rendering of a part seems a sheer impossibility. The actor may have been in some respects the playwright's tool.[2] But using to the full those two resources of voice and gesture, he was able to breathe into the plays that emotional and vital quality without which they must seem to us as cold and as dead as is now the language in which the plays themselves were written.

---

[1] So Shakespeare varied his use of rhymed verse, blank verse, lyrics and prose, according to the type of character into whose mouth the words are put.

[2] Here again Mr. Gordon Craig's theory of the function of the actor approaches somewhat to the Greek view. In his anxiety, however, to degrade the actor to the position of a marionette and to abolish, if I understand him aright, the very use of words, he seems to go to a length which Greek moderation and humanist instincts could never have tolerated.

THE THEATRE

The masked chorus stand round the altar of the *orchestra* or dancing-ring. They face the stage[1] on which are two actors in masks and buskins. Behind these rises the stage-building, with its two projecting wings and its three door-entrances. The painted imitation of a temple is hung on its front; and on either side of this are the reversible side-scenes. Between the stage-building and the auditorium is a gap by which the chorus enter the *orchestra*. The front row of seats are occupied by priests and other functionaries.

---

[1] The stage is represented as eight or nine feet high. Nearly all extant evidence, whether literary or archaeological, points to an even higher stage. But it must be remembered that such evidence refers to theatres of the second, third or fourth centuries before Christ. For the fifth century there are no direct indications at all. It is indeed quite likely that at that epoch the stage-buildings were still made of wood and not stone ; and hence no traces of them have survived. Although the plays of Aeschylos, Sophokles and Euripides seldom require an actor to descend from stage to dancing-ring, yet it may well be doubted whether their stage was in reality so perilously high.

THEATRE

XIII. AN EKKLESIA

' A jealous constituency of natural hecklers.'

A. E. ZIMMERN.

PUNCTUALLY at first cock-crow, when the sun peeps over the bow-backed rim of Mount Hymettos, and striking across the plain of Attica touches with fire the ragged grey outline of Aigaleos beyond, the City wakes in the misty flats which lie between the mountains, and there is a general stir along its streets. Bolts rattle in the doors—then voices come, first a shrill-voiced summons for staff and ' Spartans,' [1] then after a pause a second; and with lively imprecations on a sleepy slave, citizen Smithykion of the Kollytos ward is stumping out of his front door and citizen Melitides out of his, and both as they meet are asking in the same breath whether the signal is yet hoisted on the Rock. Now the Rock is the name which Athenians give to the Pnyx or Parliament Hill; and, by that same token, it must needs be the call of Politics that brings Smithykion and Melitides so early from their couch. The Athenians are no lie-abeds, and, recking little the advantages of stuffy parliaments and midnight sittings, they hold their innocent sessions upon an open hill at dawn.

It is plain enough, then, that the two honest burghers are bound for the Pnyx, there to hear the

[1] The Athenians were much by way of imitating Spartan dress—and the ' Spartan ' boot was at this time very popular.

debate and cast their votes before the sun grows hot; but what they will debate about when they are there, it is by no means so easy of conjecture. For, as all the world, or at least all Athens knows, this is none of the statutory occasions set apart in each month for the holding of debates. These days are four in number. On Sovereign assembly day, so-called, they criticise the magistrates and vote supplies; in the middle of the month religious matters are discussed, while questions of civic discipline are despatched at the end of it. There is a fourth meeting at which the reports concerning foreign policy fall to be considered. But since this morning is none of these, it would seem that there must be some special trouble in the wind. The truth is that certain ambassadors arrived from Sparta yesterday at dawn, and their business here is pressing. The Council sat in conclave till late in the afternoon, and the Public Crier was sent on his rounds announcing an *extraordinary summons* for the morrow. The citizens were not long kept in the dark concerning the affair, for as the evening crowd passed below the slopes of the Areopagos where the rude stone effigies of the Tribal ' Patron-Saints ' stare wide-eyed into the sunset, they could read placarded across the pedestals the programme for next day's debate.

So all are up betimes this morning: and Melitides and his friend are not alone in their journey to the Pnyx: every citizen, that is worthy of the name, is already moving in the same direction, from the greybeard veteran who fought at Salamis, to the youngster just out of his teens, and fresh from his year's soldiering in the frontier forts. In they

pour from all the avenues and alleys that converge
upon the market square. Here the stalls are already
opened, and while the slower-paced hobble on,
staff in hand, to climb the hill and find seats within
earshot of the platform, the younger men linger
to pass the time of day with their companions,
hanging round the perfume shops or the pastry
stalls, and chaffing the country voters, good simple
folk, as they come in from their more distant homes,
the farms of Phlya or the woodmen's huts at
Acharnae under the hills. As these tall, well-tanned
figures come swinging up from the Dipylon gate,
marching to the tune of some old war-chant, our
dainty, sallow-skinned fops let drop a sneering reference to their rustic hob-nailed boots, and sniff
with an affectation of disgust at the coarse, odorif-
erous goatskins in which the homely fellows have
lain rolled up for the night. If one of them should
by chance take a pull from the flask of sour wine at
his belt, it is thought a capital joke ; and a laugh
goes up—but the taunts do not greatly ruffle the
quiet dignity of the rustics, who are content to fling
a curse back at their persecutors and follow up after
the others to the place of meeting. For a while
the wits still linger on, but with one eye now upon
the end of the market, where at length they catch
sight of the nodding peak of a Scythian cap. That
is enough—the constables [1] are clearing the square,
and they too must be moving up ' Parliament Hill.'
Two would-be shirkers slink off towards a side exit,
only to find the barriers up, and a couple of ill-

[1] Since the task of policing the city was not becoming the dignity of
a free Athenian, the function was assigned to Scythian bowmen, who
were distinguished by their picturesque native costume.

favoured Tartars, carrying a reddened rope between them, have soon headed them off, catching them as sailors catch herrings in a draw-net. A curious dialogue ensues : the Peaked-cap gurgles some official formula to Injured Dignity in the drollest pigeon-Attic. The suggestion of a fine is waved imperiously aside—Injured Dignity agrees to enter the assembly and departs, though not without a vermilion stripe imprinted upon his shirt tail.

So, being unable to afford the penalty for non-attendance, the two pocket their pride and turn into the Pnyx. This is an open theatre, shaped in part by nature and in part by man upon the slope of a rocky knoll ; along the crest of the knoll forming an arc to the huge semicircle, runs a flat wall cut out of the solid rock, in the centre of which a great slab or table of limestone juts out. This is the Bema, or speaker's platform, and round it the audience group themselves, sitting as best they can on the rock floor and forming a vast crescent on the hill-side ; the slope of the hill drops away gently towards the lower level of the market square : and the back seats were raised somewhat by an artificial embankment. To this position in the rear the late-comers make their way nervously and unnoticed, till some one catches sight of the tell-tale vermilion on their dress, and the seated multitude stop in their noisy chatter for a moment to hoot derisively : this, however, is but a brief interruption, and soon enough the crowd falls back to its gossip. ' I can tell thee,' Smithykion is saying, ' I can tell thee what has hipped these Spartan folk, it is our scheme of partnership with Argos. They are in a hot fever about it, and what is more, they have got old

Nikias to back their cause. He is as sweet on them as cakes, and would give them back Pylos for the asking, the old mammy-suck.'

'A pox on Nikias,' retorted Melitides, bringing down his staff heavily on the stones; 'Alkibiades is our man, say I, yet I'll tell thee a strange thing too. For, if I did not see our friend hob and nob with these same Spartan envoys yesternight and they as thick as thieves with him, I'll never trust my eyes again. I misdoubt me whether they have not got round our hero somehow. There is more craft in them than meets the eye; trust a Spartan as you would a wolf.'

'Stuff and nonsense,' cried a third; 'a Spartan has no more wit in his pate than a wood block, and nowadays they have even forgotten how to fight. Only the last Dionysia I met an archer-man, a tame islander too, that had been to Pylos with Kleon and there shot down ten of the best of them. Ah, if only Kleon were alive we'd send the rascals packing!' So the talk ran on till it was suddenly cut short by the appearance of fifty white-robed councillors coming over the crest of the hill. This body represented the Council of Five Hundred, being the Committee in course for the month, and they came to take their place as Presidents of the meeting. Seats were reserved for them on the hewn steps at the top of the long rock wall. Here, after squabbling a little for precedence, they somehow settled down and sat looking out upon the vast half-moon of humanity over which, for the next few hours, they were nominally to exercise a presidential control.

'Move forward' (προίτε εἰς τὸ πρόσθεν), shouted the Herald, vigorously waving his staff. At this

summons those on the outskirts of the crowd
pressed nearer in; and another procession appeared
and this time upon the right of the assembly.
First came a priest in a long trailing robe: behind
him came an acolyte bearing in his arms, with
the most solemn demeanour in the world, the
corpse of a little black pig! These two passed
outside the gathered multitude and sprinkling
fresh blood as they went on their round. By this
curious ceremony they drew a hallowed ring, just
as a fairy-tale wizard would do, about the whole
Athenian Parliament. 'Hold ye your peace,'
bawled the Crier again when the circuit was finished.
The public sacrifices had been made and the chairman of the Council was rising to announce their
successful issue. He was, as it so happened, a
cobbler of little education, but vastly proud in the
enjoyment of his brief authority of a day—(for each
of the committee in rotation took the chair for one
day in the month)—when he came to make the
announcement he mouthed the liturgical formula
as though he were Perikles himself uttering the
famous funeral speech. 'Meet sacrifice and proper
(so it ran) has been made by us, the Presidents of
your Assembly, to the Mother of the Gods. Her
blessing be upon you!' The Herald followed
with a tedious form of 'bidding-prayer,' calling
upon all the gods of the calendar, one by one, and
begging them to assist at the coming deliberations.
And (he added) if any man in that assembly should
dare to do aught that the laws forbade, terrible
indeed were the curses that would inevitably fall
upon him, and his family, and all that was his.
These ceremonies over, the chairman read the

resolution which had been passed by the Council on the previous day. 'The Council is resolved,' it ran, 'that the Assembly having given audience to the Embassy and having heard all who wish to speak, should take such measures as seem to them best.'

These stale formalities had roused little interest and less reverence among the crowd, who were busy enough most of them cracking nuts with their teeth or munching garlic : when, however, Alkibiades entered during the saying of the prayer they all turned to gaze at him, as the wedding guests turn at the entry of the bride. When further he was seen to bring at his heels six tall figures muffled up to the chin in heavy red cloaks, and wearing travellers' wide-awakes on their sadly unkempt heads, there was some nudging of elbows and pointing of fingers. Finally when Alkibiades placed them by the side of the platform and whispered for a moment in their ears, the crowd broke out in a buzz of impatient comment. Why was not Nikias doing them the honours ? How came Alkibiades to have supplanted him ? Nobody knew : for Spartans can at least keep a secret. But the root of the mystery was this : Alkibiades had got some private talk with the strangers overnight. When they left the Council Chamber, he and every one present had understood that they had come to Athens with the fullest powers to conclude an agreement; Alkibiades had now warned them that in the Assembly such an avowal would be fatal to their interests. If they would but go back upon what they had told the Council, he promised them his support. That was enough for them and they fell into the trap. And now, when the Crier called out, 'Who wishes to speak ? ' Alkibiades himself was the first to mount the steps and take his stand upon the great rock slab. A wreath which the Crier handed to him, he took and placed on his head. Then wrapping his cloak well round him, he faced the audience. They broke into a cheer at the sight of his handsome figure. It was as if some marble effigy of Hermes had suddenly come to life, donned a cloak and descended from his pedestal. Alkibiades indeed held himself with all the grace and quiet dignity of a statue. He did not affect the furious delivery of the demagogues who ramped about the platform like ' a dog yapping on the farm-yard wall.' He spoke at first with composure. His left hand remained under the folds of his cloak ; the gestures of his right were vivid, impatient, and often somewhat supercilious. His speech was more deliberate than rapid : and often he would pause for some moments searching the right word. His style, though essentially his own, yet owed much to the rhetoric teachers of the day. And if his diction was somewhat stilted and unnatural, let us remember that with them, as with our own Eliza-bethan writers, style was still in its infancy— amused with the trick of an antithesis or the jingle of a pun, and toying with all manner of fanciful conceits. Moreover (aptly enough for our meta-phor) the speaker had a charming lisp, turning all his R's to L's. What he said was much as follows :

' Critics may cavil, men of Athens, but something I must say, though briefly, of myself, forasmuch as it behoves you with your councillors, as with your

coins, to cherish the good and current but to fling
out the counterfeit.

'Consider, I pray ye, to what end you should hear
me. Can a fine wit, think you, or the lustre of my
kin and ancestry, or a matchless stud of racers
(cries of εὖ εὖ, λέγε, λέγε), can these, I say, avail to
save from damage and dishonour our old " Kranaan
Town " ? Nay, the sole authority whereby I
speak to-day lies in my true devotion to the public
weal.

'What, then, shall be the purpose and purport of
my present admonition ? This, men of Athens !—
whatever you ordain, ordain *to-day* ! If these
Spartans come with full powers to treat, up then
with your hands and stay not for the morrow.
Such are my words of counsel. If they mislike
you—so ! (The gap explained itself by a rapid
gesture, but the grammarians have invented a very
long word to help people to understand it), but
mark me well, O Athenian men, somewhither these
words of mine will issue.' With this vague threat,
a favourite trick of speech with him, he paused, and
all looked to the Spartans to put in their word.
Their spokesman, puzzled as a ploughboy at the
quarter sessions, scratched his head, recollected
the cue he had from Alkibiades, and ingenuously
took it. ' By the Twa', sirs, we munna tak' muckle
rope.'

' How now ! ' cried Alkibiades, simulating a
tremendous rage, ' was it not but yestere'en that
they swore before the Council that they had the
fullest power to treat ? The President himself
will bear men witness that I speak no less than the
truth.' The illiterate cobbler was far too slow to

get in a word, and Alkibiades whirled on. 'And now, an it please you, in this solemn spot under these sacred vows before our People's Parliament, this false and wanton shift—"No muckle rope." So "Tongue's oath plights no troth"[1] comes from hollow Lakedaemon? And now consider well, my friends. What treatment do such traitors merit at your hands? Some there are, and full well I know them, will go about to speak of feasts in the City Hall, of a fair hearing and "all that is the privilege of guests." Scorn on all such, say I. Not so did your fathers deal with the envoys sent by the Persian king, yet honest men for all that. By the House of the Maiden yonder, if you would be true to your fathers' memory, you will not fall short of the lesson they passed down, but you will go beyond them rather, to make of these perjured knaves a grand and notable example. Aye, you shall make of them not guests in sooth, but ghosts. See how they pale even now under their scarlet cloaks. No common death should serve their turn, nor the Deadman's Pit for a grave,' and he jerked a thumb over his shoulder towards the cliffs behind him.[2] 'And, as for Sparta,' he concluded, 'she is treating with us for alliance, and we—we will treat her to a taste of war.'

The meeting was in a turmoil: and the envoys being, as they told their friends at home, 'fair mathered' by these weather-cock tricks, obeyed Alkibiades' beckoning finger and filed meekly out.

---

[1] A line which Euripides had put into the mouth of one of his characters (Hippolytos) and which had aroused much comment and indignation among the more conservative Athenians.

[2] On the farther or western side of the Pnyx Hill are cliffs or quarries where the bodies of criminals were flung.

As they went, their rivals the Argive embassy came forward. A fresh motion was framed; Athens was on the point of establishing a permanent treaty with Argos and all her allies, for one hundred years. 'Raise hands,' cried the Herald, and up went four thousand bare arms, when all of a sudden the voice of Smithykion was heard. A drop of rain had struck him on the head—it was an omen—the assembly must not proceed. Some were disposed to hold in question the value of this evidence, when a clap of thunder and a violent shock of earthquake put it beyond doubt. The meeting broke up in alarm.

'See,' said Nikias, clucking his lips in superstitious terror, as a thunderbolt fell with a crash near by, 'the god is angered against the son of Kleinias.' When the air cleared, the bolt was seen to have shattered a neighbouring shrine. 'Then,' said Alkibiades, 'may the son of Kleinias congratulate the son of Kronos on the accuracy of his aim.'

A month or two later the Argives were again present in the Ekklesia. Alkibiades was still in the ascendant. True, Nikias had made violent efforts to patch it up with Sparta. He had even made the journey to that town in person, but all to no purpose. The treaty with Argos was voted: and its terms were carved in stone and set on the Akropolis at Athens, being to the following effect:

'That the Athenians and the Argives, Mantineans and Eleans on their own behalf and that of the allies over whom they severally rule, make a peace to continue for one hundred years by sea and land, without fraud or hurt.'

To this and the numerous other provisions of the treaty, the various allies swore each in their several towns, taking the oath over the bodies of full-grown victims, and following the formula held to be most binding among their own people.

Smithykion, however, could not put from his head the memory of that drop of rain : and when some months later the new allies suffered a considerable reverse, he posed as something of a prophet—nor did he ever again record a vote for the policy of Alkibiades.

AN EKKLESIA

AN EKKLESIA

A speaker, staff in hand, garland on head, is addressing
the assembly from the Bema or platform. His violent
gestures are taken from a vase-painting. The Spartan
envoys in thick cloaks and travelling hats stand on his right.
Behind him sit the Prytanes; while the Crier stands near
by. In the foreground is a Scythian archer or policeman
with his peaked cap and trousers. The Parthenon, Propylaea,
Temple of Victory, and the colossal statue of Athena
appear on the left, Mt. Hymettos rising behind them.

XIV. A WEDDING FESTIVAL

'Qui rapis teneram ad virum
Virginem, O Hymenaee Hymen!'
CATULLUS.

AMONG the Greeks marriage was at all times and
without any disguise a mercenary matter. The
bride was bought and sold like a parcel of goods
and her leave never asked. There was no room for
sentimental courtship; and in truth a betrothal
was nothing better than a bargain. In the good
old days when the gods still walked on earth and
womenkind were rare, it was the bridegroom who
paid and the father who called the tune. It is so
at least that Homer tells of it. But when times
changed and the sex was at a discount, the bargain
was contracted in a different fashion. A father
could no longer look forward to earning a yoke of
oxen or a shekel of silver on the day he parted with
his daughter. On the contrary, it might cost him
dear even to get the girl a husband. Nobody would
take her without dowry, however great were her
charms; and dowry therefore she must have, or
remain in her father's house a spinster, a burden
and a reproach.

Here lay the manifest advantage of the young
bachelor of high birth and extravagant habits
(such as was Alkibiades). Naturally he would
consult his purse rather than his passions, and if

financial troubles could be corrected by an advantageous marriage, the son of Kleinias was not the man to stand on ceremony. Now Hipponikos had a daughter, Hipparete by name, young and by no means ill-favoured. But what was more, Hipponikos had a well-filled purse. The suitor, it is true, had small claim upon the family, for not long since he had insulted the old man to his face. But the father having died and Hipparete having passed under the care and tutelage of her brother Kallias (for every woman was legally a minor, and always remained the ward of some male guardian), Alkibiades perceived his chance. He was a frequent visitor at the house of Kallias, who kept open doors to sophists and their friends ; and he was thus able, not indeed to make the acquaintance of the lady (for young girls never mixed in male society) but at least to gauge the magnitude of her brother's fortune. In short, he broached the matter, and drove a bargain. A formal contract was concluded before witnesses, by which Hipparete was his with twenty talents dowry.[1]

It was a strange and doubtful prospect that lay before the girl, betrothed as she was, through no fault of her own, to a man whose reputation she perhaps had heard, but whom she could scarcely have known by sight, so strict was the seclusion in which her life had hitherto been spent. Year by year, indeed, she had been led forth to participate in some public festival. She had once on a great day borne a basket in the Great Procession. Once too she had gone to Artemis' precinct on the citadel and there danced the weird bear-dance along with

---

[1] Equivalent to nearly £5000, or £20,000 in purchasing power.

other children of her age.[1] But these were rare
glimpses of the external world, and she was still at
sixteen as ignorant of life as a child of ten.   For
her, as was natural, man was a mystery of mysteries ;
and as for marriage, it was at best a blindfold sort of
adventure.

The day appointed for the ceremony fell about
mid-winter ; this season for one cause or another
was held to be the proper time for weddings, and
the Greeks had even christened it the marriage
month.   So when the moon was coming to its full,
there were great preparations afoot in the bride's
home.   On the day which was the last she would
spend among her family, she bade a solemn farewell
to the old associations and the innocent pastimes
of her girlhood.   According to the quaint fashion
of the times, her childish playthings, her ball, her
doll, her tambourine, were offered with full ceremony to the goddess Artemis ; for Artemis was the
good angel of maidens, as Apollo was of boys.   Her
brother, standing at the altar side, cut from her
forehead a lock of hair and threw it on the flames ;
and by this act her life was consecrated as it were
to the service of the goddess ; and by that token
she accepted the unknown duties and dangers of
marriage and motherhood.

And now as the day was closing, a small and rather
sad procession entered the main court.   A dame
with torch in either hand was preceded by a young
boy playing upon the pipes, while behind her came
a maiden bearing upon her head a long-necked

[1] ' And then I was a bear,
     And a saffron robe did wear
     In the festival of Artemis of Brauron.'
                                   ARISTOPHANES.

pitcher. This vessel had been filled at the fountain which rises by the banks of the Ilissos and is called the Beautiful Spring. By a long-established custom every bride was washed in water drawn from that spring upon the eve of her wedding day.

Next morning the house was full of a busy confusion. The friends and playmates of the bride had gathered to bid her farewell and join in the celebrations and the singing of the chorus. The slaves were hanging every door and pillar with branches and festoons till the courtyard was as gay and garlanded as a ballroom at Christmastide, and the bride meanwhile was in the back part of the house which is the women's quarter, waiting to make her toilette. All was ready to hand, the long tunic embroidered at the hem with severe simple patterns, the mantle woven many years ago under her mother's eye, the wedding shoes of saffron hue, the myrtle wreath, and the veil, the drawing of which would presently discover her face for the first time to the vulgar gaze of man. But the bride herself sat waiting, toying impatiently with a pet sparrow. To her, thus seated, came her friends bringing small presents in their hands. ' Our Lady give thee joy,' said one, putting into her lap a small bronze mirror, ' see to it that thou use it well—or count me no judge of husbands.' ' Well said,' cried a second, ' but Alkibiades, I am told, has no eyes for a pallid woman,' and she produced from beneath her cloak a handsome box of rouge. ' I am not one to bear tales,' put in a third, ' but they say in the city, my dear, that he is a sad scoundrel and will make thee a sorry husband, mayhap this charm may help thee.' The sudden chorus of

protest which this speech provoked was as suddenly
cut short by a fresh arrival. For there entered a
dame, now well on in years, but straight and comely
as Penelope ; she was a kinswoman of the family,
and she came to act as Bride's-lady to Hipparete.
Her task it was to prepare the girl for the wedding,
and bear her company throughout the day. When
therefore the toilette was completed, she led out
her charge into the central court, where, upon the
small stone altar, sacrifice was being made. All
the deities that preside over nuptials were in turn
invoked, Zeus and Hera, Artemis and Aphrodite,
and Peitho the goddess of Persuasion. A considerable company was gathered round the altar ; and,
when the prayers were ended and the court was
still fragrant with the rich odours of burning incense, they all repaired, both the friends of bridegroom and bride alike, to an adjoining chamber in
which a repast was to be served. The ladies took
their place upon separate couches that stood on the
right hand of the doorway ; but the men lay down
opposite. Seeing that all were set down, and
greeted by a clamour of merry voices, the Bride's-
lady now led Hipparete into their midst. The
veil that hid her face was presently drawn aside,
and at that Alkibiades took the blushing girl by
the hand and placed her beside him on the couch,
and the feast began. Whatever were the feelings
of the bashful bride, there was no false decorum
in the conduct of the feast. The guests ate well
of the comfits and sesame cakes (for the viands were
of a light and unsubstantial sort) ; and they drank,
some of them more than prudently, of the wine,
well watered as it was, so that very soon the merri-

ment was at its height ; all were laughing and talking,
and in particular were ridiculing Sokrates because
in his clumsy way he had spilled the liquor down his
tunic front, when a strange figure was seen at the
door. It was Panaetios, the ancient boon-com-
panion of Alkibiades, but no friend at all of Kallias
the host. 'God rest you,' the fellow cried to the
company, and, as all heads turned his way, added
knowingly, 'Now entered Menelaos an uninvited
guest.' Some one applauded the aptness of this
tag from Homer ; but amid a roar of laughter
Alkibiades capped his sally with another : 'Right
sore was Agamemnon, the son of Atreus vex'd.'
To this Panaetios attempted no reply, but scanned
the benches, looking for a vacant seat. Kallias,
since hospitality forbade him to resent the intrusion,
motioned a slave to bring forward a stool. This
was not what Panaetios desired, and he took up his
stand by the doorway, vowing that he would not be
seated like a slave, but should, if need be, walk about
till he grew tired and then, he declared, he should
spread his cloak and lie on the floor, head on arm, like
Herakles in the picture. The company being in
high spirits were not slow to make mock at his discomfiture, and their ridicule was so galling that he
was within an ace of bursting into an ugly show of
temper, but that a diversion occurred to quiet him.
A young boy who had entered bearing a basket
of spiced bread, now extended it in the angry man's
direction, saying as he did so :

> 'From evil I fled
> And found better instead.'

This curious ceremony the boy repeated, as he went
the round and offered his basket to each guest in

turn. And by this their attention was drawn from the unwelcome visitor ; and the feast again resumed its even course. But the time soon came to break up the gathering and to convey the bride to her new home.

Outside the procession formed up : the chamberlain acting as the Marshal, a herald's baton in his hand. A chariot harnessed to four mules was waiting at the outer door, and when the pair had taken their places in it, the groomsman stepped in beside them and they got under way. The rest now set a light to their pine-flares, and the merry troop broke into the moonlit street, with a shout and much scattering of sparks. Flute and harp struck up the tune, and it brought the neighbours hurrying to their doorways when the first notes of the wedding chorus surprised the echoes of the winter night. Down the street they watched the white-robed troop go by, torches tossing aloft and feet beating to the measure, the elders a little slow and solemn, the young men excitable and boisterous, breaking in now and then upon the even rhythm with a wild and random shout, the maidens still modest and bashful, littering their path with the crimson petals of early spring anemones. The pace was sluggish, for the car strained and jolted in a laborious and uncertain motion down the unlevel roadway. At the sight of friend or stranger, Alkibiades turned in his seat and waved a hand. But whenever the street was dark and narrow, the bride wept a little, silently.

When at length the house was reached, the pair dismounted, and passing between the lane which the torchmen formed, came to the door. The groom's mother with a burning pine-stick in either hand, stood under the porch to greet them; and presently at her bidding the slaves brought trays laden with cakes, dried fruits and sweetmeats. Hipparete herself partook of a quince; which fruit possesses, so they say, much magical virtue for the newly-wedded wife. Then the doors of the bridal chamber were unfolded, and the couple passed within. The men withdrew, but the maidens lingered on the threshold to sing a parting serenade:

'Bless thee, bless thee, lovely bride!
  Bless thee, happy luver!
Lato send ye childer guid,
  Lato the All-mother.
Kypris grant that nought divide
  Love 'twixt each and other.
      Hymen, Hymen, wish us well
      In our wedding festival!

Never-ending happiness
  Father Zeus assure ye,
Living in like nobleness,
  As lived the sires before ye—
Heart to heart and kiss for kiss,
  Slumber now come o'er ye.
      Hymen, Hymen, wish us well
      In our wedding festival!

Yet be mindful to arise
  At the break of morning.
We'll renew our minstrelsies
  When the day is dawning,
And th' bright-throated singer cries
  First his note of warning.
      Hymen, Hymen, wish us well
      In our wedding festival! [1]

They were as good as their word: and daybreak saw them again before the house, headed this time

---

[1] Old-fashioned dialect forms lingered in these traditional airs. The song is an adaptation from Theokritos.

by a boy in white, and bearing in their hands sundry presents for the bride, a vase perhaps, or a shawl, a pair of saffron shoes or an alabaster casket.

The mother-in-law was present with some more substantial gift : and Kallias too was there to pay the dowry. Thus the matter ended as it had begun, upon the sober element of business.

So Hipparete has changed masters. Under the new tyrant she will know few privileges, many duties. One stands paramount. If she but bring him children, she will at least have deserved well both of husband and of state.

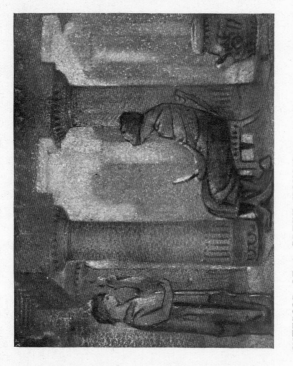

INTERIOR OF A GREEK HOUSE

INTERIOR OF A GREEK HOUSE

The lady of the house sits under the colonnade or *peristyle*, mirror in hand. A slave-girl near by is spinning wool. Houses built with such solid stone columns (note the painting on them) were a rarity in fifth-century Athens, but in the succeeding century Demosthenes complains of the lavish expenditure on private houses.

XV. A HOME IN ATHENS

'The Greeks gathered round no religious myth in which the family becomes divine.'—MR. HERBERT TRENCH.

' To see the Athenian in his true colours,' wrote a Frenchman of this century, 'perambulate the streets,' and two thousand years ago it was as true as it is to-day.   At any rate the last place to find him was at home.   He might perhaps be caught there by an early-morning caller, but unless a man was under a cloud or in some domestic trouble, or, like Timon, was a downright crank, out of patience with mankind,[1] he would show a marked preference for male society and the open air.   Both of these he could find in abundance at that most sociable of all clubs, the market-place.   Here he spent the greater part of the morning in friendly gossip : his after-noon was given to athletics, and only at suitable intervals, when requiring food or sleep, would he repair to his house : for the rest he left it to the ladies.

Such being the tastes and habits of a man of means and leisure, we shall not look in the house of Alkibiades for that comfortable homeliness which

[1] This, of course, applies only to men of the leisured class, not to the working man.   The Greeks could not tolerate men of a stay-at-home sort ; as may be read in the *Medea* of Euripides, they set such a disposition down to an arrogant assumption of superiority.   There was nothing they disliked more in the Orientals than their difficulty of access.

Northern nations prize; nor, when all allowances
for climate have been made, will it offer any but
the barest conveniences of life.

In style, no domestic architecture of our own
can produce even in broad lines its counterpart.
But in ground-plan and general arrangement it
resembled nothing so much as an old-fashioned
and secluded Collegiate House. Like this, though
on a far smaller scale, the Greek mansion lay concealed from the public street by a blank wall and
a bolted door; within, it too contained a sunny
court, round which the living rooms were grouped,
and upon which open space they had their outlook.

Coming upon the house from the street side, you
might observe, except for the front door and the
porter's lattice, no single opening or window of any
sort : there is, moreover, no upper story to the
house. Over the door, where our ancestors would
have placed a ponderous porch, the Greeks set a
slender portico resting upon Ionic columns (for
the same styles served in all buildings whether
sacred or profane), and whereas the Christian
founder, pious man, sets above the college door a
Madonna in stone to bless incomers from her
pedestal, the Greek householder found his superstitions satisfied by a rude stone pillar, set where we
should set the scraper. If it was square and had a
head, he called it Hermes; if conical, Apollo.
Why so, he no more thought to ask than a Syrian
bowing before his Asherah-pole. His father used
the names long before his day and that was enough
for him, and from time to time, by force of custom,
he hung a wreath upon the stone. Just inside the
door is the porter's cell : the careless slave is usually

fast asleep, but when roused by the rattling of the lion's-head knocker, he jumps up and puts his head through the spy-hole, ready, if need be, to loose a dog on unwelcome visitors. Access to the house is thus jealously guarded, and so impossible is it to force an entrance, that the housebreaker of those days preferred the rough-and-ready method —much simpler when a house is built of sun-dried brick—of digging through the walls.[1]

No sooner does the door (which opens outwards) creak on its hinges—the idle slave who should water them has neglected his duties—than there is a sudden patter of bare feet on the stones, and we enter the tiny court in time to see a flutter of drapery disappear through a door upon the further side. The court is empty.

Its floor is beaten mud, baked by the sun and seamed with a network of gaping heat cracks; overhead is the open sky. Bees are buzzing round the incense that smoulders upon an altar which, dedicated to Courtyard Zeus, stands out in the central space. Round all four sides of the court runs a cloister or verandah, a flat roof set upon stout pillars. Off this corridor open the rooms, small windowless chambers, as dark as cupboards. In fact, what with the bare rafters, the rough ungarnished plaster of the walls, the earthen floor without carpets and the door-openings without doors (a curtain serves), the house wears the air of a building not yet well out of the contractor's hands. Of all the rooms in it, and they are many, one alone deserves that name. It is the dining-hall, and, though it is the master's pride and holds twelve couches, its dimensions are

---

[1] 'Wall-digger' was the Greek name for a burglar.

by no means so striking as its decorations. The floor is laid with pebbles arranged in a neat geometric pattern, and the walls are done in fresco ; this is something of a novelty in house-furnishing. The painter himself, though a versatile fellow, did not like the job, and Alkibiades had kept him literally under lock and key till it was finished. What scruples he entertained against his patron's new-fangled extravagance, we cannot precisely learn. In any case, they were groundless, for in due course frescoes became all the fashion.

On the side of the court facing the street entrance is the door through which the ladies have just made their blushing exit. To be caught by strangers in the males' quarter of the house would be a grave impropriety : similarly it would be a gross breach of etiquette to follow them through that door. Nevertheless it is perhaps permissible to peep in upon their ' Withdrawing Room.' Here we may see a second and even smaller court planted with a few flowers and bushes ; upon its farther side is an open loggia or recess, nicely planned to be shady in summer, and sunny in winter. In the room to the left of this the master and mistress of the house sleep. Round the court are more cells, some used as storerooms or kitchens, one for the oil tank, but all are upon a very small scale, for space is precious in the city and a house must be planned as best may be. Indeed the next-door neighbours have been forced to build an upper story and to send their womenfolk to bed up a ladder.

The living rooms, in short, are few, very simple, and more than a little draughty, nor is the furniture designed for comfort. There is, to our thinking, very little to sit down upon. But even more remarkable than the scarcity of chairs is the superabundance of caskets, chests and cabinets. The Greeks for fear of thieving slaves kept everything locked away in boxes, and very elegant these receptacles were, often inlaid with patterns, and resting upon feet carved to represent the talons of some bird or beast. Upon the walls there were, of course, no pictures, but a few stray objects hung by nails, a harp, a lamp, or a mirror. In the corner stand a row of painted jars, and a neat row of them may look, as Xenophon remarks, exceedingly handsome. One larger than the rest is a precious heirloom. Upon its side, in red and black, is a primitive portrait of Athena striking a warlike attitude; and there is an inscription, 'I am from the games at Athens.' It is a record of the athletic prowess of some family champion, long since dead. In the bedrooms are miniature statues and a domestic shrine or two; these, together with an immense quantity of rugs and blankets and cushions, and, in the dining-room, couches and footstools, complete the inventory of the furniture. No books,[1] no pictures, no fireplaces or wash-stands: these latter are portable and are introduced at need. There are no tables, for when a Greek writes he writes upon his knee; while the dining-table comes to the diner, not he to the table, which indeed is nothing but a stool.

But, when all is said, the living-rooms were not meant to live in. The centre of family life is the open-air court. This court is the scene of con-

[1] Books (if the house boasted any, which was rare) were kept rolled up in boxes. Euripides possessed a library.

stant traffic, for there is no other means of communication between room and room. Through it slaves are for ever passing to and fro, and the street door opens full upon it.[1]

Yet, as though the ideal life were one perpetual picnic, Greeks preferred to take their luncheon here under the open sky. Manifestly in this court which served the functions of back-stairs, chapel, summer-house, and parlour all rolled into one, some seclusion from the outer world there may be, but privacy there is none.

Such then is the house, to Alkibiades a residence, but for his wife, in some real sense, a home, since within its four walls lies for her the be-all and end-all of existence. Hipparete had from her earliest years known no more of liberty than Danae in her Brazen Tower, and, as a married woman, she was still merely a minister to her lord's pleasures, a tame and useful pet, in the eye of the law a minor, in the eye of the world the merest fraction of a soul, incapable alike of deep emotion or of decent self-restraint.[2] Her experience of life would teach her the qualities of a matron and leave her the mind of a child. To be seen and not heard was held out to her as a woman's rule of conduct. Her education was shockingly neglected; for though she had heard Protagoras and Hippias at their discourses in her father's house, she could

---

[1] Visitors expected to be readily admitted, even if the master was taking his bath !

[2] This would apply less to the working-class whose necessities forbade much seclusion. And perhaps towards the end of the fifth century a movement towards the emancipation of women was taking place. This is reflected in Euripides' heroines and even to some extent in Aristophanes' plays.

barely tell a *kappa* from a *khi*, and was incapable of deciphering a line of Homer. Politics, she was told (did she dare to put a question), were none of her business. If company came to the house, she and her attendants retired within their quarters, and the door of that wing was bolted till the guests had gone. Outings were few and far between; festivals, welcome as Bank Holidays, were all too rare. In any case, to cross the doorstep she must first gain her husband's leave, or brave his anger after. On such occasions, unless she went accompanied by at least one maid, tongues wagged, and if after a taste of the outer air or the sight of her poorer neighbours at their gossip round the fountain, she was roused to some show of spirit and ventured upon some harmless escapade of her own, why, then, 'minx,' 'hussy,' 'jade'—no words were bad enough. Scandalised husbands shook their heads, comic poets descanted on the lightness of the sex. Not even Bumble himself was so deeply shocked when Oliver disclosed an appetite for food. So the poor lady would return to her former ways, become again a model of propriety and view life, like some Turkish bride, from behind a lattice, till malicious tongues, at a loss to account for how she spent her time, would declare she had taken to drink.[1]

But once she is the mother of a family,[2] time will not hang so heavy on her hands as all that. She will have her daughter to train against the day of marriage; her sons will go to school at seven, but

---

[1] An accusation constantly levelled against the sex in Aristophanes.
[2] In point of fact, Alkibiades' married life was short, for he left Athens soon after his marriage.

till then they are under the jurisdiction of the maternal slipper. She will have to see her children well supplied with toys ; tops, go-carts, hoops and dolls must be bought as presents when the Diasia comes round. A swing must be slung under the verandah for the girls, while the boys will more readily amuse themselves, cutting toy-frogs from pomegranate seeds, building mud castles, and even upon occasions bringing home a tame weasel or a tortoise. Again, with children in the house, as Medea says, 'There are diseases.' The life of a mother could not easily be dull.

Motherhood is an Athenian woman's first concern and her chief glory—after that will come her husband. Her duty towards him has perhaps no special sanctity (she did not marry him for love), but she will not fail in it. The whimsical Alkibiades is not an easy husband to please. But after having run away once at a great explosion of temper, she has done her best. Her lord values himself on her good looks ; she must spend hours daily on her toilette. Women of the best circles are blessed, by reason of their sedentary habits, with sallow complexions; for this rouge is a recognised remedy. The hair also can be dyed and eyebrows painted. Perfumes, scents and unguents she keeps in innumerable caskets, and of hairpins and combs there is a formidable armoury. Her maid is a past mistress of coiffures.

She has the more time to spend on such details, since her wardrobe is comparatively simple. Hats, for example, are, except in travelling, practically unknown. Her dress, like that of the men, is composed of an over and under garment, each consisting merely of an oblong piece of woollen cloth folded

N

in a certain way about the body, and fixed in place by brooches and pins.   Nevertheless a large portion of her life is concerned with the making of such garments; for a good housewife will manufacture, as well as ornament, the material, and she may be seen at any hour of the day seated upon a folding stool in the cool of the verandah, intent upon her spinning. In one hand is the long distaff, with its wad of raw wool—it is her pride to see that it is of the best quality from Miletus, and that the roguish dealer does not damp it and sell her under-weight—the other hand, by an occasional touch of the fingers, keeps the spindle twirling down between her feet. Under her skilful manipulation the thread draws out fine and even until the wad is all exhausted.   Then she will pass this task on to a handmaid, and, ashamed herself to sit about all day like a slave, she will pass busily to and fro among her workers, and see that they do not chew at their spinning, or idle at the loom.   And she will set the skilled hands, when the piece of cloth is finished, to embroider some lovely frieze of animals and flowers (such as in the Aegean Islands they have not yet forgotten how to make).   First and last, the garment will cost a deal of trouble, and a good mistress has stores of such, stowed away in chests, for her husband and herself; they were one of her principal concerns. She would spend much of her leisure in taking them out, unfolding, refolding, and putting them back.   One fussy old husband actually recommended this pastime to a young wife as capital exercise for the body! She might, if she were particular, go further and occupy some educated slave to make a careful inventory.   It would be a grand list, falling under the several heads, to wit, every-day clothes for men, ditto for women, special holy-day garments, men's sandals, women's sandals, weapons, utensils for baking and washing, sacrificial utensils, silver plate, gold plate, earthenware : not to mention the furniture of which, in Alkibiades' case, a list has actually survived. The items though incomplete are as follows :—

> Cabinet with folding doors.
> Ditto with double set of doors.
> Sofa with Milesian tapestry.
> Tables.
> Pallet-bed with head-piece.
> Linen curtain.
> Alabaster box.
> Stools.
> Divan.
> Wicker basket.

At noon all this business would stop : the Milesian sofa would be pulled out ready for her husband's return. When he came there must be a slave waiting to wash his feet : and when he lay down, she would sit upon a stool to watch him eat and recommend this delicacy or that. In the course of the meal it would transpire that he had asked such and such company to supper, and although Hipparete would not be present to play the hostess (for the only feast a woman ever attended was her wedding banquet), yet it would rest with her to order the dinner and make other arrangements. She must send to the myrtle-mart for garlands, borrow extra lamps from a neighbour, and set a whole regiment of slaves upon their several businesses.

It is the management of this large domestic staff
that most taxed the young housewife's powers.
The slaves are very numerous : no self-respecting
family keeps less than a dozen, and how the next-
door neighbours contrive to exist on two, surpasses
comprehension.   Besides, slaves are, strange to say,
averse to work and require much driving.   The
females are docile enough ; the men are obsequious
to Alkibiades, for he once killed one in a temper :
but he is not always at home and then they are
quarrelsome and cantankerous.   The ' market-boy '
is jealous of the ' water-boy,' whom he believes to
have the lighter job.   The latter answers his insults
by swearing horribly in his native Phrygian lingo.
The ' secretary ' looks down upon the rest, pluming
himself on a smattering of knowledge picked up by
listening at the schoolroom door in his young days
when he was acting ' tutor.'   Sometimes the slaves
will be impertinent.   The new lackey, for instance,
is far too free and easy—his previous master liked
to be amused by chatter when they were walking
out, but Alkibiades will not tolerate his loquacity,
and the fellow has been in a pillory a dozen times
this month past as the price of a jest.   As a result,
the ' lamp-boy ' has caught the habit and is never
tired now, when the oil splutters, of repeating the
stale joke about the lamp wick.[1]   It will not be long
before his mistress has him sold, for he is forgetful
into the bargain ; last March, for instance, when
there was a late fall of snow on the hills and all the
beggar men of the town were crowding round the

[1] What precisely the humorous aspect of a lamp wick was we do not
know, but it tickled the Athenian mind so much that Aristophanes is
full of it.

stoves in the public baths, the careless fellow had not enough charcoal for the braziers.[1]

The eldest and most trustworthy of the slaves has just bought his freedom. Alkibiades was loath to part with him, but his savings (deposited at Delphi) had covered more than his full price in the market, so the master made a virtue of necessity and gave his consent. His fellow-slaves are jealous of his luck, and affect not to understand how he can leave the warm house and the good barley-mash to bury himself in a hovel, a wretched place, they say, with a straw bed full of fleas, an old barrel-end for a chair and a dinner off radish ends and mallow. It is all put down to ambition. There is a wager among them that within the year he will have grown his hair long to hide that tell-tale scar where he was branded in his youth for a runaway. Soon, no doubt, he will worm his way on to the roll of citizens and change his name like that notorious rogue who started life as Sosias, blossomed out as Sosistratus on campaign, and now cuts a popular figure in the Pnyx under the democratic title of Sosidemus.[2] The worst of it is that no money can replace the steward. Alkibiades would gladly give three or four minae but, since the war began and so many went over the frontier, there is a dearth of good slaves. Just lately, however, the captives have been coming in from Melos, and at the new-moon fair the market may easily be glutted.

[1] As in most modern Greek houses, there was no fireplace ; a portable brazier was brought in on the rare occasions when it was really cold.

[2] It would be easy enough, but invidious, to find modern parallels to this changing of names with condition or ambition.

All the slaves will pilfer shamelessly; and it requires as many eyes as Argus to spy upon the lot of them. The plate chest and the store cupboards must be kept under seal; but however intricate the signet is, they will forge it down to the very worm-holes or the smallest crack. There is no keeping them out; and if they are taken in the act, they will swear the cat did it, and when no one is looking, be off over the roofs and claim sanctuary at the Temple of Theseus. It is upon the mistress rather than the master that the supervision of the slaves devolves. The husband will perhaps see that the bastinado is properly administered, or, if a slave is more than usually intractable, threaten him with gang work in the mines.[1] But the brunt of the management will still fall upon the wife. A lazy husband will even leave to her all the minor services of religion, the offering of the ' first-fruits ' of a meal, the monthly wreath for the domestic altar, or the visit paid to the family tombs.

Nevertheless, it was the received opinion that women were the drones of the community. And in the Greek's eyes a land like Egypt, where men sat idle and women did the work, seemed utter topsy-turvydom. When the wits said, as they were fond of saying, ' Do not ask a lady : she is far too busy,' it would be ' meant sarcastic.' A few men were found, perhaps one in a thousand, some stray philosopher or poet, to entertain a lurking sympathy and deplore the injustice done to the sex, but they were misunderstood and could scarcely command

---

[1] Of the working of the Laurion silver mines by slave labour and the brutalities equal to the worst atrocities of the slave-trade, an excellent description may be read in Zimmern's *Greek Commonwealth*.

a hearing. Yet it would be an error to suppose that all Athenian wives were despised and down-trodden creatures. Sokrates, we know, was married to a shrew.

The brightest days in the woman's calendar were those great festivals of the State in which she played a part, and often an important part. Girls carried baskets in the grand procession to Athena's temple, and remembered it all their lives. The women congregated yearly on the roof-tops and conducted mimic funerals in mourning for Adonis. Many such rites were specially confined to women, and all males were excluded with rigour.[1] One of these, which took place at the fall of the year, was carried out with exceptional secrecy. The greater part of the festival, which lasted several days, they spent in mourning and lamentation, beating their breasts, tearing their hair. They sat all night fasting upon the ground with torches in their hands, and in general rehearsed, by pantomime, the Descent of Persephone to Hades and the wild grief of her distracted mother. On the last day the ritual took a more cheerful strain, and, like the greater Mysteries of Eleusis, symbolised a re-birth and triumphant return of life. During all these days and nights the women congregated in the precinct of the temple. It was, in effect, a manner of 'retreat,' and they broke away for once from the tyranny of home-life. For some time previous also they were in the custom of forgathering to rehearse the dancing-figures which were so important a feature of the ritual and required no little

[1] Compare the Dorsetshire women-clubs and their festivals mentioned by Thomas Hardy.

practice. This opened the door to the forming of friendships, and it must not be imagined that a wife was totally debarred from female society. Calls were paid, upon one pretext or another, and often, no doubt, one young Athenian lady would pay her confidante a visit and take her off to view some public gala. And, on such occasions, there would be the usual time expended upon the comparison of husbands and the typical feminine gossip. Praxinoe would retail to Gorgo her man's latest folly : how he had gone to market for soap and rouge, and come back home with salt. 'Mine,' cries the other not to be outdone, 'is just such another. Yesterday he bought five mangy fleeces, utter trash, and oh such a business spinning, and actually paid eight drachmae down, the great big booby ! '—' Hush, madam,' whispers the first, ' don't speak so with the baby by ' ; then to the baby, ' her not mean papa.'—' La,' cries the delighted mother, ' but it understands. Nice papa, then.' So they carry on till the hour presses and it is time, in the guest's opinion, that they were starting. ' Ah,' sighs the lady of the house, wishing it to appear she cannot spare a moment, ' to folk of leisure, life 's all pleasure,' and with that puts on her shawl. The maid is told to bring soap and water : the water she contrives, the wasteful huzzy, to spill all down her mistress's dress ; she is scolded and told to clear the floor of the litter of wool, and finally the key of the cabinet is safely pocketed ; the child wishes to be taken too, is easily scared out of the idea by awful threats, ' Bogy ! Gee-gee bites ! ' and off they go discussing the price of a new bodice ' that cost—don't speak of it—two minae, solid cash.'

So women talked in antiquity.[1]   Thus is the gap of twenty centuries curtailed, not to say annihilated, by an elegant trifling upon the two eternal topics, the ineptitude of husbands and the price of dress.

Change indeed, if not a pure illusion, is at least a growth incalculably slow.   A woman's life was full then, as now, of the business of engrossing trifles, of small opportunities for piety and kindness and of formed affections.   Marriage, it is true, was never, not even in the imagination of the poets, a romance.   Yet it is not always the love match that works the closest tie.   And the marriages arranged by parents must have often produced in ancient, as in modern Greece, a relationship of mutual dependence and regard.   At any rate, there was to be found, even in the less ideal husbands, not chivalry perhaps, but at least a fine consideration for their wives.   One we know of who put himself to a grave discomfort and migrated to the upper loft of the house to save his lady a dangerous climb. Men would check in their women's presence the coarse language of male society,[2] and however much we pity their enforced seclusion, there is something beautiful in this ideal of Athenian womanhood, sheltered as if in some high-walled garden, and protected in a measure from the gross and flagrant coarseness of the times.

Nor did the woman fail of her part.   She too was capable of a close fidelity ; many a marriage

---

[1] This conversation is drawn from the dialogue between two ladies of fashion which Theokritos wrote in Alexandria ; this might have been quoted in full, were it not that it is much of it stamped with a sophisticated and supercilious affectation, which is typical of Hellenistic over-civilisation and foreign to the direct and plain-spoken fifth century.

[2] In Dorian Syracuse such an offence was punished by a fine.

contracted as a bargain and begun without enthusiasm grew with the process of years into an ingrained devotion and a tie, the sundering of which, when Death rattled at the door and the man was picked for Hermes' passenger, would leave, we cannot doubt, one blank life and one bitter heart behind. The world at large watched with mere contempt the ugly excesses of her grief, the torn hair, beaten breast and shrieking dirge, and all the outward liveries of mourning,[1] and subscribed, in its general judgment, to the opinion of the dying Sokrates, who, with an almost painful brutality, dismissed the womenfolk early in the day, because he said they could not be trusted to behave.

But that man perhaps had a deeper insight and a sounder faith in the companionship of the home, who carved upon wayside tombstones those controlled but sad-eyed scenes of parting, or he who wrote this quiet and tender epitaph [2] :—

'O Atthis, mine through life, mine to thy latest breath,
    Thou my past happiness, my present sorrow!
Lost one, in what lone sleep now sadly slumbereth
    That hallow'd head, none from my breast might borrow.
For me, when thou didst pass down the dark way of Death,
    Dead lay life's hopes ; to Theios comes no morrow.'

---

[1] A law of Solon which forbade such extravagant hysteria seems from the evidence we possess to have been a dead letter.

[2] In fact the practice of Athenians was, as in much else, in advance of their theory as regarded women. The same was certainly true of their treatment of slaves.

ATHENS FROM LYKABETTOS

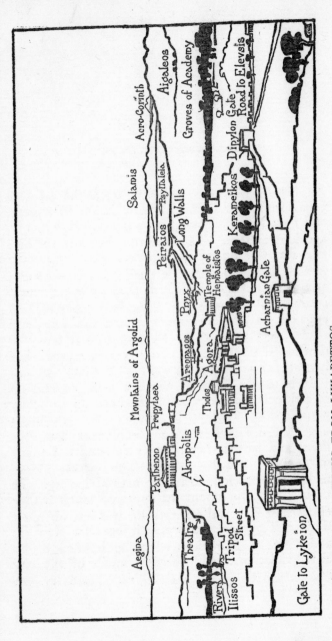

KEY TO VIEW OF ATHENS FROM LYKABETTOS

XVI. ATHENS

'Who has not seen Athens is a blockhead.'
(ANCIENT SAYING.)

AT Megara the wise traveller from the Isthmus calls a halt. It is the half-way house to Athens, and from here the second stage is a full day's march, and long at that. The road runs between the hills and sea over dusty, sun-scorched flats. First the frontier is passed, then the small hillocks of Eleusis, and at length the traveller is pushing up the steep incline and through the straggling pinewoods of Aigaleos,—till there comes a moment when the road sweeps clear of the trees, and, as it takes the downward slope, the eye may catch, spread wide beneath, the first sudden vision of the Attic plain.

It is such a sight at which a man, coming on it suddenly and for the first time, might justly pause. Yet, though it chanced one summer's day that a Greek traveller arrived at this very point and halted there, that vision did not touch nor at all hold his mind. The Greeks indeed had little conscious taste for natural beauty. To their minds the mountains appeared much as they appear to the animals which wander on their slopes. They took scenery, as it were, for granted: and even an Athenian, when he boasted of his city ' violet-crowned,' thought much of the city and very little of her violet hills. Moreover, this

particular traveller was moved by no such sentiments. He was a Spartan; and Spartans had no
call to feel much love for Athens.

For ourselves it must be different. If then we
wish to study the natural topography of Attica,
we can do no better than linger at this point,
while our Spartan goes jogging down the winding
road to meet the open plain. Here, from our
Pisgah summit, we may well take stock of this, the
Promised Land of the scholar's pilgrimage.

The plain is long and narrow. From range to
range of the hills between which it lies, the distance
is something short of ten miles, the length from
sea to mountain perhaps twenty. Confronting us
across the plain rises the bold blunt outline of
Hymettos; in contour like our Sussex downs, but
higher, grander and less smooth. Farms nestle
on its fore-slopes; sheep are grazed on its summit
where the heather, they say, is the best food for
bees in all the world, the land of the Alazones
alone excepted (wherever that may be). Far away
on our left, the north end of the plain is closed
in by a mountain of lively angularity. This is
Pentelikos; its marble has no equal; the white
streaks on its sides are the famous quarries. The
mass of it is misty blue in the summer haze; bluer
still with a full rich colour that startles Northern
eyes, the sea stretches away on our right. There
are islands in it, and ships with gay sails making
for Peiraieus. The plain fixed between these limits
is not rolling like the Weald of Sussex, but quite
flat. Here and there are rocky knolls thrust up
nakedly from the grey-green sheet of olive orchards;
and you may count among the tree-tops perhaps a

score of hamlets from Kephisia under Pentelikos to Phaleron down by the sea.

Just below us, where the muleteers have reached the bottom of the slope, and are already plunging under the shade of the olives, our eyes can trace out the line of the white road where it cuts direct across the plain between its avenue of trees. It seems to lead towards a huddle of low hills, sunburnt and treeless ; and dominant among these is a great square rock—such a rock as would have roused the envy of your feudal baron—from the top of which comes a hard white glint as of marble. You may know it even at this distance for the front of a temple. It is the Parthenon, and Athens lies beneath its shadow.

There are, when all is said, fairer views in the world and grander views even in Greece. Considered from a calculation of mere distances, how insignificant and puny is this little strip of fertile plain, gleaming like some slender green streak of precious ore in the mountainous limestone bed of the Attic peninsula. Yet this little country nursed a great race. We cannot but honour the fields that were tilled by this brave small people, the world's pioneers in Thought and Art, and we can find only praise and reverence for the hills that stood about so beautiful a city. And now it were better to avoid the historian's besetting sin, and instead of making a map and putting in the names (and how clearly from a Greek hill-top does the map lie plotted out under the eye), to rise and hurry after the mule-train. We may yet catch our traveller upon the outskirts of the city.

Lining the road outside the gates is an avenue

of stately tombs ; they are of marvellous diversity, big tombs with brazen bulls above them, little tombs with no more than a modest pillar or a long-necked jar of marble ; slabs sculptured with peaceful scenes of domestic happiness and tender partings ; [1] pompous cenotaphs blatant with the names of the unremembered, and here and there a single line carved as a simple record of the great dead. Where stood the farthest of these monuments, carved for some latest victim of the plague, the traveller was accosted by a slave who had been posted here for the purpose by Alkibiades, his master. After a brief greeting the two pass on through the leafy suburb, down that line of mournful mild-eyed sentinels in stone : and presently they come to the so-called Dipylon or ' Double gate.' There they find the usual crowd dawdling, conversing and passing in and out, and the usual scene of leisurely aimless bustle, of which the Greek knew so well the secret. What a strange confusion of gay colours, and strong smells and high-pitched voices ! Cloaks of white or green or brown or with purple trimmings ; yellow shawls over the women's heads ; arms naked to the shoulder, incessant in gesticulation ; legs naked to the knee and grimy with the dust ; the sunburnt shoulders of the men and the sallow cheeks of the women ; the whole air full of a dry stench of dust and carrion and the salted bloaters borne on the fishmonger's tray. The fortune-teller and the inevitable beggar haunt the gate ; naked children play and tumble in the sand. A Megarian peasant, with a couple of pigs in a sack, is shaking his fist

[1] Most of these farewell scenes date, it is true, from the fourth century.

at the Keeper of the Tolls and swearing loudly in his native brogue, when the Spartan comes under the gate. A nod from the official to the slave, and the pair enter unmolested as they passed within the great town-walls which Themistokles built after the Persian sack, the silent stranger looked up at this stout masonry and made his first sardonic comment. 'Heigh wa's for auld wives, a 'm thinkin',' he said. For, Spartan-like, his respect for fortresses was small, and as a Dorian his accent was exceeding broad.

Just inside these walls and adjacent to the Double gate is the quarter known as the Pottery. Here, some while ago, you might have seen the manufacture, from start to finish, of Athens' famous export-ware. But the street has been broadened and planted out with an avenue of plane-trees. Stately buildings and brazen statuary line its sides, and the potter has retreated into those winding shadowed alleys to left or right of the main street. Here, if you care to penetrate, you may see the workshop of some famous painter of vases, and watch all his assistants at their tasks, the potter, clay in hand, standing at his wheel, the painter with his colour pots of black lustre and violet and white, the fireman stoking the furnace and the slaves packing the finished pot for Tuscany or the Nile. Up one such alley the Spartan's guide now turned upon his right. The Spartan, however, was not yet of a mind to follow. He was still standing open-mouthed in the avenue of the planes. He could not have stared harder had the streets been paved, like London in the story, with slabs of pure gold. His astonished eye surveyed the lofty buildings of the market square towards which this roadway led,

travelled up to the Citadel aloft and the glittering
Temples that crowned it, and finally passed with
evident relief to the gaunt cone of Lykabettos, a
waste untenanted crag standing there like the
Akropolis' younger brother, awkward, idle and over-
grown.   But the guide would wait no longer ; and
the Spartan was led to his lodging, and there—for
it was now dark and Alkibiades was from home—
he was housed for the night, not far from the hill
known as the Areopagos, and near to the Temple of
Hephaistos that lies under the hill.

It was no accident that had placed just here the
shrine of the god of Smithies : for it was in this
quarter that the blacksmiths plied their noisy trade.
And it was to the ring of the anvil that the Spartan
awoke next morning.   He rubbed his eyes with his
fists, and, his toilette being thereby both begun
and ended, he stepped to the street door.   There
he found his guide of yesterday already awaiting
him, and the two set out into the street together
to find Alkibiades.   The great man had been out
in the country hunting on the previous evening,
and had now sent for the Spartan to follow him to
the market-place.

As the Spartan strode along behind his guide,
he seemed a grim and alien figure among the sleek
and merry townsfolk.   The naked urchins stopped
in their game of knuckle-bones to stare after him,
half frightened by this apparition of tattered
homespun, tousled hair, ferocity and dirt.   He for
his part frowned upon the passers-by, despising
them all in his smug Lakedaemonian way.   No
Puritan could have been more clean out of his
element in the streets of Vanity Fair.   Their

shops, their scented hair, their free and easy manners
vexed his self-righteous conservative soul. The sight
of the public baths roused his contempt. A soft
degraded folk! Worse still, there came the sound
of a man singing aloud in his bath, a blatant breach
of good manners even in this godless town. The
Spartan shuddered too at the new-fangled songs he
heard, so different were their strange indecorous
trills from the sedate and solemn chants of his own
land.[1] Nor do I think that he paid much heed to
the Temples, the paintings and the statues that he
met with in his passage through the streets, many of
them the masterpieces of their age. Yet to Endios
(for such was his name) it was all one : for he
knew less indeed of art than he did of letters, and of
these, as he often boasted, he ' kent but little, and
that little ill.'

Nevertheless it was an inscription which presently caught his eye and brought him to a standstill.
It was carved across a marble base which supported
the figures of two men in a warlike posture. Their
names were already well known to him and their
story also. Indeed it was famous throughout
Greece. Nearly a hundred years before this,
when Athens was under the heel of the usurping
house of Peisistratos, two injured citizens, who were
sworn friends, had plotted to kill the tyrant princes.
It was true that they failed dismally : after killing
the younger brother, one was cut down by the
guards, his accomplice caught and racked. But
despite the pitiful issue of this foolhardy scheme,

---

[1] As a ragtime chorus differs from the Scottish Psalm-chants. The
Spartans regulated their music according to a strict sense of decorum
and moral values.

their endeavour had caught the fancy of freedom-
loving Athens.[1] Their names had become a household word to later generations : and over the cups
there was no song which fetched a more rousing
chorus than the ballad of Harmodios and Aristogeiton. The Spartan stood for a moment looking
at the champions of Athenian liberty, and as he
did so, a careless slave swept round the corner ;
there was a yoke over his shoulders, such as milkmen
sometimes carry nowadays, and swinging at either
end of it were two brim-full pails. Endios was not
used to impudence from inferiors, and expected
the fellow to behave like the cringing Helots in his
own streets at Sparta, and to give him a wide berth.
So he did not budge : and when he received a large
quantity of the unsavoury contents of the pail
upon the skirts of his cloak, his reflections upon the
glories of Democracy and benefits of Freedom
were vigorous to a degree. True that, Spartan-like,
he did not utter them ; but if he had I do not doubt
that they would have done credit to the most
choleric British colonel that ever visited London
after a ten years' absence in the East. Yet there
are those who believe that Tories date from somewhere in the seventeenth century.

If you stand, as this indignant stranger stood,
by the statues of Harmodios and Aristogeiton, there
is upon your right hand a rocky path that leads up
the slope of the Areopagos and so to the entrance
gates of the Akropolis. To your left the road
descends abruptly into the market-place, and down
this the two now turned. The market, or Agora,

---

[1] It would seem that, so far from being democratic champions, they
were in reality creatures of the Tyrants' court.

was an oblong space surrounded by stately buildings.
Two public halls, one round and one square, filled
the south side near which he stood. The other
three sides were framed by rows of pillars which
supported lofty and spacious colonnades. Even
at this early hour the market was already full, and
the statues dotted here and there about the space
appeared to walk upon a veritable sea of heads.
A moving and restless sea it seemed, and stormy
too, such a constant roar of voices rose therefrom.
Every one was talking at once : for no Athenian
could hold his tongue and yet be truly happy.
And coming there, as they did, for many different
purposes, their talk was of many things. Those
at the farther end were shopping : this was a great
business, for there was to the Greeks no pleasure
like that of spinning out a bargain ; to cut it short
would be a grievous shame, so that round the stalls
of the ' bazaars ' men stood higgling over some
paltry purchase till half the morning had sped by.
' Obol ' and ' drachma ' seemed the only words
current, and these were bandied to and fro with
indefatigable fury. Friends of the disputants stand
by to listen and admire, or if they flagged, to egg
them on again : others who have business to trans-
act in the public offices near by, are glad to be
amused during the time of waiting. Here is a
pale young student, hanging round the entrance
to the King's [1] Colonnade. As he waits, the young
man is accosted by a squat, middle-aged man with
a very flat nose, to whom he eagerly explains his

[1] Lest this should seem an incongruous title to be found in democratic
Athens, let it be said that the office was a survival of old times, and the
official a sort of pontifical sheriff, or if you prefer it, a lay archbishop.

case. His father, so he avers, has been keeping
some worthless murderer in custody but has allowed
him to die of neglect : this, good son as he is, the
young man cannot in conscience allow to pass
unpunished, and feels himself bound to prosecute
his parent for homicide. So he waits and talks
outside the offices of the king till the doors are
opened and he may file his quixotic and somewhat
original suit.

There let us leave him and turn to the buildings
which line the eastern border of the square. One
of them is a magnificent and lengthy hall, the side
which faces us is open to the air ; it is full of men
and wears the social aspect of an eighteenth-century
pump-room. Some are strolling idly about, or
standing to talk in groups, some who are out for
exercise walk up and down with a more determined
manner, conversing as they go and wheeling with a
military precision when they reach the end. On
the stone benches sit elderly men, glad to escape
from the sun's heat, and above the benches the
walls are covered with painted scenes. These are
of a simple but grand design, quaintly innocent
of the laws of perspective. Look at Kassandra
among the well-greaved Achaeans, and admire
especially the pallor on her cheeks. Beside it is
another, a historical piece. In this ' battle at the
ships ' the cicerones will point you out Aeschylos
the poet, and the famous Marathon dog barking
at the Persians ' in their trews.' In front of this
' Painted Colonnade,' [1] as it is called, stands a

---

[1] Being known as the Stoa Poikile (*i.e.* the Painted Portico) and for
short Stoa, it afterwards gave its name to the Stoic Philosophers who
taught here.

group of dandies, gossiping round the base of Solon's statue. Their jests and language are such that, for all his imperturbable demeanour, I fancy the old legislator is itching to make a posthumous addition to those laws of his, which stand in the building just across the square. They are carved upon strange little pyramids of wood, similar to those which hold the journals in our public libraries, and turning on a pivot.

Towards this group Endios and his guide were now elbowing their way. But as they approached, one of the companions stood out and began to deliver an interminable harangue, waving his arms as he did so in an excited fashion. The Spartan stood by, at a loss to know what it all meant; but by and by the speaker paused to drink a cup of cold water brought him by a slave, and Alkibiades who was among the listeners, turned round and, catching sight of his own servant, came forward to welcome the visitor. 'A'm thinkin',' said the Spartan pensively, 'what for will yon callant be bletherin' a' the live-long day?' Alkibiades laughingly explained that the speaker was a well-known professor, and that he was engaged in delivering a homily upon Love, a topic which had formed the subject of their previous discourse. 'It's a' aboot luve!' cried the Spartan contemptuously. 'Aye, but it is only a daft souter wad be makin' sic lang shoon for a short foot.' This remark was not lost on the rhetorician, who had begun again, and recognising in it a broad hint to stop, he turned upon the stranger and said half in jest, 'I know that you Spartans set much store by silence, but we have a saying here that speech is golden.' 'Then, stranger,' was the curt reply, ' if thou 'lt stop thy gab, thou 'lt no fetch a boddle.'

Luckily at this instant they were interrupted. A door opened in that round building of which we spoke above—and which was given by reason of its shape the nickname of the Parasol—and out of the open door trooped fifty commonplace little men strutting along with an air of conscious self-importance. Their heads were very much begarlanded, and their cloaks were exceptionally clean, as indeed befitted the dignity of their office. They were, in short, the Prytaneis, the standing committee of the Council,[1] now upon their way from the Rotunda, their official residence, to the Council House next door. They were preceded by the chairman for the day, who dangled somewhat self-consciously a strange metal instrument which resembled a small gridiron, but was in reality no less a prize than the key of the State treasury. Their colleagues, the other four hundred and fifty senators, have already entered the Council Chamber. The Session is about to begin.

Once inside, the chill air of legal formality sits somewhat heavily on the lively spirits of the open-air Athenian. The councillors stand mutely round while the prayers are being made. The Clerk scratches his head wisely with his little bronze stilus, waiting till he may use it by and by on the black wax of his folding tablet. Two trousered policemen hailing from the Balkans [2] stand yawning in front of the barrier; while a listless public, such

[1] The Council of Five Hundred was divided into ten sections; each of these sat during a tenth part of the year as an executive committee in permanent session.

[2] Freedom-loving Athenians would not undertake so undemocratic a function; so Scythian foreigners were employed instead as policemen.

snappers-up of unconsidered trifles as would forgo
the pleasures of the outer day, gossip immoderately
behind it. Even when business is well begun it
deals for the most part with dull details of routine :
it is no great matter to hear them preparing business for to-morrow's Ekklesia. For the Council
has little real power ; and the Senate House is
merely the ante-chamber to the Pnyx : the Council
may propose, it is the People that disposes. To-
day's topic, as it so happens, is the exchange of the
Spartan prisoners taken captive at Pylos : and
since that pessimist Archeptolemos is not here to
wring his hands and whine about this wicked war,
there is nobody present that cares a rush for the
debate. The tedious business is long since stale
to every ear, so that not a flutter of interest is per-
ceptible when the word goes round that Alkibiades
is about to introduce a new deputy from Lakedaemon. Endios puts forward his proposals. The
discussion drags wearily on, and the business is less
than half completed and the constables are more
than half asleep, when an adjournment is proposed.
No one objects ; the motion passes, and the five
hundred solemnly withdraw to ' arm the inner
man,' as they say at the banquets.

At their departure the audience melts away.
The trousered constables retire to their quarters
in the square. But Endios, following Alkibiades,
went in the wake of the Senators ; for he was
entitled, in his quality of foreign deputy, to share
their midday luncheon which was provided at the
Guild Hall or Prytaneion. Here they fed daily,
but the meal, to do them justice, was a modest
affair. The Guild Hall lay somewhat up the

slope of the Akropolis hill, and upon its northern side, and there they found a large crowd already gathered. Many persons were entitled to a meal, being for one cause or another pensioners of the State. Here is a young athlete, victor at last year's Olympic games; there two orphans whose father had died gloriously in an attempt to rally the rout at Delion; all had some claim, whether personal or vicarious, upon the gratitude of the State.[1] Presently the doors opened, the crowd flocked in, and the pantler was soon busy serving out the doles. Coarse barley bread is the chief part of the day's ration—wheaten loaves are reserved for festivals. In the evening there will be a fuller diet: large bowls of broth, collops, cakes and comfits, garlands for the head, and wine. Now, however, the fare was simple enough, and Endios' meal at least was soon done.

Now if there be one thing more admirable than another in the habits of Athenian gentlemen, it is their constant zest and energy for walking. The distance covered by your man of leisure in five days' walking about town, would have taken him, so it was computed, half the way to Olympia. Even the landowner of middle age when he visited a country farm would send his mount back home without him, and make the return journey on foot. Often, as he neared Athens, he would break into a trot by way of whetting his appetite for supper. Nor was Alkibiades any exception to this rule. So when their meal was done, noting how his guest

---

[1] Sokrates, when condemned for the new teaching he had spread in Athens, claimed that he was in reality a benefactor to the State, and that his proper recompense should be a share in this public meal.

was out of humour with the town, he proposed a turn outside the walls.

Skirting the northern slope of the Citadel, they headed for the eastern gate. The street they traversed was like most streets in Athens, dark and narrow. So narrow that the houses on either side could be touched by stretching out the hands. These houses were built of mud-brick baked in the sun, covered, in some cases, with a film of plaster. They formed one continuous wall, which but for the doorways was quite blank. No window looked out upon the street, except for an occasional balcony projecting overhead, and by each door a grated peep-hole through which the porters would scrutinise a visitor before admitting him. One door stood open as they passed, and through its frame they caught sight of a cool, pillared court and a leafy vine rambling up the painted columns. An aged housewife sat under its shade, spinning wool and crooning a song. It looked so clean and tidy, that after the sight of it the streets seemed by contrast doubly foul. In Athens there was no regulated scavenging : there were no drains : a hole dug by the door served as receptacle for unspeakable refuse ; and often the passers-by must turn aside to avoid some carcase black with swarming flies. Happily the Greek's nose was dull, so that all this could not spoil the pleasure of his eyes. For some streets in Athens were as fine as others were squalid ; and as the two rounded the north-east corner of the Citadel they entered one of these, splendid with monuments and shrines and statues—not here those uncouth blocks of stone, fitted with men's heads, that line every street as frequently as lamp-posts, but in their stead gaily tinted figures of Pentelic marble, and bronze stools set upon bases delicately carved. The tripods, as they were called, have given the street its name. For often, when a man had won a prize of this sort in some dramatic contest, he would set it here with an inscription to commemorate his triumph. Where Tripod Street passes outside the gates, there are four crossways. And here stood another monument of a ruder sort, a simple cairn of large smooth stones. It is sacred to Hekatê, goddess of the underworld, and as the two friends passed by, a superstitious rustic was lingering at the pile ; he took out a flask of oil and poured a humble offering on the stones. They left him there mumbling his prayers and went on into the fields.

The country beyond was pleasant with green trees. Tall poplars stood up in front of them, and at their feet flowed the Ilissos river, now dwindled to a tiny rivulet, trickling down its broad dry bed of rocks and shingle. Among the poplars, and equalling their height, rose the gigantic columns of a temple half in ruins. For eighty years or more this temple had stood unfinished. For it was planned and half completed by the Tyrants, and, after their fall, was left as it stood, to point the warning and moral of their tale. Passing beneath its columns, the two now joined the stream, where it was dammed into a wide shallow, in which a group of slave-girls were rinsing linen, and scrubbing it clean on the smooth flat stones. Away from the banks the country was parched with summer heat, a tract of low brown hills, burnt scrub and yellow rocks ; beyond them rose the blue mass

of Mount Hymettos. The sun was still high in the
heavens; and the shade of the poplars was more
pleasant than this arid waste. So, stopping first to
cool their feet in the shallows, the pair turned up
the course of the Ilissos, enjoying the delightful
scene. It was the fairest spot near Athens; the
margins were green with oleander, and from the
spare grass peeped here and there a head of cyclamen
or crocus, or a cluster of late anemones nestling in
a bed of thyme. The air all about them was 'full
of summer scents and sounds, the blossom of agnus
castus dropping,' and the throbbing chirp of innumerable cicadae in the grass.

After a few hundred paces, they struck off to
their left hand and headed for the steep sides of
Mount Lykabettos, and so came presently into the
grounds of the great training ground called Lykeion.
Within the walls men were at exercise of every sort.
In one wide space a troop of cavalry were drilling.
When that was ended, there was a match of quoits
to watch or a wrestling-bout. So the two men
whiled away the afternoon, Endios staring and saying
little, as was his fashion. Once indeed he broke out
angrily against a boy who let a slave untie his shoe-
lace, 'as though he hadna hands.' He had his
mock too at Alkibiades himself. The young man
had taken a turn at quoits, and when he came in all
hot and dusty to receive his bath, the slave gave
him a warm douche; and as he was about to call
for a second, Endios burst out impatiently at this
extravagance. 'Was he sae awfu' foul?'[1]   Alki-

[1] These sayings of Endios are all attributed by Plutarch to various
Spartans. If not strictly historical, at least they show what Spartans
thought of Athenian habits.

biades was still laughing at his prejudice against warm water, when evening began to fall, and they both turned home for dinner.

The sun set in a clear and radiant sky; from where they were, they could see Salamis, a line of purple hills floating in a sea of gold. The sun dropped with a rush behind the pine-groves of Aigaleos; and it was dusk. Endios watched it go, and thought in his heart how over that hill the road to Sparta lay: and I make no doubt whatever that, like another sturdy patriot of another country, he thought that particular view the finest in all the land. Better than all the wonders of Athens would be a sight of Taygetos once again. And before next day dawned, Endios was out upon that road, shaking the dust of Attica indignantly from his feet.

When he was back again in Sparta, his friends were curious to hear about his journey. What manner of city, they would ask, had he seen beyond the hills? Then weighing well his words, he would answer with a wise air and ambiguously, as an oracle, ' In yon toon, I wot, ilka mortal thing is dacent.' They might make of his meaning what they pleased, but not for the kings and all their council would he add another word.

Alkibiades meanwhile thought little enough of his guest's abrupt departure, setting it down to the inscrutable workings of the Spartan mind. But the truth was that Endios was deeply incensed by the young man's arrogant behaviour. And, when next he comes to Athens to treat about the prisoners, he forsook the usual course of international etiquette, and employed as official go-between,[1] not Alkibiades as heretofore, but the man who was Sparta's best friend but Alkibiades' enemy, the General Nikias.

[1] Alkibiades served as Sparta's consul (or 'proxenos,' as he was called) at Athens. It was customary for a Greek city to select some friendly native in each foreign state who should look after the interests of her own citizens residing there.

THE PROPYLAEA

THE PROPYLAEA

The west front of the Akropolis is entirely masked by
the Propylaea, with its two massive wings and its pillared
central porch, above the gable of which may be seen the
colossal bronze statue of Athena.

The projecting bastion upon the right holds the little
Ionic temple of the Wingless Victory. Behind is the
Parthenon which, according to strict perspective, should
be somewhat farther to the right. The distance between
it and the Propylaea is about one hundred yards. The
Panathenaic Procession is winding up the zigzag approach
to the great porch. The steps leading downwards to the
left descend by a steep slope to the market-place. The
roofs of Athens are seen below, and beyond them rises
Mount Lykabettos.

XVII. PANATHENAEA

'He beheld the city full of idols.'

THE Calendar-maker, that misguided man, was never so ill-inspired as when he fixed for us our New Year's Day. This arbitrary appointment of his, too late to be appropriately connected with the close of autumn, too early for the coming of spring, has no visible link with the annual revolution of men's natural labours. It has in it neither intelligent logic nor poetic fitness. The Greeks went differently to work, and being in these matters still nature's priests, they contrived things better, choosing for their New Year's tide that pause which comes immediately before the harvest,[1] at just that moment in the height of summer when the labours of preparation are over; and the labourer, having bid farewell to the Old Year, may fairly promise himself to reap the fruit of his toil, drinking of his wine, and eating of his fig-tree, at the advent of the New.

Upon this lull or brief period of respite the people of Attica seized naturally enough, to celebrate what was for them a yet more significant anniversary. They reserved for this season the

---

[1] True the corn harvest was reaped a little earlier in the year, but this was in Attica at least a matter of minor importance. Corn came for the most part from abroad. The Panathenaea was celebrated at the end of Hekatombeion, roughly our July.

chief festival, the Name Day of their City—the famous Panathenaea.

Nor was this a mere holiday of one summer afternoon. On such high occasions, the pagan world, being innocent of the regularities of a weekly rest and a recurring Sabbath, compensated itself by a whole week, as it were, of accumulated Sundays. For nine successive days, towards the close of their first month, the entire town kept holiday and made merry to the honour of Athena. Her glorification was, for that matter, a glorification of Athens too, town and goddess being merged for them in a close identity. No town perhaps, except Jerusalem, was ever loved with so vehement a pride, and whereas the religion of the Hebrews, by the mouth of its preachers and prophets, strove to curb a worldly patriotism and to humble an undue pride of country, the worship of Athena was designed rather to uplift her people's hearts towards a supreme conviction of their own miraculous and momentous importance.

Every fourth year the Panathenaea assumed a magnified significance. It ceased then to be a merely local or municipal celebration ; it became Imperial. Delegates from the colonies and Island allies flocked across the Aegean to pay their duties to the mother city and sacrifice two sheep and a cow to the common divinity of all true Ionian folk. Visitors too from every corner of the mainland were present to witness the spectacle or to enter for the Games. They called it, by a simple addition, the Great Panathenaea.

It happened in a certain year which followed close upon the patching up of a peace with Sparta, and in which Alkibiades was at the high pitch of his popularity, that the Great Panathenaea fell to be observed. Never perhaps had there been promise of a pomp more splendid, and never certainly had spirits run more high. Herself too, Athens stood, as it were, at the midsummer of her splendour, though the decline of autumn was for her likewise only too near at hand; and with fruit bitter enough—Syracuse, Dekelea, and in swift culmination Aigospotami and the Conqueror within her gates; all this was to come within how short a space, and all this was now how distant from her fancy, as she kept the feast with a tragic, but magnificent bravado !

All the open-air peoples of the South have a passion for processions. In Italy it will be a poor hamlet indeed that does not produce once at least in the year some worn old grimy image, and per- ambulate the streets with chanting and copes and candles. So in their Panathenaea the Procession was the most considered part of the ceremony. It was the crowning function of the festival; but by way of prologue there came seven days of games. These began with certain trials of skill between flutists, harpists, and the whole tribe of makers of music—under which head were included those grand reciters (I had almost said actors) of the Homeric legend to whom they gave the name of Rhapsodists. Homer read and Homer recited are two very different matters.[1] In the old days poetry was still a living thing, and the enjoyment of it a

---

[1] Of this fact, if there be any doubt, it will be enough to invite the local scholar in any district of the Morea to recite in the racy intonation of his modern dialect a passage from the *Odyssey*.

real and popular emotion. Homer had not then become a business of the folio and the fireside, and they would listen to the Rhapsodist as men listen to a play, and the story warmed their hearts like wine, as they sat there drinking it in. Choosing for recital some great episode from the Homeric saga, he would roll forth the verses with such vehemence of emotion, such apt accompaniment of dramatic gesture, that the old legend seemed there and then to spring into life under the magic of his art. He would tell (till you might fancy Odysseus himself the speaker) of that hero's coming to the Cyclops' cave, of his strange reception there, of the cannibal feast, and, finally, of the ruse whereby he planned his grim revenge and ultimate escape :

> ' Then up and spake I, nothing loath
>   At Cyclops' side to stand,
> The dark, dark wine in the ivy-cup,
>   And the cup in my two hands.
>
> *" I prithee drink, Sir Cyclops,*
>   *Of man's meat thy wame is full.*
> *But 'twere good to see what this liquor may be*
>   *Doth line our good ship's hull.*
>
> *For thee have I filled and fetched this stoup,*
>   *That thine heart may yet know pity,*
> *And thou, for all thine utter wrath,*
>   *Mayst send me to my city.*
>
> *Hard, hard oj heart, in time to come*
>   *What mariner may be*
> *Shall sail to thee from the world of man*
>   *Who hast dealt so wrongfully ?"*
>
> At this my word he hath taken the cup,
>   He hath taken the cup and quaff'd,
> Full fain hath he been of the sweet wine,
>   For he calleth a second draught.

" Birle out, birle out, nor stint nor stay,
And tell me straight thy name,
So I may give thee for thy pleasure
Such boon as a guest may claim.

O rare, rare is the wine, I trow,
When the rain of God gars the red grape grow
In the field of a Cyclop lord.
But this is a sup from Zeus his cup,
And a bite from Zeus his board!"

A second time I birled the wine ;
    And dark it gleamed at the brim.
Yea, thrice I took and I served him thrice,
And thrice he drank in his heedlessness ;
    But it stole the wits from him.

I spake him soft, I spoke him fair.
    " Wouldst learn my doughty name ?
An I tell thee sooth, wilt keep thy troth
    With such boon as a guest may claim ?

By his own proper name they call
    Each mortal born of woman,
Both father and mother, and comrades all,
    And mine have callèd me NOMAN."

Yet cruelly he answered me,
    " Now when I have eaten the lave
On NOMAN *last will I break my ȷast ;*
    And that is the boon I give."

He laid him back, he laid him down,
    He laid him along the floor,
And sleep it took him prisoner
    In the grip of its sovran power.

His lusty swyre was thrawn awry ;
    His queasy paunch did puke,
Till bloody gobbet and gouts of wine
    His thrapple gan to choke.

Then I thrust the brand in the ember-heap,
    So it waxéd hot the while,
And cheerly I spake to my merry men all
    That none should quake nor quail.

Slow to burn was the green olive-brand,
  But or ever it caught the lowe,
I took and pluckt it from the fire ;
  All grimly did it glow.

Then into our heart God breathéd might.
  My merry men stood by,
And all set hand to the burning brand,
  And drave it into his e'e.

Then I gat me abune to tirl it round,
  I tirled it with a will,
As he who into a good ship's board
  Doth featly tirl the drill.

Below the haft with a twisted thong,
  Men yerk it to and fro,
They hale to right, they hale to left,
  But aye the spit runs true ;
E'en so in his e'e we tirled the tree
  And drave the hot point through.

Then O to see the red blood run
  About the red-hot stake,
To see his e'ebrow roosed wi' flame,
  His e'elid seared and black,
And O beneath the burning ball
  To hear the e'eroots crack.

Shrilly, I trow, doth the axehead sing
  That water cold hath kisst,
When a smith doth keel the temper'd steel
  ('Tis the mettle of steel, I wis),
But shriller far beneath the bar,
  The e'e of the Cyclops hisst,

Then a waeful groan did Cyclops groan,
  And an eldritch thing to hear.
With the hollow groan the rocks made moan,
  But we shrunk by in fear.

The brand all bolter'd thick wi' blood,
  He pluckt it out of his e'e ;
And syne he flung it from his hand,
  So wud with dule was he.

Then long and loud did Cyclops call,
Hailing his feres that round him dwell
  On the cliffs where the high winds blow.
And east and west, and north and south
From their dens they came to the cavern mouth,
  To learn what ailéd him so.

" *O Polypheme*," quoth they to him,
  "*What bitter dule dost dree,*
So sair to chide, in the soft night-tide,
  And banish our sleep away?

God send there be none who in thy despite,
  Thy sheepfold plundereth,
Ne yet by subtlety, ne by might
  Thyself would do to death."

Then from his den the wighty man,
  To his feres thus answereth :
"NOMAN *by subtlety, ne by might*
  Myself would do to death."

Lightly, lightly they answer'd back,
  " *Sith no man doth thee scathe,*
Thy sair pain thou must thole alone,
Since none may mend what Zeus hath done,
Yet pray thy sire to save his son,
  If the Ocean-lord can save."

Thus answer'd they, and went their way,
  And my soul with laughter fill'd,
By my false name and brave device,
  To see him so beguiled.'[1]

When this episode was finished, another reciter
would take up the tale; and the audience would
hear perhaps for the twentieth time (like the lessons
in Church) the story of Odysseus' home-coming; how
he passed safely the perils of Skylla and Charybdis,
the blandishments of Syren maidens and the en-

---

[1] If there is some mixture of dialects here, so is there in Homer.

chanted island of the witch Circe, till voyaging home to Ithaka at last, he found his palace and his wife beset by the band of 'overweening suitors.' Then came the climax—and what suspense the listeners would endure, as the hero entered his own halls in the trappings of a beggar. How they would wince as the ox-foot, flung by some cowardly suitor, went hurtling past his head. And finally what a shudder would run round the ranks at the 'apparition of Odysseus, leaping forth upon the floor and casting his arrows at his feet.' The man on the stage too felt the story at its full strength, his heart throbbing, his hair erect, and the sweat gathering on his brow : and 'as he went over some tremendous passage there would come upon him the spirit of the ancient men and a voice as of Homer himself,' till at the sound of that voice the whole audience was seized and elevated by the uncontrollable passion of the lines. This lasted till nightfall, and the morning after, by a curious contrast, the same crowd would be cheering with equal energy the efforts of the naked runners at Echelidai down by Phaleron beach. Incomparable Athenians !

At this spot, upon successive days, the whole athletic programme (on the model of the Olympic festival) had to be gone through. Horse-races followed, and then by a pleasant rustic touch a competition was provided for good looks. All the prizes, with something of the same simplicity, were paid in kind. Each winner received jars of olive-oil to a stated number. The olive was, according to tradition, Athena's special gift to her people, and as the oil stood them instead of soap, butter, and many other valuable commodities, the prize was designedly useful. The jars were ornamental into the bargain, one, at least, of them being painted in the old-fashioned black silhouette, with Athena's figure on one side, bull-eyed and belligerent, on the other a scene of wrestling, boxing, or what not, according to the nature of the prize. The jars, moreover, were immense, and a successful athlete must have needed a capacious cellar.

The eve of the Procession was spent in further contests : rival companies of men danced in a ring ; teams of youths ran torch-races in the gathering dusk. Far into the night the whole town kept vigil and observed a solemn feast, only to troop out the more happily and gaily on the morrow, shiny and scented, in their holiday clothes. Every one had some part to play, even if it was merely as spectator, in the Great Progress up the Burg.[1]

The marshalling of the Procession takes place at dawn in the old Potters' Quarter outside the walls. Hither has been brought a monster ship which glided upon rollers. There has been much ado piloting it from its permanent home on the slopes of the Akropolis.[2] And when at length it is in station, the sacred mantle or Peplos is hung from the yard-arm at its mast. This mantle is the special gift destined for the goddess, and is woven of wool, dyed a deep saffron and emblazoned at the hem with a frieze depicting in bright colours Athena's warfare against the giants. With the great

[1] The Athenian name for the Akropolis was the Polis (= town or burg). In early days the Citadel *was* the City. Compare the survival of the term 'City' for that part of London which originally bore the name.

[2] One is reminded of the progress of the Bullock Cart so eagerly attended by Florentines on Good Friday morning.

ship at its head the Procession makes for the market-place, where sacrifice is offered, and the cavalry performs some preliminary evolutions to the great consternation of the ladies. When the escort have at last wheeled into place, the ship again moves on, lurching and rumbling on the rollers, the Peplos waving and jerking at its mast. It sails first under the lee of the Areopagos, and then passes up the hollow that lies between this knoll and that of the Pnyx. The clumsy hulk towers above the mean houses of the narrow street, and presently emerges at the foot of the Akropolis slope and, swinging round upon the left hand, begins to mount towards the great rock above. Across the western front spreads the wide Portico, massive as a fortress ; its two wings lie like guardian watch-dogs of the hill, and by their side is perched the dainty little temple of the Wingless Victory, thrust forward on a jutting promontory of rock, and squatting there like Impudence at the side of marble Dignity. As the Procession passes below this bastion, the gradient becomes more decisive, and the ship must be left behind. The drive zigzags steeply towards the great gates, and up it the train goes winding back and forth, dragging out its vast length like some huge unwieldy serpent.

Processions are to us Northerners a foreign and uncongenial ceremony, and to walk well in proces-sion is an art long lost to England. The Athenians rejoiced in that art, and were masters of it ; in no way self-conscious, still less mechanical like the drilled supers in a tragedy, they carried it off with a certain ease and informality, not afraid to give a word to a neighbour, a nod to the crowd, and yet wearing throughout an air of grave preoccupation, like children intent upon some game of make-believe. This gravity was most to be remarked at the head of the Procession, where the sacred Peplos moved under the jealous eye of priestly greybeards, clad in spotless robes like a surpliced choir. In the wake of the Peplos followed a train of girls, dressed also in robes of white long enough to be passed over the forehead and still fall in straight folds about their feet. The four leaders carry nothing in their hands. They are the weavers of the Peplos. The rest walk two by two, bearing this pair a censer, that a wine flagon, and a third baskets of scents or sweetmeats that fill the air with heavy fragrance. It is the proudest moment in the girl's whole life, and, though half abashed at such publicity, she walks with a conscious pride in her great privilege, demure and stately as the figure on a monument, her eyes fastened on the ground.

The girls are no sooner well within the gates when there follow at their heels a string of sleek white bulls, tugging impetuously at the cords bound about to their gilded horns, as eager as though they were aware of the honour to be done them and impatient to be killed. Two youths are told off to each; and the more they pull and struggle with their charges, the more do the beasts plunge and bellow, to the great confusion of the band of pipers and minstrels that follow in their rear. These in their turn are succeeded by a train of Outlanders, or foreign residents, shouldering great trays of sacred cakes; their scarlet cloaks lend a dash of colour in the general white. Their wives by an odd privilege are there also, bearing sacred parasols.

After them come boys, some with stools, some with great earthen pitchers; then staid old burghers, solemn as apostles, with branches of olive in their hands. Next a corps of charioteers with a marshal at their head. It is the picturesque that tells in a pageant : for military purposes, chariots are as antiquated as are Beef-eaters to-day. Each is drawn by four horses and carries a warrior in full panoply, and beside him a groom whose long robe sweeps the floor.

Close behind them come the cavalry, corps after corps, in a continuous and turbulent stream. Their mounts are unbroken, obstreperous creatures, very deep in the neck and all the while spoiling for a gallop, so that more than half the time they are reined in upon their haunches. As for the riders, they sit them without stirrup or saddle, as easily as a sea-bird rides the stormy waters, and imperturbably erect. They are a fine sight for the eyes to follow, with the sun flickering on the golden bits and their cloaks tossing with the violent commotions of their steeds ; they also pass out of sight under the Portico, and on the farther side their noisy clatter bursts in upon the silent level before the Temple front. By what right, one wonders, does this boisterous cavalcade invade that sacred precinct. Yet upon the friezes of that Temple are they not prancing in immortal marble yet ?

There are some works of man upon the first vision of which the spectator is, in a literal sense, staggered ; it is as though something immeasurably grand and dazzling had risen from the ground and struck him in full face. Such is the vision of the Parthenon, even to-day, and if it is still so in its age and its decay, what must it not once have been on the first morrow of its completion?

There is a peculiar fascination in this attempt to pry into the past, and to conjure before our minds the outward appearance of antiquity. There is no peep into the future that could be compared, for pleasure or for interest, against a walk behind Pepys down Whitehall, or a rendezvous with Cicero on the Palatine. Here a clever painter might perhaps render us some aid. Research can do much, and imagination more. But there are some scenes that baffle us still. If we could call upon the screen a picture of the Parthenon, as it stood in the first bloom of its perfection, we are in this way utterly at fault. We can, it is true, doctor the dilapidated ruin of it, and, by the eye of faith, piece the fabric together bit by bit, mending that skeleton of a façade, and patching the gaps in the forest of its pillars. But how can these dry bones live without the hot bright breath of the sun upon them, glancing down between the columns as down an avenue of trees and by a play of variety tricking the eye into an imagined lightening of their ponderous weight, and a softening of their stiff monotony? Without the brilliant Attic air to work this transformation, our mental image is as unreal and vacuous as is a cheap print after some masterpiece of Titian.

Or what again of the colours? Can our dull Northern eyes conceive this mellow ruin, blazing out as it once did, with blues and crimson, with greens and purples and gold, a rainbow set against a ground of winter snow ? Can we imagine its now ragged outlines as whole once more, each of them as firm as porcelain, and in every carven detail as delicate ? Granted that imagination might heal the ravages that have been wrought, in turn, by Time, explosives, and the archaeologist, yet our modern mind, trained to admire the grand disorder of York or Winchester, can scarcely grasp, much less visualise, such unity of plan wrought out in such infinity of detail ; we cannot follow the master-mind that took count of all, nor even left to chance the imperceptible convexity given here to the temple step, or the premeditated curve of some fluttering skirt up there among the gable groups. We know nothing of a workmanship like this, infallible, both in the handling of the sculptor's chisel, and the humbler tool of the mason. Plato (had he been less Philistine a critic) would fitly have praised the mathematical precision of its proportions, and found some mystic significance in their planned ratio. He would then, we may be sure, have added the art of building to arts of astronomy and cubic geometry, and all other studies which he held to be essential to the attainment of true knowledge. Better still, he might have left us yet another of his great allegories and told how the spirit of Athena herself had conquered the brute matter of the stones and passed into the very architecture of her house. Nor is this mere empty fancy. For while other buildings age with the passage of the centuries, yet over the Temple of the Maiden there broods still (much as it too has suffered) a freshness as of youth. Its frowning brow has caught, like the brow of the goddess, the inscrutable and ageless beauty of the Sphinx. Its ruin, like her name and memory, is now as a ghost strayed out of the past, a derelict on the drifts of time. Yet never did a ruin call for our pity less. For it remains, like her, proud and unbending, scornful, as it were, of man's small passions and aloof from the havoc and pathos of life. Our fallen minsters or ruined castles have each their individual character and human tale, for the spirit of their builders has passed into these friendly stones. But the Parthenon has no history ; in those Greek marbles there is a cold perfection which seems like the goddess herself, impersonal, and more than human, and yet for that very reason (shall we say ?) less than divine. There is more to touch man that way in the darkened and vaulted chancel of the humblest roadside church.[1]

Within the gates a spacious way runs along the heart of the citadel, dividing equally its broad and level top. Upon the right or southern side of this way (and so not quite centrally), where a swell in the natural surface of rock has given to the builder a master-station for his edifice, the Great Temple rises. On either hand the approach is lined with statuary ; indeed the whole precinct teems like the field of dragon's teeth, with a prodigious company of figures, statues in stone, in bronze, and in marble, set singly or in groups, massed in an un-

[1] After this it would seem a trifle imprudent to attempt a reconstruction in monochrome of the Parthenon. Pausanias, in describing the scaly texture of Athena's aegis, remarks that those who have not seen a dragon have at any rate seen a fir-cone. Sometimes we must put up with a fir-cone.

premeditated scheme of orderly disorder. Here sailors and soldiers, statesmen and poets stand side by side with gods and legendary heroes. Here is, so to say, an epitome, in stone, of all Attic history and Greek mythology. Yonder stands Theseus, Samson-like, strangling his lion. There Athena challenges Poseidon for possession of the soil ; and there again she is flinging the flutes, in contempt, at Marsyas' feet. There are a score of such legendary scenes, which have come to be, as it were, the People's Bible, colouring their beliefs and forming no small part of their mental furniture ; they are the companions and familiar symbols of the nation's daily life, moulded in miniature upon its coins, and traced even upon the patterned surfaces of its domestic crockery.

Nor are there wanting the more modest tributes of private piety or affection. Here Pheidias set up a thankoffering for his favourite slave who fell from a roof-top, but by a miracle escaped with his life : the fellow is seen crouching on his haunches and blowing upon the embers of an imaginary fire. At no great distance stands Leaina's monument, a lioness cast in bronze, not without passing allusion to her leonine fidelity : for, being mistress to the man who killed the Tyrant, she refused even under torture to compromise her lover by a word of evidence, and in token of her heroic silence, the artist, so they say, has cut the tongue from the animal's mouth.

The marbles seem, for the most part, the work but of yesterday, and their paint bright and fresh.[1]

[1] Some statues of the antique female type here described have been discovered, their brilliant colouring as fresh as on the day when, after the Persian inroad, they were dug into the foundations of the new defences.

But some are old and weather-worn; yonder female figures with the dainty garments and simpering mouths stood through the Persian sack, and their colours are smirched with fire. Whom they commemorate is doubtful: Athena's priestesses, some say; but others Athena herself; this, with some show of reason, for it is Athena's ground and the precinct is well peopled with her likenesses. One —a bronze colossus—stands sentinel over the whole hill, a mountain of metal, the point of whose uplifted spear flashes a welcome to mariners far out to sea, and beneath the shelter of whose mighty shield the city may well boast itself to lie secure. This giant stands just within the gates; and as the multitude of worshippers press up the central roadway, they pass like a pigmy people under the shadow of her outstretched arm.

When the farther limit of the central pathway was reached, and beyond the eastern end of the Great Temple, there lay an open space. Here the head of the line came to a halt. The sacred garment was taken down from its pole. It was placed in the High Priest's arms. There was a cry for silence, the crowd stood still, and a great hush came over the hill-top. So still was the air that the piping of a shepherd boy could be heard rising from the rocks below, and the song of a slave-girl as she filled her pitcher at the fountain sounded faintly from the deserted town. The whole wide plain lay under the noonday sleeping like a wearied man; there was nowhere either breath or motion; only the blue waves laughing in the distance and the blue hills shimmering in the haze. Even the very swallows, perching on the painted cornice overhead, would take fright at the sudden silence, and dive down under the lintel of the great east door.

Through that doorway there flashed and glowed, in the cool half-light of the sanctuary, the form of the golden goddess, more exquisitely wrought than a well-cut jewel, yet as monstrous and majestic as Dagon on his pedestal. The mantle that covered her was from neck to hem one sheet of beaten gold ; the helmet on her head and the angel of victory that floated on her palm were wrought in gold; the buckler, set at her side, was a crusted field of golden shapes. Her face only and her hands and feet were of ivory inlaid. Pheidias made her : and Perikles caused her to be set here in his new temple, dreaming perhaps that *his* Athena might one day receive the supreme homage of the city. Perikles was now dead, and Pheidias an exile, but still the great gold image waited in vain ; and the Peplos went elsewhither.

The priest who held the garment in his arms did not enter by that open door, but moved to where there stands, close to the northern brow of the rock, a second shrine. It is far less grand, less massive and less masculine than the Great Temple. It is fresh from the builder's hands, and much of its carving is still unfinished. But the site on which it stands holds for the people of Athens all the memories of an ancient and hallowed past. Here Athena's house had stood beyond the memory of living man. It was the house of that old serpent which outlived the Persian sack, and of the sacred olive too, the charred stump of which had sent forth a fresh sprout on the morrow of Salamis. The sacred emblem which it contained was a wooden idol, very hideous, but immensely old, so old that some declared it to be the self-same fetish that was carried off from Troy.   Ugly or not, it was in Athenian eyes a very sacred thing,[1] and not for all the sculptors or statesmen in the world would they abandon their old persuasion.

So here the Peplos was carried in.   The ceremony of the presentation was held in secret, and as the people waited outside, the sacrifice was begun. The oxen were led before the broad rock slab that served for an altar, and slaughtered there on the spot.   Select tit-bits were laid upon the fire, and soon great columns of odorous smoke were pouring skywards, through which sounded the droning buzz of pipes and the chanting of priestly choirs.   Meanwhile the bulk of the flesh was cut in portions and equally distributed among the twenty city wards. All day long the smoke rolled upwards ; but when the sun, low over the mountains, was already bathing the hill in a golden light, the priest stood forth and, stretching his hands to heaven, prayed a prayer which the whole throng repeated with one voice, a solemn and final invocation of Athena's blessing for the year that was just begun.   The last libation was poured ; the last words said ; and then they departed homewards to break their now lengthy fast.   Each family roasted and with the evening meal devoured, like the Hebrews at their Passover, its separate portion of the sacrificial meat.[2]   So

[1] Wundertätige Bilder sind meist nur schlechte Gemälde.—Lessing's Laocoon.

[2] The Greeks ate meat seldom except on feast days.   Of this habit one is reminded by the modern custom in connection with the Easter lamb.

the great day drew to a close and (though there was a regatta in store for the morrow) the best of the feast was now over. The townsfolk, loath to think their pleasures at an end, made merry far into the night. But by and by the sounds of feasting died away ; one by one the last lights dropped out ; at length only the owls could be heard calling from the Temple eaves, the lamp which burns continually before the sacred image blinked sleepily over the brow of the rock, as though even Athena slept at her post. It was not indeed her final slumber ; but on Olympus was already falling the Twilight of the Gods.

XVIII. PEIRAIEUS

' Themistokles, though thou art dead,
Still at thy tomb, when sails are spread,
    Goes up the merchant's " Ave " ;
And when the battle lines are drawn,
Come wings that whisper through the morn,
    Thy spirit 's with our navy.'

PLATO.

HARD by the quay, and conspicuous above ware-houses, factories, arsenals, boat-sheds, barbers' shops and fish-stalls of Peiraieus, rose a marble colonnade ; it stood close to the water-side, but despite the lowness of this situation it commanded within a single prospect the whole circumference and sweep of the great harbour. Under this colonnade, with the wide expanse of water stretching almost at their feet, four men sat talking in the still of the evening. It was early summer, and at the hour when men are naturally tempted to leave behind them the heat and vexations of the city, and wander down—an odd forty furlongs as the crow flies—into the cool, free, restful atmosphere of the port. The breeze which, according to its summer habit, had held steadily throughout the day, was now dropping : and there came, as always at this time, a lull and a silence. The tiny ripples lapped more and more drowsily against the land ; the ships rocked less and less rudely at their moorings : then the reflections quivered and stood still, and in a flash the whole roadstead was turned to a serene and shining lake.

Under the peaceful influence of this moment, even the four talkers paused and looked away into the sunset.

Out, beyond the harbour bar, the open water still danced and sparkled under the burning west, like a live thread of dazzling silver. Beyond lay a range of hills, now in the soft evening light pale and transfigured, though in reality the distance was a trifle : a ferry plied across the strait and, even as the four men watched, the boat was setting forth on its last passage for the day. In mid-channel lay a long shelving rock, barren and seemingly without inhabitant : at the boat's approach, however, a vast flock of sea-fowl rose circling and vociferous. This rock was Psyttaleia : [1] and the hills towards which the boat was steering, were the hills of Salamis.

At this hour, so indolent and so peaceful is Peiraieus that it might well be taken for some sleepy, half-forgotten port. But, if it sleeps now, it has at least earned (better even than the city) a period of repose. The day has been a busy one upon the wharves ; since early morning the ships have come and gone : there have been many fresh arrivals : and as each ship puts in, the same scene of brisk commotion is repeated at the water-side. At the first hint of approaching sails, a hundred idle fellows scramble down to the foreshore ; a dozen crazy shallops are launched and there is a race for

[1] On the morning of the battle of Salamis, Xerxes disembarked on this rock a picked regiment of Persian infantry. Before nightfall these were cut off and slaughtered by the victorious Greeks.

the vessel's side. Men who own no boats plunge
into the water, and stand waist deep shouting
advice (to which nobody listens) or wrangling over
a rope (which, as it turns out, nobody needs).
Others more wisely, but no less heatedly, conduct
on shore a debate over the ship's identity, disputing
whether she sails from Cyprus, Rhodes or Sicily,
whether she carries wheat or wool, what her name
may be and who her captain. These points once
settled, there is a fresh activity. If, upon closer
view, she proves to be a corn-ship from the Euxine,
the news spreads rapidly on 'Change, and down
come the merchants to inspect a sample of her
cargo. Still more eager is the rush, when, upon
more rare occasions, an Oriental trader makes the
port. While she is still in the offing, the barbaric
cut of her rigging marks her for what she is, the
gorgeous blazon on her main-sail may even proclaim
her nationality in advance, so that before she has
dropped her anchor, half of the population is down
on the quay ready to waste an hour or so in staring
at the swarthy, jabbering, trousered Tyrians, and
watching them unload their gaudy knick-knacks,
their gay parti-coloured carpets, jewelled drinking-
cups, ivory dolls, nuts and dried fruits, pomades
and aromatics, and perhaps (in half-anticipated
climax) a live Barbary ape.

But by and by even this brief interlude is ended ;
the banker returns to his counting-desk, the loafer
to his broken slumbers, the shipwright prepares to
give his boat another coat of pitch, the fisherman
falls to mending his nets again ; and the port
contentedly resumes its interrupted music. So
the day passes, and business goes forward—until

towards evening, the squabbling of the merchants suddenly slackens. The customs-master closes his office, the money-changer packs up his broad gold Darics in one bag, his plump silver drachmas and obols in another, and sweeps together a handful of iron tokens (the clumsy coinage of Byzantium), and, flinging them to a roadside beggar, departs for home. The beggar too shifts to a more profitable station. The hum of the factories dies away ; the slaves troop into the open streets ; the shouting and hammering in the arsenal sheds ceases ; the evening ferry-boat puts out for Salamis : work is over, and the hour sacred to the homely god of gossip has begun.

The four men stirred and resumed their broken discourse. 'You mind the proverb?' said the youngest of the group : 'If the vine-prop breaks, down comes the vine.' The speaker was an Ionian of Miletus : and like most Ionians, he was a fleshy man with a shifty eye, a sleek handsome face and an indolent habit of body. He wore a coarse brown tunic which was smeared with pitch, and smelt abominably of the bilge. For he was a ship's captain fresh from the sea, and only that morning had brought his vessel into port. It had been an easy, uneventful voyage. For to an experienced pilot a cruise on those inland seas is the merest child's play, calling for no special skill or hardihood. To calculate the currents without a chart, to know the stars, to use a following wind and none other, to spare the oar as much as may be ; lastly, and as if life depended on it, to hug the land, and at the rising of the wind run for a sheltering shore—these were the simple elements of the Greek navigator's

science.   For the rest, each day was exactly like its
fellow : a cloudless summer sky above and a waveless
summer sea beneath (for no prudent mariner would
ever venture out of port till the Pleiads were well
up and winter over) ; each morning (as surely
as the sun rises), a breeze out of the north ; each
evening, by the same immutable decree of nature,
a breeze out of the south.   All day long he could sit
lazily at the tiller, and watch the dreamy islands
float by, and pass away behind him, losing themselves
at last in a blue shimmer of the sky-line.   Often at
noon, to vary the monotony, they would beach the
vessel in some sunny bay and eat a meal there,
washing it down perhaps with a jar of sweet white
wine purchased from the friendly islanders.   At
nightfall, too, if possible, they would put in again
and bivouac on shore.   For, like the rest of his
tribe, the worthy skipper was never wholly recon-
ciled to the discomforts of his ship.   Indeed his
temperament was more suited to a road-tramp
than a mariner, and he would rather miss his market
(though of that there was no great risk) than consent
to violate a lifelong habit or to spoil the pleasures
of a voyage which, if it were to be worth the making,
should be conducted ' decently and in order.'
Despite these easygoing methods, the skipper is no
fool : he is known for a shrewd man of business,
who, if he needs capital to finance a venture, can
tell precisely where easy terms may be met with,
and for what sum his vessel or his freight will stand
him security.   He can predict the best market for
Athenian crockery, and estimate to the fraction of
an obol what Attic olives will be fetching at Ephesus.
His calculations are invariably made for the ' double

voyage ' : so that on his homeward beat he never
fails to take in wheat at Byzantium, or it may be a
load of timber on the Thracian coast. His caution
is proverbial : and though he has shipped perhaps
a hundred cargoes in his time, he has only once lost
a vessel : and even then (since the capital was
borrowed at the lender's risk) he was not above
suspicion of having profited by the catastrophe.
Sometimes, if his word is to be trusted, he has made
more adventurous cruises to yet more distant
shores ; and he is well known at the home port
(where he spends the long winter months in snug
inaction), for marvellous stories he can tell of the
outlandish corners of the world, stories of one-eyed
cannibals, of men with feet as large as pumpkins,
of countries where for whole months at a stretch
the sky rains showers of feathers ; or, if he has a
mind to make his audience shudder, he has hideous
tales of Scythian tortures and of savage men who
can transform themselves at will into the shape of
wolves. Even now—though it is of no such uncanny matters he is speaking—the spell of his
racy eloquence holds fast his three companions,
who listen with something like consternation in
their faces.

' If the vine-prop breaks,' he repeated in the
added emphasis, ' down comes the vine. A rift
in your precious League, a successful insurrection,
and, by the dog of Egypt, there 's Athens in the
dust. It is not a month since I was in Chios, and
what they are talking there, and in open market,
if you please, is rank treason every syllable. Come
next Dionysia, and, if I am not much mistaken,
these islanders will be buzzing round your heads, like

flies over a carcase. Leastways, should Sparta break the truce, there will be no holding them, and then you may whistle in vain for your freights of foreign corn. I tell you I know foul weather, when I see it—as sure as when clouds gather on Hymettos, there is a storm brewing. For my part I have done with Athens; I shall buy a boat and sail with Alkibiades to-morrow. I 'm for the west, my masters, and it may be, who knows? that even the cruise to Sicily will prove too short for me. I met a man once—he was a merchant from Tartessos —that told me of wonderful lands out in the great sea beyond the Pillars, lands where they gathered gold in the ship's buckets, and loaded up with silver for ballast—rivers of amber, mountains of tin . . .,' and the man's voice positively failed, such was the gusto of adventure that seized upon him, even as it seized on the men of Raleigh when first they listened to tales of the illimitable riches of the Eldorado.

Before he was able to continue there came an interruption from his neighbour, a stout, serious man who set more store by one solid fact from Chios than by all the fairy stories of Phoenicia. He too was a man of commerce, but a merchant rather than a trader. His origin and parentage were as obscure as his wealth was obtrusive : and for both reasons his fellow-citizens heartily disliked him. Nor was his position bettered, when the story was put about, that he had shirked his service with the infantry. It was of no avail to plead the privilege of exemption allowed by law to all bona-fide merchants. In vain he had lavished the most generous benefactions on an ungrateful country :

he even equipped and furnished a State galley,
voluntarily, and at his own expense. But men still
called him a coward : and when the boys at the
wrestling-school took to laughing at his figure, he
was true to that reputation and began to stay away
—a remedy which, however, only served to aggravate
the defect. His appearance, in short, was as vulgar
as his manners ; he kept his hair perfumed, and
very long, affected a wide border to his cloak, and
wore on his right hand an enormous signet which
he used with ostentation for sealing his bonds.
His speech was loud and pompous, and though he
had listened with more than his usual patience to
the rumours from Chios, he now burst out into
noisy expostulation.

'Plots and treachery and sedition,' he cried :
'it is always the same story ! And where is the
wonder ? We have nobody to blame for it except
ourselves; we pamper these allies, I tell you, with our
trade concessions, our treaty rights, our privileges
at law. Allies forsooth ! Old Kleon (he at least
knew black from white) had a shorter name for them
than that. "Skin the flayed dog," says he, "tax
them double, make them pay, keep them weak !"
Name of a name,[1] but there's a deal of sense in
that. What said that pale-faced sophist, Kephalos,
yesterday down at thy house ? "Might is right,"
says he, and never man spoke truer word. Yes,
my friend, Mercy is a bad master, and well the
knaves know it . . . I tell you they need Master
Kleon back. True, if he cared to, Alkibiades

[1] A favourite form of swearing at Athens consisted in stopping short
of the god's name intended, ' By the . . .' This modern expletive I
take to be the nearest equivalent ; at any rate, a superstitious reluctance
to mention the name is the origin of both.

could manage them—Melos will testify that much—but now he's off on this giddy new dance of Westward ho ! It's Syracuse to-day, Carthage to-morrow ; why, the town can talk of nothing else, and every raw apprentice in the shops is drawing maps of Libya on the sand. I'm not saying, mind you, but there may be something in the scheme. There is a grand field for us out West. Corinth has had it her own way there all too long : and if there's not cash in plenty for those that join the venture, then I am no prophet. I would sail myself were it not for my duties here . . . but what will you ? I'm not free to travel. I have three corn-ships in the Euxine, a couple more in Cyprus, a cargo of silphium due this day month from Cyrene, two carrying pots and metal to Tarentum, to say nothing of a pretty little craft I have chartered for the Lycian coast which as between friends, you know, spells slaves. Still I shall have a finger in the game, trust me. In any case I shall send my son ; we have fitted out a galley, and we have a merchantman ready to follow ' (and he pointed away to the left where lines of vessels lay hauled up on shore). He continued with some heat : ' Unless, that is, Nikias cancels the whole excursion. Plague take him for a canting meddler ! What's Sicily to him, the sly intriguing spoil-sport ? Every fool knows where he has his own little nest-egg. I will wager, if he owns one slave in the Laurian mines, he owns a thousand. God send his soul to Hades, and his carcase to the crows.'

At the sound of Nikias' name, a third member of the party, who had remained hitherto rapt in gloomy contemplation, now slowly raised his eyes. His

name was Stilbides : a soothsayer by profession, and,
it was commonly asserted, in the pay of Nikias
himself. The general appearance of the man, his
pinched and haggard face, his unkempt beard, his
cloak weather-stained and threadbare, all presented
the strongest imaginable contrast to the wealthy
merchant on whom he now turned a bright, indignant eye. 'My friend,' he began in a shrill,
rasping voice, 'thou dost wrong, grievous wrong,
to the most righteous and scrupulous of men. If
the fleet sails, then blame the Evil Genius of our
country—but pity Nikias. Last night, I dreamed
a dream which, did not piety forbid me to disclose
it, would fully convince even thy darkened mind.
In truth, sir (this to the skipper), thou errest
strangely to think this voyage can prosper. I can
scarce believe that thou hast heard what awful
catastrophe has of late befallen the city. Did they
not tell thee how, not many days since, we awakened
from our beds to find the holy emblems at our very
doors insulted and defiled—aye, grossly cut about
and mangled while we slept—Zeus in heaven have
mercy on us all, and may he visit the omen on the
true offender's head. Men declare (though nothing
is yet proven) that the hand which did it was the
hand of Alkibiades the son of Kleinias, and they say
that he is already denounced. It is like enough he
is guilty. Which of us has forgotten the dark deeds
that he committed years ago, against our Most
Holy One ? Therefore is the plague come upon
us. Verily, his life is an offence to Heaven. He
bears on his head the curse of Kylon. Ruin cannot
but fall on the fair crowned city of Kekrops,' and
the maudlin fellow, in the fervour of prophetic

utterance was positively breaking into the conventional metre of his craft, when the venerable gentleman at his side cut him short. He was very old and spoke with the mild dignity of a patriarch. Kephalos (for such was his name) had begun life as a citizen of Thurii; from that town he had at Perikles' express invitation removed to Athens,[1] where he was now spending his declining years in a green and prosperous old age.

'My friends,' he said, 'forgive me if I speak with warmth, but I am from western parts myself: and I know something of the temper of that island. Remember, I pray you, that those brave men are Hellenes like yourselves, not in name only, but in spirit. I know full well that they will never yield to your armies. The whole country will rise as one man against you. As for Segesta [2] and her promise of support, trust it not. Her boasted wealth, of which your ambassadors have told, is a fairy-tale, and a delusion. Her strength is as the strength of the fig-tree that breaks under the hand. As for Corinth, why would you meddle with that unhappy town? Has not the poet said that of all earthly plagues wealth is the worst; in God's good time the insolence of her riches will work her own destruction. Nay, my friends, consider that city happy which meddles least with her neighbours'

[1] Kephalos belonged to the class known as Metics or Outlanders; a class which Athens, unlike some Greek states, encouraged by various privileges.

[2] The citizens of Segesta had dazzled the eyes of the Athenian embassy by a simple ruse. Inviting them to dinner at a certain house, they had collected thither all the gold and silver plate of the township. The guests were much impressed; and still more so when the same process was repeated the day following at a different house.

business, and take to heart the saying of the good Sokrates, that no man should ever pass beyond his country's border except at his country's bidding.'

To this last doctrine, the two first speakers were about to offer a strenuous opposition : but Kephalos waved them aside. 'Let us speak of that another day,' he said, 'the sun is setting and I have a sacrifice to perform,' and with that he left them to continue the argument alone.

The sailor now declared that he must sleep that night in Athens ; and the merchant undertook to see him on his road, finding occasion by the way to suggest an advantageous loan, at two drachmae on the mina [1]—a rate of interest which (since the Greeks reckoned by a system of monthly payment) represents the modest proposition of twenty-four per cent. Meanwhile Stilbides, being left to find his own way home, did not follow them along the shortest route to Athens, but took the other road that led outside the Long Walls and entered by the Dipylon gate. This track, as it neared the city, passed close under a deserted quarry where the dead bodies of criminals were thrown after execution. Stilbides, on approaching the spot, must suddenly have been reminded of this uncanny circumstance : for he turned sharply in his tracks, rapidly retraced his way to the Peiraieus, and entered Athens by the direct route between the walls. Truth to tell, the prophet's nerve was already badly shaken, and little wonder ; for despite his own dark forebodings and his vision of the impend-

[1] One drachma on the mina, viz. one per cent., was the usual rate of interest, which being reckoned on monthly payments amounted to twelve per cent. per annum.

ing doom, he had that very day given an undertaking to sail with Nikias to Sicily.

Next morning, very early before sunrise, the road
by which Stilbides had entered overnight was filled
by a great and noisy throng of people passing
down to the port—not sailors only, men-at-arms,
and merchants, but every man in Athens, were he
citizen, slave or stranger, who had either a relative
or friend on board or a desire to see the Grand
Fleet sail. With high wall on this hand and high
wall on that, the road they followed ran dead straight
across the level plain,[1] until at last it reached the
abrupt slope of a rocky eminence, at the foot of
which lay the suburbs or outskirts of the port.
Here the two walls parted to enclose and protect the
town. Although comparatively new the town of
Peiraieus was of large extent. Like the mushroom
cities of the new world, it was laid out according to a
severe geometric scheme. Its square-cut tenements
and rectilineal streets stood in odd contrast to the
winding lanes and haphazard planning of Old
Athens. The citizens themselves were vastly proud
of their brand-new chessboard town ; but, just as
the old-fashioned Londoner might prefer the dark
and squalid alleys of Old Smithfield to the broader

[1] The space between the walls was about two hundred yards.
Originally it would seem a third wall had run farther to the south-east,
enclosing a far wider area of country, and taking in the broad sandy
bay of Phaleron. This bay was in early days the only harbour of
Athens. But Themistokles, seeing it much exposed to enemy raids,
had persuaded the Athenians to employ the natural rock-harbour of
Peiraieus. So the bay of Phaleron lost its importance as the industrial
activity of Athens grew. It became merely a haunt of fisher-folk, and
the third wall which had been built by Themistokles' short-sighted
successors was suffered to decay.

spaces of Piccadilly and the Mall, so the Athenian's heart still warmed to the less sanitary byways of the mother city. The area upon which the town stood was a point or peninsula west of the Phaleron bay. This peninsula is a gigantic knob of rock, on the seaward or eastern side robbed, as if by some ocean monster, of two small circular bites (these were the harbours of New Phaleron [1] and Munychia), while the side that looks towards Salamis had suffered more considerable indentation. This bay was known as the Great Harbour, and it was here upon that morning in early summer that the ships of the fleet had been launched and rode at anchor.

They were a brilliant spectacle, and worthy of the city that sent them forth. The men on whom had fallen the fitting and equipment of the triremes had vied with each other in a loyal prodigality. The lithe black bodies had each its new coat of pitch ; the gilt on the prowheads was newly burnished ; and the great square main-sails were dyed with new devices in yellow and brown and crimson. All told, there were more than six-score galleys, and four thousand hoplites were to board the transports, while over and above these, many merchantmen had been fitted out by private enterprise. Such a fleet had never before put out from Athens, yet, such was the public ardour for the expedition, there was not a place unfilled. Every petty adventurer who had two drachmae to his credit had paid [2] his passage, and flattered himself that his

---

[1] Not to be confused with the sandy bay above mentioned.

[2] Passenger rates were very low in Greece, two drachmae, for example, took you to Egypt. Presumably you had to provide your own food.

fortune was as good as made. Against the extravagance of this light-hearted confidence, and the mad
lust which urged Athens on to western conquest,
no saner counsels could prevail. Many politicians—
especially those of the landed interest, the adherents
of the old régime—had denounced the whole undertaking from the Bema; others had cited oracles
and portents which revealed the god's evident dis-
pleasure. But neither carried weight with the mob.
Even the horror which was roused by the mutilation
of the sacred stones was soon forgotten, and all
investigations concerning it were postponed. In
vain did Theodoros the priest of Eleusis call down
curses on the head of Alkibiades. In vain did
Meton the old astrologer, frantic to prevent his
son from sailing, exhaust all the devices of magic
and divination : till, all other expedients failing, he
went home and burnt the house down over his head.
Most pitiable of all was Nikias, chosen to command
the expedition and yet inwardly persuaded of its
folly. A prey to both a wasting physical disease
and the forebodings of a superstitious mind, he
suffered during those days an agony of fear : he
was ready to grasp at every straw ; and stooped to
the most humiliating shifts, if only to delay for a
little the imminent departure. A pathetic figure,
helpless in the hands of Fate and King Demos, he
deserved less than any the miserable destiny that
was in store. And now as he went down to the sea,
aloof and melancholy as was his fashion, he shuddered
to hear the flippant banter and loud laugh of his
rival. For Alkibiades, though a grave charge and
a priest's ban hung over him, yet went his way
cheery and boastful as ever. He rallied Nikias for

his baseless fears, and when a friend pointed out
to him a gathering on the housetops, and recalled
how, on that day, the women of Athens were to
sing the Death-song and commemorate the Passing
of Adonis, he scoffed at the superstitious implica-
tion—'Dear hearts,' he cried, 'bid them to grieve
not overmuch for their Adonis, he will be back in
Athens with the spring.' Stilbides, who was walking
within earshot, noted the omen and spat in his
bosom.

On the quay there was an indescribable confusion. Thousands were clasping hands and saying
their farewells, many were weeping. Others helped
the sailors to coax the horses up the gangways,
watched the troops as they filed on board their
transports, or cheered the rowers as with oar and
cushion on their shoulder they were ferried out to
their galleys. When every one was aboard, a trumpet
sounded and there was silence. The Herald on
the flagship recited aloud the prayer for victory and
a safe return, the crews repeating the words after
him and those on shore joining in. When the
prayer was ended, each captain called the men-
at-arms about him (while the rowers stayed
below) and taking a vessel of gold or silver in
his hands, he poured a libation on the upper
deck. At length, this last ceremony performed
(as upon ships newly christened), the order was
given, the blades struck water, and the grand armada
moved out in silence with the great crowd standing by.

They passed the harbour bar in line, then, spreading out, they hoisted sail and the faster vessels raced
each other as far as the island of Aegina. The fore-

most ship flew the admiral's pennon : and the rumour ran round that Alkibiades led the line. 'Bless him,' said Timon the hermit as he retired to his solitary tower, 'he will ruin the city yet.'

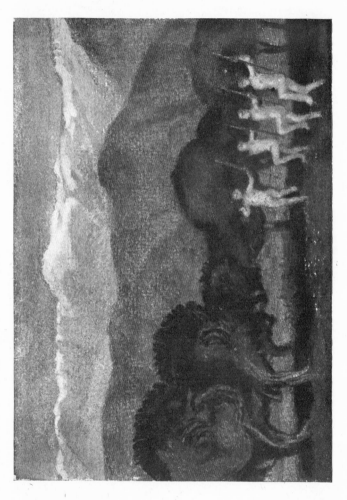

SPARTA: A PYRRHIC DANCE

SPARTA : A PYRRHIC DANCE

The snowfields and foothills of Mount Taygetos rise behind. The Langada pass, which leads over the mountain
to Messenia, runs up the ravines upon the right.

XIX. SPARTA

'Stane wa's do not a city make.'
(SPARTAN MAXIM.)

ABOUT Greece, and especially about the natural features of Greece, the poets have blundered terribly. The strangest tricks have been played with that land's geography in the name of literary tradition, and thus it is that for an accurate appreciation of its landscape nine readers out of ten are utterly at fault.

It would be a fair revenge to take some writer of glib pastorals and lead him up into a certain bleak and elevated region, so deplorably flat that its marshes must lie stagnant all the year with no stream to drain them, so caught in and ringed about by cold high hills, that the whole landscape has a feeling as of something utterly remote and banished from the world. There from some wizened Corin, who sits under a stunted thorn-tree, tending pigs, the stranger at length might learn that these are the 'flower-strewn hills of Arcady.'

It should be his next business to take the Sparta road and go in quest of some wind-swept upland province, still more comfortless, and fit (as he fancies) to have bred that people, whose perverted taste it was to bathe all the year round in the river and exercise without clothes in winter time.

The journey will be long, but a traveller, 'well-girt ' and starting at dawn, may cover the distance in a day. At sundown the track, which has been winding hitherto among steep desolate moors, takes a sudden downward plunge; the hills fall away; and there, beneath his feet, lies nestling, like some sheltered creek among high mountains, a warm leafy plain. It is the very garden of Greece. Taygetos, the guardian monster of the plain, sprawls mountainous across the west, dividing the sky with snows which even in summer sprinkle his jagged spine. Close under his sheer flanks lies the vale, a narrow strip indeed, but fruitful, deep-coloured, pleasant with rippling streams, and clothed for the most part with orchards of low trees, olives, figs, and pomegranates, apple-trees and mulberries, while here and there a tall cypress or poplar thrusts up a head. The broad track of a river may be seen as it threads in and out among the trees, winding deviously southward; and though in summer the Eurotas' waters dwindle sadly between wide beaches of barren shingle, yet the stream is always strong.

' This plain,' says our pastoral poet, being a man of education and blessed with some smatterings of science, ' this plain must always have been the curse of its possessors. The warm climate would surely sap their strength, the soil so easy of cultivation, so rich in production, would teach luxurious and lazy habits. It cannot be but the people led a soft and idle life.'

Yet such was not the life that Alkibiades found when he came to the Spartan plain, flying from the anger of his countrymen. To the fine gentleman from Athens the change was rude; but being at their mercy, he must be at some pains to win his way among these people, with whom it was a point of pride to dismiss intruders without ceremony and be churlish even to their friends. Therefore, much as he hated physical discomfort, he adopted their strict habits, washed in cold water, wore a short cloak and shaved his upper lip. It must have been a strange and bitter contrast, after the free and easy liberties of Athens, to submit to this barrack life of military routine. But he had no choice in it. He was admitted on sufferance as a declared enemy of Athens, though even so not without suspicion, and by the patronage of a friend (for his family was well known in Sparta) he was introduced into a mess or club. The formalities of election were performed, a large bowl was handed round in which each of the fifteen club-men dropped a pellet of bread. When none of the pellets were found flattened by the thumb, Alkibiades was admitted as member of the mess.[1]

It was the rule at Sparta that the men should live, not at their homes, but herded together soldier-wise. It was also a rule that each member should contribute to his mess a fixed quantity of food, to wit, eighteen gallons of barley meal, sixty pints of wine, and a small quantity of figs and cheese. After a successful hunt a member might give an extra feed and claim special credit. Alkibiades, as honorary member, was excused these duties : he could hardly have performed them, and failure was normally followed by exclusion from the club—a sad

[1] This sketch of Spartan life must necessarily represent Sparta as seen through Athenian eyes—doubtless a somewhat one-sided and exaggerated perspective. The Athenians regarded Sparta (as Professor Bury somewhere says) as, like a Doric temple, dignified but uncomfortable to live in.

calamity which left the defaulter, as it were, a social
bankrupt, neither citizen nor slave. The meal
was eaten every evening in a bare hall decorated in
the rudest fashion (for law forbade the use of all
tools save the axe), and the food was most unpalat-
able. The staple dish, besides pork, was the
Spartan 'Kail,' famous mainly for its nasty taste,
and so nauseous that it was said nothing short of a
plunge in the Eurotas could give an appetite for it.
A certain satirical gourmand, upon a bare recital
of its qualities, declared the broth to be a sufficient
reason why no Spartan was afraid of death.

If the Spartan was not a dainty feeder, he was
by no means a pleasant table-mate. Let alone his
Doric dialect, which to Alkibiades was often unintelligible (he lisped his ' th' like a Frenchman,
and leant upon his vowels broadly like a Scot),
there was no knowing what to make of him, so queerly
compounded of contradictions was his character.
His clothes, for instance, were foul beyond words :
yet he was in some points inordinately careful of his
person, and his toilette before battle had astounded
even that ' grand monarque' the King of Persia.
He lived the laborious life of an over-trained
athlete, but he would not lay a finger to any manual
task, holding such work to be fit for none but
slaves. He was as dull as a routine could make him,
which was all ' play' and no headwork. But with
all his dulness he had a well-established reputation
for wit. This showed best in those abrupt out-
bursts of repartee, of which the point was often
neither subtle nor polite. ' Who is the best of the
Spartans ? ' a stranger was heard to ask, mimicking
a question which Spartan elders loved to put to

boys. 'The least your like,' was the quick retort.
A Spartan was not himself easily moved to mirth ;
he was not apt to seize a point, nor was he quick
in conception ; but (and in this as in the last respect,
he resembled strongly our Northern countrymen)
he was canny to a degree, and possessed of much
broad common sense. Lysander was once offered a
choice of two garments for a present to his daughter.
'A'm thinkin',' he said, 'I'll tak baith : the
bairn'll best ken her ain mind.' They might have
made shrewd men of business, had they made it
their object to amass wealth, but with a currency
of iron ingots this was hardly practicable. It was
said that nine or ten minae (the cost of an expensive slave) would have filled a large-sized wagon.
This cumbrous device, which was designed to prevent trading and so banish the ' root of all evil ' from
the State, was typical of their methods. In like
manner they ensured the integrity of their officials
by the simple expedient of an empty treasury. But
not even by such discipline will the human being
be made perfect, and Nature, soon or late, will out.
The tiger's taste for blood may be starved, but it
cannot be eliminated. Once the old environment
is left behind, the old conventions and restraints
removed, the lust returns the stronger. So with
the Spartan : after an excursion into the outer world
you might detect even in him a smug self-satisfac-
tion : and if you know the way about his house,
somewhere above the rafters you will find a hoard
of money that, curiously enough, is neither bars nor
iron.

Alkibiades, we may be sure, found them dull dogs.
For a day or two, maybe, he was diverted by the airs

they gave themselves, but he very soon grew weary
of their everlasting cant. They were constantly
boasting, like self-satisfied Puritans, of their contempt
of pleasure. Whatever Alkibiades specially wanted
was declared illegal : ' Lykurgos had forbidden it,'
was the invariable answer to his protests. Indeed
it seemed a man's body was scarcely his own at Sparta.
So things went on, till one evening, shortly after his
arrival, thay had asked him for a song, and a harp
had been brought out, but since it was an old-
fashioned affair with only seven strings, Alkibiades
would have none of it, and demanded a proper
instrument with its full complement of sheep-gut.
He was told that this could not be : Lykurgos had
ordained that a harp should have seven strings and
there was an end of it. Alkibiades was bursting to
speak his thoughts about their Lawgiver and shock
these narrow-minded slaves of dull convention.
But having no desire to risk his precious neck, he
held his tongue, yawned in disgust, and presently
—an unpardonable breach of manners—fell sound
asleep at table. There was no understanding a
folk of this sort.

The next thing he knew he was alone, and an old
man of immense age and portentous gravity was
beckoning him to the door.

' Young man,' said the stranger, who was blind of
one eye, ' you marvel at my countrymen. They
are in sooth not as the men of other lands. If you
would know why they are thus, I will show you.
Come.'

As they quitted the hall, they saw ahead of them
a troop of boys going down the road. ' Listen,'
said the old man as they followed in the same

direction. ' I am a man of few words, but hear me.
Would you know the man ? Then mark the boy.
The son of a Spartan is silent, but he is tough. We
do not love your young Attic crickets. From his
seventh year he quits his mother and knows no
home ; that year he joins his ' troop ' ; he lives
always with his mates. The Eiren [1] watches him,
the Master schools him ; but none of your books
and figures here. Two lessons he learns, to obey
and to endure. It is a rough life : the river is his
bath, reeds and thistle-down his bed : one cloth
shields him in sun and rain : he goes often naked in
the snow. There is scant fare at the club dinner.
If more is needed, there are the farms. But he will
suffer for his clumsy thieving if he is caught ; also
if he brings back nothing they bite his hand. It is
a hard life : but it makes men.'

As he was speaking they had followed the boys
into a Temple close : this enclosure lay among the
olives close by the bed of the river : the space was
thronged with people, intent upon some ceremony.
' See of what metal they are made,' said the old
man once more. And Alkibiades saw. Before the
temple front was a long structure like a low stone wall.
It was an altar on which charred offerings were
smouldering. Beside it stood a boy, naked and half
fainting. A priest in robes was laying on the lash.
Alkibiades heard a pipe screaming : he heard a ghoul
of a priestess (she nursed a hideous wooden idol in her
arms) cry out, ' Lay on ! Lay on ! Why do you bate
the blows ; the goddess grows heavy to my touch,'
but he never heard the boy, and presently the
victim swooned. A second and a third took his place

---

[1] A sort of prefect, and an integral part of the system.

at the altar, till all had received the scourging. Each bore to the uttermost of his strength this barbarous ordeal,[1] and they were proclaiming victor the boy who had borne it best, when Alkibiades' guide again said, ' Come.'

This time they arrived at another suburb of the town, where was a plot of ground thickly planted with plane-trees. A stream had been diverted and the plot turned into an island. Two bridges had been thrown across the stream on opposite sides of the ground, and now at either bridge a band of youths was gathered. ' This,' began the old man once more, ' is no chance meeting that we witness, but a fight of note. The teams are picked lads. Last night they did sacrifice. Follow the road that leads to Tegea, and you come to a shrine by that road. It was opened last night, but at no time else. Also to the god of war they offered a puppy : a black female, if I remember right. Now look ! '

As he was speaking the two teams began to advance across the bridges, and at a sudden signal they launched themselves in a combined rush upon their opponents, whom they strove by fair means or foul, kicking, biting, fisting, scratching, to drive or pitch into the moat.

All the while that the naked figures went darting in and out among the tree trunks, the red-cloaked men stood on the banks, noting this boy and that : they were watching the soldier in the making.

Before the fight was finished his guide led Alkibiades away, and this time he took him high up

[1] This ordeal, which took place in the precinct of Artemis Orthia, and which was probably a survival or substitute of human sacrifice, was voluntarily undergone. The victor, called the Altar victor, was rewarded with a sickle.

among the foothills of Taygetos, where a steep
mountain track leads over the rocky pass into
Messenia. A young Spartan stood against a rock
hiding. Presently a man came down the ravine.
He was driving a mule laden with farm produce
and he did not see the Spartan. As he passed, the
youth drew a dirk from under his armpit and killed
him at a blow. 'So,' said the stranger, 'the boy
grows to a man: he is eighteen and for two years,
more or less, he serves. It is the Secret Quest.[1]
He will go southwards to Methone and the sea;
he will go west among the valleys of the mountain and through the Messenian plain beyond.
Wherever he comes, he seeks and he kills: in search
keen as a dog, in killing swift and silent as a hawk.
Whichever of the enemy is sly, stubborn or strong,
he will die: only the weak may live. The enemy
—if you would know—is the serf. Now you have
all. You know why we are not as other men;
why we possess the land, but not its pleasures.
It is not our own. When our fathers came out of
the North and conquered it, they left a semblance of
freedom to the men that dwell in towns, cobblers,
smiths, weavers and suchlike, but of the country-
folk they made utter slaves.[2] "See," they said,
"the land is fat; for us these shall sow and for us
they shall reap." So they turned to ease and
pleasure. They made merry, crying "peace" when
there was none. They were blinded of heaven.
But to me the God gave sight, and at my word they

---

[1] Krypteia.

[2] The conquest of both the Perioeki and the Helot peasantry was, of
course, a long and gradual process. The Greek mind would naturally
represent it as a single act.

left their vain ways, and I made for them new laws.
Have you not seen? Their life is ceaseless toil,
their youth they spend in the expectation, their
manhood in the exercise of war. They prefer
duty before pleasure, they choose law rather than
liberty. Nor is it in vain. The enemy are many,
we are few.[1] Yet with us lies the mastery, and
will lie so long as there is honour for the laws, the
laws of me, Lykurgos.'

With that the bearded stranger vanished, and
Alkibiades awaking found himself alone. Day was
faintly dawning and, as he pondered over his
visitor's strange words, he saw a group of strangers
pass the door. They were certain envoys from
Corinth and Syracuse, whom he had joined at the
Isthmus, and with whom he had journeyed down
to Sparta. They came thither to appeal for assist-
ance against the Athenian army then in Sicily.
For religious reasons, however, their audience at
Sparta had been postponed, a festival standing in
the way of political transactions. Now at last the
day for discussion had arrived, and the assembly
was to meet at dawn. Alkibiades therefore rose
and passed out in haste to the market square.
He found it already empty. There was no one but
a hunter starting for the hills, and holding in leash
a hound, more fox than dog; under a doorway a
Helot bickering with a hot-tempered dame: he
swearing that the crop of beans had failed, she that
he had brought less than his due proportion.[2]
The Athenian left them squabbling and turned
down the long straggling street that led to the river.

---

[1] The Helots outnumbered the Spartans by fifty to one.
[2] A Helot owed one half of the produce to his master.

The township was no more than a large rambling
village, meanly built and badly kept, like a town of
the very poor ; it was, as they were never tired of
boasting, utterly without walls or defensive works
(in truth, with the 'enemy' coming and going in
the city every day, much use would walls have been),
nor was there a single building conspicuous for beauty
or dimensions. The most remarkable perhaps was
the Temple of Athena. It stood on a hill which,
though a mere mound, bore the title of Akropolis,
but the queer thing was that the Temple was com-
pletely cased, like a man in armour, with solid bronze
plates. It was in this 'brazen house' that Pausanias the king had met his end. Accused of high
treason, he had taken sanctuary inside, when the
magistrates ordered the doors to be blocked and
the king was left to starve. So had Sparta served
the victor of Plataea. 'And so would Athens
have served me,' thought Alkibiades as he went by
that way ; and as he entered the Assembly, he
vowed that very morning to satisfy the restless
craving for revenge.

When therefore the envoys had said their say,
he begged leave to address the people. He knew
it would be no easy matter to win a hearing, and
he set about to prove that Athens was his enemy
no less than theirs. But, for all he might say, it
was clear they were still suspicious. He therefore
played his second card. He described the ambitions
of Athens, her schemes of conquest in the West,
predicting by a strong exaggeration how they would
annex Libya, would pass the Pillars of Herakles,
and possess the utmost limits of the world. Sparta
would be crushed like a toad beneath a plough.

At this the Assembly quailed visibly. They were ripe for his advice now, and he gave it—send a man to Syracuse, build a fort on Attic soil. Then the vote for war or peace was put. The war-party gave a loud shout : their opponents followed with still a louder, and the meeting broke up in eager discussion whether ' ayes ' or ' noes ' had it.

This was a matter of merely academic interest, for the final decision lay with the eight-and-twenty elders, who now retired to their council chamber and there proceeded to over-ride the sense of the Assembly, browbeat the kings, put even the ephors in their place, and pronounce decisively for war.

And for war the time was ripe. The spring was even now breaking, the snow was off the passes, and at the New Moon, when the ephors issued their monthly edict calling on all good Spartans to shave their moustaches and obey the law, they added to it an order for the preparations of the march. Then in truth the Spartan took on, as it were, a sudden glory. He stood taller under his shield by an inch at the very least, and though grave to all appearance, his heart within him sang. Yet the town was unperturbed as ever. At Athens there would have been much running to and fro, burnishing of shields and whetting of spear-points. At Sparta mobilisation was like going on parade ; a thing they did each morning of their lives. If they showed their feelings, it was only by an added curtness in their speech, or a grimmer turn to their wit. One humorist had painted upon his shield, not the customary Λ which stood for Lakedaemon, but the diminutive figure of a mouse. His friends protested it would not be seen from afar on the field of battle. 'Wha'll fecht wi' me,' was the retort, 'will blink it near enow.'

Nor was there, as it happened, any need for hurried preparations. The Hyakinthia was due, and during the feast, which would occupy some days, the start could not be made. But the religious ceremonies will presently be over, and then away they will go, a dense and formidable troop, accurate in drill, moving as one man; and behind them a large but looser company of Helots, also under arms, who will act as bodyservants, carrying their masters' shields upon the march, and arranging the bivouacs at night. Across the bridge of the Eurotas and up through the hills northward they will march, singing some chant of old Tyrtaios, or perhaps that famous chorus used at the festival:

> *Old men.* Lusty chiels were we lang syne.
> *Men oj middle age.* Sic be we before your eyne.
> *Youths.* Braver blood sall yet be mine.

So they swing away, and at the end of a long day's marching they will trace a circle upon some level spot, and pitch their camp within it, the king's tent being erected at the centre.

The king too, like the rank and file, has found his true self with the stir and the presentiment of war. Once away from Sparta, he is no longer a puppet-prince, a figure-head receiving as a regal privilege a double portion of daily victuals. On campaign, at least, he is lord of creation. But though his powers are unlimited, he is even now hardly out of reach of mischievous interference; the ephors have their spies among his very guard, and at any moment may bring a fresh despatch from home—

queer scratches on a parchment, the key to which, and the only key, is a wooden roller of a particular pattern. On this roller the parchment was wound spirally before the despatch was written, and upon it the parchment must again be rolled before the words can be deciphered. Of this roller both king and ephor possess duplicates. It was a wise king that left his duplicate at home.

A third day's march will bring them across the Argive frontier, and now their only thought will be, not what force the enemy can muster, but where he may be found and fought. The two armies will camp face to face, and on the morrow the sacrifice will be offered, the pipes strike up, the quickstep given, the charge delivered—and, after one sharp moment of conflict, the enemy will have been swept, like chaff, from off the face of the plain, and one more triumph will have been won by the seasoned troops of Sparta over her neighbour's miscellaneous levy.

That battle never took place. The Spartans met an earthquake on the way, and, like the pious men they were, turned instantly back for Lakedaemon.

Upon his return from war, if on no other occasion, the warrior would perhaps unbend and shyly indulge some secret tenderness for home. He might even offer—though I doubt it—to give his wife a kiss : it is certain he would be scolded for his weakness, for the womenfolk of Sparta could not tolerate a husband who did not play the man. The housewife was not a person lightly to be crossed. Taught, like Plato's monstrous ' regiment ' of women, to run and wrestle in the open field, she was no shy, ignorant, indoor creature such as her Attic cousin was. In her own home she was very much the mistress and would stand no meddling from the man. She was austere even to hardness, and if her own son played the coward, she would call curses on the traitor out in the public street : if he fell in battle with wounds upon his back, it would be, ' Och, nae son o' mine that,' and never a tear in her eye.

But shrews as they often were, these ladies had a fine cast of feature and a very noble bearing ; their charms soon took the young Athenian captive —and it was the pleasure which he found in their society that brought his stay in Sparta to an abrupt conclusion.

He was just learning, painfully and slowly, to take his part among the men ; he had ceased to take offence at their incivility or to resent the ' borrowing ' of his personal possessions ; [1] he was even accustoming himself to shout outside a door instead of knocking, as he was wont to do at home ; all in fact was going well, when he aroused the jealousy of King Agis. ' I doot,' said his Majesty, ' yon callant has been makin' e'en at my wife.' The culprit pleaded that he had meant but common politeness. It was all in vain, and when he took an injured tone, declaring Spartans did not know what good manners were, the retort was ready. ' Aye, we are the ae folk has no learned yon Attic tricksies.' He had no choice but to go ; one way alone lay open and he went to the East, and to Persia, the old enemy of Greece.

[1] The Spartan code of morals did not recognise the distinction of ' meum ' and ' tuum.'

XX. A TRIAL BY JURY [1]

'In Athens wise men plead cases—fools decide them.'
(SAYING OF ANACHARSIS THE SCYTHIAN.)

ALKIBIADES the younger, so far from adding lustre to the name he bore, dragged it sadly in the dust. His father, even when he broke the law like a reckless boy, could at least defy it afterwards like a man. But the son had never the spirit to do either. Having first played the defaulter upon active service without incurring the technical guilt of running away, he then at the close of the campaign, when a summons was threatened for desertion, must needs play the coward a second time, and skulk within his own house walls. For a time indeed he was thus able to defeat the object of his accuser, who, though permitted to sit all day upon his victim's doorstep, was forbidden by law to force an entrance to the house, but Archestratides had patience, and soon enough his opportunity came. Alkibiades, being not only a knave but a fool, ventured out one evening to dine with that notorious blackguard Archedemos. The watchful enemy waylaid him in the street, and there and then did summon him to appear in five days' time before the magistrate. To make assurance doubly sure, two friends

---

[1] The ridiculous side of these processes-at-law is doubtless somewhat exaggerated in what follows. The picture which Aristophanes gives of Athenian juries (and upon Aristophanes this sketch is partly based) must naturally correspond to Dickens' parody of English legal methods.

were fetched out of a neighbouring bath-house to bear witness to the summons.

Now this Archestratides was not, as might be fancied, a salaried official with cap, badge and baton. He was a plain, undistinguished citizen, and he was only exercising in this matter a common legal privilege. For criminal prosecution, like much else at Athens, was left to private enterprise. If a law were evaded or a magistrate took a bribe, there was invariably some one ready to come forward and denounce him. Too ready it seemed to some; for there sprang up in Athens a class of human jackals who made it their business to inform against honest men, and lived upon the pickings of such processes. These amateur detectives drove at this time a prosperous trade: for all democracies are by nature suspicious, and the Athenians, jealous of their judicial privilege, and doubly jealous of their juror's pay, had a taste for litigation and lent a ready ear to such 'sycophants.' [1]

In the case of which we speak, however, the motive was neither private gain nor public spirit. Truth to tell, Archestratides was acting to gratify a grudge. There was an old feud between his house and that of Alkibiades, and he had been long biding his time before the occasion came.

The circumstances of the occasion were these. Sparta, who throughout the war had posed as the champion of Hellenic liberties, proceeded upon the fall of Athens to give the allies a taste of uncompromising tyranny. As a consequence, she very

[1] 'Sycophant' was properly the name given to these public informers. The origin of the name is thought by some to have been connected with the detection of smuggled figs.

soon had set all Greece by the ears, and the first
state to take up the challenge was Thebes. Thebes
was the traditional enemy of Athens, but in their
hurry to take revenge on Sparta, the Athenians
forgot their ancient quarrel and in an optimistic
mood concluded a treaty of alliance with their old
enemy ' for ever and ever.' Before however they
could put their forces in the field, Boeotia was
invaded by two Spartan armies. One of these,
commanded by Lysander, was surprised under the
very walls of Haliartos, and was heavily defeated,
leaving the commander dead on the battle-ground.
The second army under Pausanias presently arrived
and set about bargaining for the dead body. So
when the Athenians also appeared on the scene, they
found that Lysander's body was to be granted to the
Spartans, upon the single condition that they should
instantly evacuate Boeotian territory. Thus, as things
turned out, the Athenians were forced to march
their forces home again without a fight, an event
highly satisfactory to all but Alkibiades the younger.
He had been ' pricked ' to serve among the heavy
infantry, but he had preferred to come out among
the horse. This preference might easily be con-
strued by an ill-wisher into a confession of cowardice,
since the horse ran a distinctly smaller risk than the
foot. The case against him was further strengthened
by the discovery that he had never properly qualified
to serve among the cavalry. Here then was Archestratides' chance, and he took it.

Five days after the summons had been served,
the two met in the presence of the Marshal.[1] As

---

[1] The Strategoi, ten in number, filled many functions beside those of
military command, hence General is a title that gives a false connotation,

a military offence, the case came under the jurisdiction of this magistrate : notwithstanding that,
as a criminal process, it would eventually be decided
in the public courts. The Marshal accordingly
received the application, took the prosecutor's
cautionary fee, and bound over both parties to
appear on a day which he fixed for the preliminary
hearing. The Writ (γραφή), as they termed it,
was made out, and that evening there appeared on
a whitened board near the market-place, the
inscription 'Archestratides *versus* Alkibiades for
Desertion.'

In due course the two appeared once more in the
Marshal's presence : and this time things were
meant to begin in real earnest. The clerk accordingly
spread a parchment on his knees and prepared to
take a procès-verbal of the evidence, while the
Marshal, for his part, settled down to a nap in his
comfortable chair. First of all, the complainant
took an oath by every god and goddess imaginable,
declaring that his cause was just, and praying that
he and his family might perish miserably if his oath
proved false. Then the accused swore a precisely
identical oath, attesting the justice of his cause,
and might *he* and *his* family perish miserably if *his*
oath were false. Were the gods attentive to their
business upon earth, it is a melancholy reflection
that every lawsuit must by rights have blasted the
lives of at least one family in Athens. Having thus
cleared the ground, and incidentally exposed themselves to an action for perjury, the pair then passed
to the production of evidence. Before proceeding
further, however, it was open to Alkibiades, had he
so wished, to raise legal objections showing cause

why the case should not proceed ; as, for instance, that his opponent was not competent to bring the charge at all, being, as he, Alkibiades, was prepared to prove, an alien and no true citizen. Or he might submit that the question did not properly fall under the Marshal's jurisdiction : nor would that official have been sorry perhaps to get rid of a tiresome piece of litigation so early in the day. The decision of these points would in any case have to go before a jury : but they would serve at least to delay the bringing of the main action, and the defendant would benefit to that extent. Or again—and although this final method would involve two simultaneous trials instead of one, it was the most gratifying of all—he might rebut upon his adversary the charge levelled against himself. Alkibiades, however, either from inability or from negligence, attempted none of these temporising tactics. He evidently relied on cajoling the jury, when the time arrived. For such evidence as he did produce was of little account. He even neglected to score an obvious point by offering his slaves as witnesses ; for by an odd and inhuman practice, the evidence of these unfortunates might be taken under torture. Perhaps he felt it doubtful what they might reveal. In any case, Alkibiades' evidence was soon taken, and Archestratides was called to present his. He had come fully armed. He brought with him two burghers who had served in the campaign and were ready to swear that they had missed Alkibiades from the ranks. A third swore to having seen him in a cavalry cloak. The clerk meanwhile scratched away at his parchment, taking down the substance of their deposition. Next Archestratides produced from under his cloak a lengthy scroll, which he unrolled with some pride, and disclosed a copy of the Cavalry List—the names, that is, of all who had qualified as 'Knights.' Alkibiades' name was not among them, for though accepted by the Marshals, it appeared that he had never secured the approval of his tribal officer. Finally Archestratides put forward a tablet of wood on which was scratched a copy, carefully made from the Archives, of the law concerning Desertion. These documents, together with the clerk's procès-verbal, were put in a metal box. The Marshal woke up in his chair, set his seal to the box, and dismissed the two men for the time being. The first or preliminary hearing was over. The case was now ready for the second. This was Trial by Jury; for in all cases the court of the Sovereign People was the final arbiter of Justice.

Accordingly, one month after the first posting of the 'writ,' the case comes up for trial. In the interval both parties were kept busy. There were speeches to prepare. These were, in most cases, drafted by professional speech-writers, and the parties then got them by heart. For, by a legal fiction, the principle of 'every man his own advocate' was the rule of the Athenian courts.

Although it was winter time, the courts sat at daybreak; and in the dark hours of a chilly December morning the jurymen might have been seen hurrying to the market-place by hundreds. All of them were past thirty years of age, and many were infirm old men, complaining of their chilblains and cursing the bitter cold; others, more youthful, were hungry ne'er-do-wells, who hugged them-

selves closely in their threadbare wraps. The juries
were, in a word, composed either of those who were
past work or of those who preferred the juryman's pittance to an honest job—they were the
Unemployables and Old Age Pensioners of Athens.
All of them would be well content to sit the whole
day and draw three obols for their pains. But it
is not as yet so certain that all will be wanted. In
fact, it is an anxious moment for many, when they
approach the office. Each carries a badge bearing
a letter of the alphabet. This letter has reference
to the panel to which he was originally assigned
when he applied to serve on juries and first took
the juror's oath. One fellow now presents an
Alpha badge. Panel Alpha is occupying the
'Scarlet Court': and he is given a red staff and
told to join his fellow-jurors there. A second
who produces a Gamma is told that the Court
which his panel should occupy has no cases to try
to-day : so he is sent empty away. A similar fate
befalls a third whose letter happens to be Delta.
The Delta panel are sitting in the 'Greater Court,'
but the jury is only to number 201 : and 201
'early birds' having already appeared, no more
need apply. The late-comer has himself alone to
blame, for the morning is now well advanced, the
signals are already hoisted over the courts ; the
Scythian policemen are bustling about the entrance ;
the Court Crier announces that if there be any
juror yet at the door, he should enter and be quick
about it. The benches are filled, the jurymen's
wicket [1] is closed, and the sitting begins. Mean-

---

[1] The jury-box was divided by a railing from that part of the court
to which the public were admitted,

while others besides disappointed jurors are to be seen hanging about in the purlieus of the market. These are the plaintiffs and defendants, waiting for the opening of the courts accompanied by their kinsfolk and supporters. One man is shepherding a bevy of miserable children clothed in filthy rags, and to all appearance in an extremity of destitution and despair. At the right moment our provident friend will bring them forward in court and appeal to the jury's tender feelings on the ground that he is a family man. The best of it is that they are his nephews and not his sons, for, though the jury may not know it, he was never married.

About the hour when the market begins to fill, a considerable crowd has gathered round the doors of the court which goes by the name of Frog-green. Up till now it has been engaged upon a tiresome quarrel over a plot of debatable ground which the litigants, according to their respective claims, have variously described as a road, a water-course, and a garden ! It is a nice point for decision, but when it is once decided, the Frog-green doors are again thrown open and the case of Archestratides *versus* Alkibiades comes on. The crowd which has assembled enters. The jurors, who have been specially selected for the case (they are all men who took part in the campaign in question), number no less than 501, the odd man being added to preclude a tie in the voting. Their place is upon the benches at one side : while the Marshals, as presidents of the court, sit upon carved thrones. Behind these is set a statue of the god of Justice (presented in the likeness of a wolf), while to right and left of the central altar are the two enormous voting-jars.

There are platforms for the witnesses and speakers. The whole court is open to the sky.

At a signal from the chair, the Court Crier calls on the two parties to appear, and both come forward. This is not surprising, since any defalcation would cost them dear : the accused would lose his case, the accuser forfeit a cool thousand drachmae. The Crier steps before them to the altar, where he offers some incense and a prayer. After these formalities the charge is read and the accuser mounts the platform to begin his speech. He is supposed, by a legal convention, to be his own pleader, but the speech, as all the world very well knows, is not of his own composition. The jurymen have all this while been chattering as merrily as crickets, and one of them has already spread the rumour that the speech is by the hand of Lysias, an immigrant litterateur from Syracuse. This piece of news is eagerly taken up by the juryman's neighbour, a prig who plumes himself upon a taste in style, he opines that in such a case the speaker will be primed with a string of periods as bald and plain as one of his own Sicily cheeses. The reference to that island Sicily roused the quick resentment of the third. His father had died in the quarries at Syracuse, and he laid the whole blame on Alkibiades' father and all his mad schemes of conquest in the West. He would not acquit the son now, no, not for all the silphium in Cyrene. He was cut short by the first speaker, who had no such prejudice. It was all one to him which party had his vote, so long as he got a good morning's entertainment out of the process. In the last case he served on, he well remembered the humorous speech of Kresphontes the actor, and the recitation from the 'Knights' to which the jury had been treated after his acquittal. If Alkibiades supplied them now with half as good a laugh, the rogue should have his vote, and welcome !

'Let the water run,' said the Marshal, and the keeper of the water-clock set his instrument in motion. The case must be concluded within the day : and therefore the speaker's time is strictly limited.

Archestratides put forth his arguments, backing them from time to time with the evidence which the clerk read out from the procès-verbal, taken at the preliminary hearing. As the evidence was read, each witness came up to the altar and formally swore to the truth of his testimony. During this procedure the water-clock was stopped until such a time as Archestratides was ready to resume ; so it went on, and when at length his speech was ended, he stood down, but the case for the prosecution was not yet closed. A near kinsman of his was now put up, primed also with a speech (by the hand of Lysias likewise), which he proceeded to deliver in his friend's support.[1]

'I do not think, gentlemen,' he said 'that you will expect us to explain why we have brought Alkibiades into court. There is nothing in his whole Career which might incline you to regard him even in his public Capacity (and all Private Prejudice apart) with any feelings other than

---

[1] Considerable extracts from this speech (still extant) are here given, partly to illustrate the kind of argument that 'went down' with an Athenian jury—partly to give some idea in equivalent English of the style prevalent among the Athenian speech-makers.

Disgust. Nor are his Misdeeds of such a trivial or venial Character as to allow any expectation of Reform. His Depravity is so decisive, that many of his proudest exploits would put his very detractors to the blush.

'But in my case, gentlemen, this is not all. The Difference between us goes back as far as our parents; so that long ago I have learned to hate him. Now, however, that I have a special grievance, I shall with your aid endeavour to bring the rogue to book for all his past Offences.

'With the other Counts of the Indictment, Archestratides has already dealt in full. He has directed your attention upon the Law, and it devolves on me to instruct you in those points which he has left untouched.

'This case, sirs, is the first of its kind to come before you since the Declaration of the Peace. So it is not a simple verdict that you will be passing here; but a Precedent you will be laying down. For you may be very sure that the country will hereafter be guided by your Judgment in its treatment of similar cases. Nor can I but consider it the bounden Duty of an Honourable Citizen, as of an Upright Judge, to define the Law having regard to the future Interests of the Community.

'It is an argument with some that no charge can stand here for Cowardice or Desertion, because no Battle has been fought, and that the Law enacts that "whosoever shall be guilty of cowardice shall leave his post and be tried before the Marshals." But the Law plainly includes "those also who absent themselves from the Lines." Please read the Law.'

(Law read by the Clerk of the Court.)

'The Law and the Facts,' the speaker continued, 'are beyond dispute : but when they mount the Platform, we shall have passionate Appeals, they protesting that Cowardice is no Charge to bring against a man who has Alkibiades for father, as if Alkibiades had been the Hero and not the Villain of the Piece, whose timely Execution at the outset of a mischievous Career would have spared the Nation manifold disasters. And now despite all that is laid against his father's door, they must needs make a Virtue of his crimes, and talk about his Power—a Power exercised to so ruinous a Purpose. Why, what man is there among you so ill-informed of national affairs, but he might, if he had a mind to it, instruct his country's enemies to the seizure of Strategic Points, discover to them her neglected Frontiers, or indicate which of her Allies was ripe for Revolt. A strange Power this, which as long as his Exile lasted was capable for Harm, but which, as soon as his Intrigues had brought him back with a Fleet at his command, was quite helpless either to eject the Enemy, or to recover Chios (for the loss of which he was alone responsible), or indeed to do you any Service whatsoever. In Power it is plain he had no monopoly, in Crime he had no Master. . . . He knew your weaknesses well enough to sell the Secret to the enemy, but when his own turn came to take command of your Forces, he was powerless to retaliate. He might promise you subsidies from the King's Exchequer : but he, in fact, relieved you of 200 talents. And lastly as a Climax to his Crimes, he actually engaged with Adeimantos in the betrayal of your Fleet into Lysander's power. If you still grieve for the Victims of that Battle, if you reproach yourselves with the Fate of those Prisoners, if you resent the Demolition of your Walls, if you have not forgiven Sparta nor forgot the Thirty, you may set all this to the charge of the defendant's father. And remember that his two ancestors, Alkibiades on his father's, Megakles on his mother's side, were both of them dismissed the Country for a term of years, while the elder among you were concerned in passing Sentence of Death upon his Father. Regard him therefore as your hereditary Foe, and return an adverse Verdict, allowing no thought of Pardon, Pity or Indulgence to weigh against your Obligations to the Constitution or the Pledge of your sworn Oath.

'What right indeed has such a family to Mercy? Can they claim that apart from political Miscarriage their Conduct has been one of Decency and Order —as though they had never been guilty of all manner of nameless Crimes, never defaced the Hermae, never profaned the Mysteries, never insulted Heaven or betrayed their Country, lawless and without scruple towards their own Party as towards the world at large, stopping short of no wickedness and innocent of none. There is no Depth of Degradation to which they have not descended. For Vice is to them a Thing to glory in, and Virtue a Reproach.

'For you it remains to make an example of Alkibiades, an Example to the world, and an Example to his friends, whose one ambition is to defy authority and imitate his model. As for me, I have done my best—yet I am well aware that while the rest of my

T

hearers are admiring the detail in which I have catalogued his Crimes, he will be laughing in his sleeve because I have not recited the barest Fraction of the whole.

'Now let there be read the Laws, the Juror's Oath, the Text of the Indictment—and with these in mind do you return an honest Verdict.' He then stood down.

The court had followed with close attention the thread of his argument and applauded his invective ; at the vigorous attacks on the elder Alkibiades there had been lively signs of approbation. Many of the jury stamped and waved their staves, while the man whose father fell at Syracuse shouted abuse in Alkibiades' direction. 'We'll not so much as hear him!' he cried excitedly. 'Let us cast our votes forthwith.'—'What ?' said his literary neighbour, 'before we have arrived at the parsley and the thyme,' which was his way of signifying the fringe of the matter. These demonstrations were, oddly enough, allowed to pass unchecked, and the Crier now called upon Alkibiades to make his speech.

Being little of a speaker, he made a poor job of it and was soon ready to give place to a more eloquent supporter. This man was a terrible ranter : and his speech began with a flood of cheap invective, in which no near relative of Archestratides (whether male or female) was spared from the grossest imputations. Neither was he more scrupulous than his opponents in adhering to the facts and legalities of the case : for he soon wandered off upon an elaborate justification of Alkibiades the elder, whose exile, according to his theory, had been through no fault of his own, but was the outcome of a plot, hatched by an unscrupulous gang of the aristocratic extremists. His recall, on the other hand, by whatever dubious means it was secured, had proved the undoubted salvation of the State.

As for his having been a danger to his countrymen, had not their arch-enemy, King Agis, desired the Spartans to have him put to death? Finally he pointed with triumph to the noble part which Alkibiades' ancestors had played in the expulsion of the tyrants. Of these great family traditions he declared the defendant to be the not unworthy heir.[1] The jury (who were no sticklers for relevant discussion) had been highly delighted with his vigorous rhetoric : but this last claim was so ludicrously wide of the mark, that it called forth nothing but a derisive jeer. Thus the whole effect of the speech was spoilt.

Alkibiades himself was highly indignant at this blunder—and told his friend roundly that he had made a mess of it. But the time was now past for such recriminations. The Crier called on the jury to cast their votes, and they, rising from their seats and taking the mussel-shells served out to them, advanced towards the two large jars that stood in the centre of the court. As each man went forward, the fatal shell held daintily like a pinch of snuff between forefinger and thumb, Archestratides watched their demeanour for some indication of their mind. Whatever confidence he might feel in the justice of his cause, there remained behind it

---

[1] These arguments are drawn from an extant speech written by Isocrates on behalf of the younger Alkibiades.

the disconcerting thought of the thousand-drachmae fine.   Should less than one-fifth cast their votes in his behalf, he was a ruined man.   Alkibiades too looked them narrowly between the eyes, indicating by his glance that an acquittal might well be worth their while.   Had it been in his power, he was not the man to stick at wholesale bribery : but such was the secrecy observed in the selection of the jury, that bribery in advance was not to be considered. A token of gratitude delivered after the event was as much as could be accomplished.   The penalty for this offence, however, was very heavy, and Alkibiades had, it appeared, few friends among the voters.   ' After all,' he said carelessly, ' supposing they have a mind in the matter, they will choose the wrong jar as like as not.   A voting pellet, as my father used to say, is not a thing to trust one's own mother with.'   Though Alkibiades might talk big and conceal all traces of anxiety, it does not follow he felt none.   Condemned, he would be a political outcast, forbidden to take part in Assembly or Festival, to make a will, contract a marriage, or even, by a nice touch of irony, to appear in the ranks as a soldier.   In fine, he would be a mere inhabitant of Athens, and no Athenian ; as well almost change places with his slave !   Neither could there be any appeal against such a decision.   The vote of the people's court was final.   The only loophole of escape was to convict the witnesses of perjury.

' Has any juror failed to vote ? ' bawled the Crier, and started pouring out the contents of the jars. He had barely time to make the count, before the jurymen had declared what the penalties should be and were hurrying off from the court.[1] At the door each received a leaden tally; and a crowd of them was soon collecting round the cashier's office in the market, where they might receive their three silver obols in exchange. Then off they went, the nasty old men, wheezily chuckling over the fine day's work they had done, counting up on their crooked fingers the victims of their votes, and boasting to their friends what smart wits they had and how powerful an instinct in scenting out a rogue.

It remained for the scribe to record the verdict on a brazen slab, which was thereafter stored among the archives of the City Hall; and this (should it ever come to light) will reveal which party won.

[1] The sentence in this and similar cases would be prescribed by law. In some cases, however, a second discussion arose over fixing the amount of the fine or the nature of the penalty. Both parties in the case offered suggestions, and the jury was called on to decide.

XXI. BARBARY

'Persicos odi, puer, apparatus.'—HORACE.

AMONG the uplands of Phrygia, where men bow to
the rule of Artaxerxes the king, Pharnabazos the
satrap had built for himself a summer-palace. He
had planted round about it a *paradise* or pleasure-
park, which he laid out cunningly in garden terraces,
and palm groves, shaded walks and canopied bowers,
with here and there a leaping fountain or a still
lagoon where fishes swam and wild-fowl sported.
Near the middle of the park stood the palace itself
among a clump of stately holm-oaks, and seen from
afar, its painted cornice showed above the dusky
green, as vivid and various as a pagoda. The archi-
tect, an Ionian Greek, had suited himself to his
employer's taste and had imparted an exotic flavour,
as it were, to his customary style : so that the decora-
tion of the palace inclined rather to an Oriental
exuberance than to the sterner delicacy of Grecian
art. This outer brilliance was matched within by
an even richer, though more subdued, magnificence.
The interior was dimly lighted, and the walls
heavily hung with tapestries, upon which the fantastic shapes of birds and animals and fishes were
repeated in every imaginable conjunction. The
floor was spread with soft rugs and carpets, glowing
with a thousand harmonies of delicate colour such
as Eastern dyers alone know how to match. In the

centre stood a pair of luxurious couches heaped with cushions and draped with silken coverlets. Upon one of these, during a summer's day in the reign of Artaxerxes the king, a man lay sleeping.

The summer was at its height, and notwithstanding the exertions of two negro slaves, who plied large long-handled fans without cessation, the room was hot and airless and, to make matters worse, heavy with the sickly fragrance of strong Arabian perfumes. The man who lay stretched upon the divan stirred uneasily in his sleep : presently he threw back the coverlet and, raising himself amid the pile of cushions, addressed a brief order to the nearer slave. The fellow left the room, and presently returned in company with the High Chamberlain of the palace. This solemn flunkey seemed burdened with an excessive sensibility of his elevated rank : he moved with a slow majestic step, sweeping the ground as he advanced with the wide skirts of his voluminous attire, and at the same time brandishing his staff of office with the ludicrous pomposity of a drum-major. When, however, he approached the couch, this grand manner instantly fell from him : with obsequious humility, he bowed his turbaned head in a low salaam, and taking the hand held out to him, kissed it reverently. Then, prefacing his speech with all the fulsome titles of address which, according to Eastern etiquette, are the prerogative of superior station, he inquired the wishes of his master's favoured guest. Alkibiades (for it was he) felt a strong desire to laugh at the man's ridiculous posturings, but checking the impulse, and assuming as grave a demeanour as he was able, he answered in a tone of lofty condescension such as would have been considered outrageous in the society of Greeks, but which alone commanded a due respect among their Oriental neighbours. It was his wish, he said, to despatch a letter to Pharnabazos upon a matter of importance. At the mention of the name the Chamberlain made a sign of the deepest reverence, and, producing a wax tablet from somewhere about his ample person, he prepared to write at Alkibiades' dictation. The letter began with an elaborate exordium which deplored in the accepted manner the unworthiness of the sender, and extolled by way of contrast the boundless virtues of the satrap. Then passing to more serious business, it announced that Alkibiades intended (with due permission) to hunt next day in the vice-regal game preserves. It concluded with an undertaking that one half of what fell to his spear, bears, buck,[1] wild-fowl, ground-game and what not, should go to replenish the stores of the vice-regal larder. When this letter had been duly signed and sealed, Alkibiades again extended his right hand; as before, the Chamberlain gave it a deferential kiss, inclined his head in low obeisance, and passed noiselessly over the soft carpets to the outer door, where he resumed his first ridiculous air of self-importance, and disappeared.

Once more Alkibiades beckoned to the slave. This time the order was to seek his mistress and inform her that the hour of supper was fast approaching. After a brief interval, the curtains were drawn aside from an inner door, through which entered two female slaves, and behind them

[1] Big-game hunting, as Mr. Zimmern remarks, in comparison with the smaller animals of Greece.

Timandra, the renowned Sicilian beauty. For a
Greek, her toilette was inordinately pretentious.
It is true that Alkibiades himself affected the
native style of dress, wearing the softest linen,[1]
and even enveloping both head and chin with the
unmanly wrappings of a Persian 'mitra.' But in
this dame's attire there was no single item of Asiatic
finery omitted, from the golden bracelets and
jewelled rings upon her arms and fingers, to the
flaunting cosmetics which adorned her brow and
cheeks. Indeed, her appearance would have been
shocking beyond measure in the eyes of all respectable Athenian matrons; but as if to show still
further her complete emancipation from the con-
ventionalities of Greece, she now took her place
on the second divan at Alkibiades' side.[2]

No sooner was she seated than a veritable army
of slaves appeared, bearing gold and silver dishes,
and supper began. First came a variety of fruits
and lighter condiments, dates, raisins, dried figs,
almonds and salted filberts. Then followed all
manner of baked meats in so interminable a procession, that Alkibiades from sheer satiety begged
that the flow might cease and wine be brought.
Timandra laughed at his early discomfiture. 'These
barbarians make poor warriors,' she cried, 'but by
Osiris, they are better trenchermen than we.
Your true Greek, they say, would always rise hungry

[1] It was considered in Greece to be a wasteful and luxurious habit to
wear linen, which required (like white shirts) an almost daily washing.
They preferred woollen cloth which only needed an occasional visit to
the fuller. The 'mitra' was a kind of turban which enveloped the
head, chin and all.

[2] No modest Greek woman ever lay down to a meal in company
with men.

from the board.'—'Aye,' replied Alkibiades, 'but the fool would mix good wine with water, and we, Timandra, have learnt to better that.' So saying he drained off a pint of the rich syrup, without a drop of that undesirable admixture [1]

Supper being over, the slaves withdrew; only a dark-skinned Hebrew, the cup-bearer, remained, filling and refilling the cups as fast as they were emptied. Meanwhile from the outer night came the low sounds of soft seductive music, the mellow note of flutes and the gentle tinkle of bells and tambourines. For long the two sat there, listening as they drank, until by and by the minstrels ceased, and a tall white-robed figure appeared in the doorway. It was a wandering stranger, a professional teller of tales, who had come that morning to the palace and begged leave to appear before the Greeks after they had dined. He now seated himself, cross-legged, before the couches, and was about to begin his story when a noise of shouting was heard in the outer court. Timandra asked in some alarm what this might mean. But Alkibiades reassured her; it was nothing, he said; the huntsmen were doubtless preparing for the morrow's expedition; let the man proceed to business. So the teller of tales began and the tale he told was as follows :—

'Once upon a time, in the heart of the world, in the place where the four winds meet, there dwelt a people whom the gods loved, and to whom they gave their choicest gifts, not gold, nor abundance of corn or of wine (as they give to other men),

---

[1] When a Greek took to drinking his wine neat, in imitation of foreign habits, he was thought to be past praying for (cp. Thukydides' story of Pausanias the Spartan).

but knowledge and the secret of all arts ; in these the people wrought, honouring toil, and despising idleness or ease. Therefore, though their land was narrow, the people grew and prospered : their old men were strong with the strength of youths : their young men were wise with the wisdom of the old : and in that country, so men said, it seemed always to be Morning.

'Now there was one among them in whose heart the gods had set insatiable desire. And when he had come to manhood, he must needs know the source of all happiness : " for," said he, " in all this land, none shall be happier than I." So he went his way into the market and sought out a merchant who was accounted the richest of all, who bought and sold in that place, and of him he inquired, saying, " Wherein doth happiness consist ? " and the rich man answered him, " In gaining wealth enough and no more." Then he left the rich man and came to the chief ruler of the country, to whose counsel all men hearkened ; and of him he inquired as before, " Wherein doth happiness consist ? " and the man answered him, " In gaining power enough and no more." Lastly he came to a philosopher, who was accounted the wisest man in all the world, and of him he asked the same question, and the wise man answered, " In gaining wisdom enough and no more." Then the young man said in his heart, " This is but the prating of fools ; for as the whole is greater than the half, so surely is *more* better than *enough*. When I shall have surpassed all other men in riches, in power, and in wisdom, on that day shall I in very deed be happy." But the people, when they were aware of it, declared that he had passed the boundary of desire, and they drove him from the land.

'So he journeyed abroad into the world.

'Now there was, beyond the seas, another land where was corn in abundance and much gold. And the people of that land loved ease and idle luxury. Therefore though their land was broad as ocean, yet were their hearts narrow as the kernel hidden in the nut : the strength of their young men was as the feebleness of the old, and the wisdom of their old men was as the folly of babes, and in that country it seemed always Afternoon.

'So he came and sojourned in this land, saying within himself : " This people are wise for they live as gods, knowing neither want nor grievous toil. Here will I take my fill of ease and taste the pleasures of life, for it may be that therein lies happiness " ; and when he had tasted of ease and pleasures, lo, they were but emptiness mocking his desire.

'Then was he fain to return and come again to his own people and the bright land of Morning. But his enemies, when they heard it, were afraid and sent messengers desiring that he might be slain.'

At these words Timandra cried out, 'O Alkibiades, it is thou ! The omen is against thee.'

'What does Hippokleides care ? ' [1]   he answered ;

---

[1] The origin of this saying is given by Herodotos as follows : A certain Kleisthenes, tyrant of Megara, had a beautiful daughter, Agarista, and he invited the nobles of Greece to come and compete for her hand. The others having exhibited their proficiency in music and song, one, Hippokleides, called for a table and, bidding the piper strike up, began to dance thereon.   After giving examples of the more modest and conventional steps, he suddenly stood upon his head and 'gesticulated' with his legs in the air.   Kleisthenes, profoundly shocked at this extravagance, cried out, 'O son of Tisander, thou hast danced thy wife away.'—'What does Hippokleides care?' was the retort, and the words became a proverb.

and he bade the man continue the tale. But scarcely had he spoken when great flames lit up the doorway and the room was filled with smoke. Then he rose from his couch and gathered in his arms the pillows and coverlet and threw them upon the fire, and going out he stood at the threshold. But he knew already that his life was forfeited, and, as he stood there, he fell pierced with arrows. So he died.

'It is well,' said the wandering prophet. 'Morning bringeth toil to man, and the Afternoon satiety: but of the Night no man can say whether it be good or bad.'

Printed by T. and A. CONSTABLE, Printers to His Majesty
at the Edinburgh University Press